*An Anthology
of Nineteenth-Century
Women's Poetry from France*

Texts and Translations

The Texts and Translations series was founded in 1991 to provide students and teachers with important texts not readily available or not available at an affordable price and in high-quality translations. The books in the series are intended for students in upper-level undergraduate and graduate courses in national literatures in languages other than English, comparative literature, ethnic studies, area studies, translation studies, women's studies, and gender studies. The Texts and Translations series is overseen by an editorial board composed of specialists in several national literatures and in translation studies.

For a complete listing of titles, see the last pages of this book.

An Anthology
of Nineteenth-Century
Women's Poetry from France
In English Translation,
with French Text

Edited by
Gretchen Schultz

Translated by Anne Atik, Michael Bishop,
Mary Ann Caws, Melanie Hawthorne,
Rosemary Lloyd, J. S. A. Lowe, Laurence Porter,
Christopher Rivers, Gretchen Schultz, Patricia Terry,
and Rosanna Warren

The Modern Language Association of America
New York   2008

For information about obtaining permission to reprint material from
MLA book publications, send your request by mail (see address below),
e-mail (permissions@mla.org), or fax (646 458-0030).

Library of Congress Cataloging-in-Publication Data

An anthology of nineteenth-century women's poetry from France :
in English translation, with French text / edited by Gretchen Schultz ;
translated by Anne Atik ... [et al.].
p. cm. — (Texts and translations)
Includes bibliographical references.
ISBN 978-1-60329-029-6 (pbk. : alk. paper)
1. French poetry—Women authors. 2. French poetry—19th century.
3. French poetry—Women authors—Translations into English.
4. French poetry—19th century—Translations into English.
I. Schultz, Gretchen, 1960– II. Atik, Anne.
PQ1167.A58 2008
841′.5—dc22   2008021378

Texts and Translations 24
ISSN 1079-252x
ISSN 1079-2538

Cover illustration: Édouard Manet, *Nina de Callias Villard*. Gouache,
graphite. Louvre, Paris. Photograph: Réunion des Musées Nationaux /
Art Resource, NY

Printed on recycled paper

Published by The Modern Language Association of America
26 Broadway, New York, New York 10004-1789
www.mla.org

CONTENTS

ACKNOWLEDGMENTS

I would like to thank Martha Noel Evans for initially proposing this project to me and, with good humor and great skill, guiding me through the initial stages of its review. I am also grateful to those at the MLA who have encouraged my work and shared their insights: the director of book publications, David Nicholls; the anonymous outside reviewers; and the members of the Texts and Translations series editorial board. Their feedback helped me shape this volume into the form it now holds. Michael Kandel copyedited the manuscript with careful attention, and I am obliged to him for his expertise.

Brown University supported the preparation of this anthology with research grants, for which I am appreciative. Thanks also to my research assistants, who helped in identifying and tracking down source texts and compiling the manuscript.

To my undergraduate and graduate students who read and took apart many of these poems with me: our discussions enriched me. Thanks for putting up with photocopies and course packs, prototypes for this anthology, in order to do so. Patsy Baudoin, Dominique Fisher, Tamar Katz, Dian Kriz, Evie Lincoln, Henry Majewski, and

Sonya Stephens all played important roles as sounding boards, aesthetic advisers, writing coaches, and expert consultants: thank you for your erudition, friendship, and encouragement.

I would like in particular to express my appreciation to the translators of the poems that follow, for their good-natured collaboration, their patience over the long haul, their hard and fine work, and for all they have taught me about translation. It was a pleasure to work with you.

Finally, hearthside: my love and gratitude to Alissa and our three little boys, who provide poetry in motion.

INTRODUCTION

This collection presupposes that a poetic canon—any canon—is ideological rather than disinterested and, as a result, inevitably limiting. The art historian Griselda Pollack has criticized canonicity as an "impoverished and impoverishing filter for the totality of cultural possibilities" and a "version of the past [that] ratif[ies] a present order" (4, 10). Anthologizing, a practice that often contributes to canon formation, involves the politics of choice; it establishes selection criteria and asks questions such as, What deserves to be included and what should be left out? What is a good poem, a challenging poem? What kind of reader is assumed by these choices?

This anthology does not intend to enlarge an existing canon or to propose a parallel one; instead, by reinstating long-forgotten textual resources, it aspires to expand our understanding of what poetry meant in and for nineteenth-century France.[1] Male and female poets wrote in dialogue with themselves and each other; poetic values and movements developed in gendered environments. To presume otherwise is to misunderstand the political, cultural, and personal contexts of poetic production and to overlook intertextual relations that open up our readings. The poems in this anthology allow for new modes of reading both with and against—and sometimes regardless of—other poetic texts that are more familiar to twenty-first-century readers.

The nineteenth century is arguably the richest period of lyric production in France since the sixteenth century.[2] From the Romantics through the symbolists and beyond, innovation marked its poetry. Victor Hugo's monumental oeuvre, Charles Baudelaire's modernist aesthetic, Stéphane Mallarmé's poetics of silence, and Arthur Rimbaud's quest for a new language all contributed to revolutionizing poetry and shaping the works of following generations. But literary historians have tended to focus on these four poets and a handful of others to the exclusion of work by women, leaving both lay and academic readers with the impression of an era largely confined to a male-authored corpus and masculinist aesthetic. Indeed, although many nineteenth-century women poets achieved critical and popular prominence during their lifetime, only a few are known or republished today. Most have been out of print for over a century, and nearly all are unavailable in English translation.[3]

A reckoning of nineteenth-century French poetry that takes women's work and subjectivity into account is therefore overdue. This anthology illustrates the wide variety of forces that motivated women to write and counters received notions that contribute to the relegation of their work to the footnotes of literary history. Here we find poets actively involved in—and many marginalized from—the poetic circles of their time, others on the vanguard of poetic change, as well as some whose innovations were overlooked because they were women. Throughout the century, women were involved in important stylistic revolutions, from the birth of elegiac Romanticism to the inauguration of free verse in France. Literary critics are only beginning to study the prosodic and rhetorical strategies employed by women that diverge from dominant models.

Women participated in the literary debates and intellectual inquiries that marked the period. During a time when poetic transformations paralleled political and cultural upheaval, women writers also included social reformers and radicals who countered the apolitical stance of art for art's sake by writing about battles played out in the public sphere. Women poets, moreover, reconfigured love poetry by unsettling the I-thou relationship, defined by convention as that between a male subject and female object. In a genre traditionally devoted to male depictions of heterosexual love, they provided the other side of the story by addressing male love objects. And they broadened the boundaries of poetic intersubjectivity by writing of and to mothers and children, female friends, and women lovers.

The recognition of sexual gender points the way to a reading practice that enriches our understanding of poetry. Although femininity is central to poetry in which muses and female love objects abound, representations of women remained a largely male construct in nineteenth-century France. But women also wrote lyric poetry, a genre devoted to subjective inquiry, and in so doing demanded the right to full presence and authority, the right to answer for themselves the question, How does the "I" trace its contours?

The renewed visibility of women poets allows readers to reimagine what and how poetry means in any number of ways. It necessarily highlights the limitations of conventional literary histories, which tell stories of an almost exclusively masculine poetic tradition in nineteenth-century France. It can be argued that the dominant tradition depends on the exclusion of women's poetry because of what *woman* means in a masculine poetic culture: an aestheticized, malleable object of desire that poets seek to control and perfectly render in their quest for recognition from a male literary elite.[4] Literary critics from the nineteenth century until today have therefore targeted women poets with greater virulence than women novelists.[5] For example, the writer Paul de Molènes (1821–62) asserted in 1842, "Tous les hommes qui ont reçu du ciel une verve originale et un esprit vigoureux . . . ont été d'accord pour condamner les tentatives des poètes femelles" (75; "All men blessed by God with originality and a vigorous mind have united to condemn the endeavors of female poets").[6] "La poésie féminine" ("feminine poetry"), as women's poetic production was often patronizingly labeled, has consistently been represented as minor, derivative, sentimental, and lacking in compositional rigor. The nationalist poet, critic, and polemicist Charles Maurras (1868–1952) decried femininity (which he equated with Romanticism) as a threat to French masculinity, proposing that "le vrai *féminin*, c'est bien de se cacher éternellement" (196; "real femininity means hiding oneself forever"). The metaphor of unveiling recurs persistently in discussions of women's poetry, suggesting that to write poetry is comparable to self-exposure. Jean de Gourmont (1877–1928) insisted:

> Toute femme poète fait un peu le geste . . . de l'amante qui se déshabille pour son amant. Mais c'est une impudeur plus

complète, puisque ces femmes porte-lyres nous révèlent ce
que l'amant le plus perspicace, le plus curieux, ne saurait
découvrir: les secrets mouvements de leur horlogerie sen-
timentale. (28)

All women poets reenact the gesture of a mistress undress-
ing for her lover. But their immodesty is greater, since
these lyre-carrying women reveal to us what the most per-
spicacious and curious lover could not discover: the secret
workings of their sentimental clockwork.

Such relentless disapproval had the effect of discourag-
ing women poets from writing and even moved some of
them to embrace the interdiction themselves. For exam-
ple, Louise Ackermann, who abandoned poetry during
her marriage, later wrote:

Mon mari n'eût pas souffert que sa femme se décolletât,
à plus forte raison lui eût-il défendu de publier des vers.
Écrire, pour une femme, c'est se décolleter ; seulement il
est peut-être moins indécent de montrer ses épaules que
son cœur. (53)

My husband would not have allowed his wife to wear a
low-cut dress, much less to publish poetry. To write, for
a woman, is to expose herself; indeed, it is perhaps more
indecent to bare one's heart than one's shoulders.

The perception that writing poetry was an unbecoming
occupation for women doubtlessly inhibited many oth-
ers from writing or seeking an audience for their work.
    There are many reasons for such furious attacks against
women's poetic production. Foremost among them, it

would seem, is the defense of poetic masculinity. With an aura of genius and grandeur, the prophet-like poet, charged with the momentous task of sounding the limits of the self, of nature, and of the universe, was nothing if not a man. The figure of the poet was above all linked with masculine exceptionality and mastery. Hugo makes that linkage clear in this apostrophe, which associates the poet with both mastery and the sowing of seed: "Ô poète, ô maître, ô semeur" (1: 421; "Fonction du poète") ("O poet, O master, O disseminator" ["The Poet's Function"]). For women to assume a poetic voice imperiled the modern brotherhood of poets. Indeed, it was metaphorically castrating, since it represented women's adoption of the creative function and men's surrender of poetic potency.

The conventions of French poetry, which rely on stringent rules of composition, rendered lyric expression particularly problematic for nonelite women, who had unequal and limited access to education and thus were sometimes poorly equipped to master the structures of French prosody (laws enacted in the early 1880s finally made primary education free and compulsory for girls). Because the novel—unlike poetry, whose genres were centuries older—had a relatively recent tradition, it beckoned to women writers. "It is as if the French female tradition had come into existence in order to create the modern novel" (DeJean 8). Poetic subject positions were also firmly fixed by convention, thus making it more difficult for women to break out of the passive roles of muse and beloved assigned to them and to assume the functions of poet and speaking subject.

While the socioeconomic context and exclusivity of the male literary establishment conspired to discourage women poets, they clearly did not prevent all women from writing. It is perhaps not surprising to discover that, in addition to being verbally gifted,[7] those few women who succeeded in publishing their work often led atypical lives that allowed them to navigate a pathway to achievement despite so many obstacles. Some had fortuitous access to education or were encouraged to write by strong mothers, and occasionally fathers. Most possessed extraordinary drive and did not fear nonconformity. They all braved criticism that was frequently withering. And they had friends.

As the biographies of the poets in this anthology show, literary connections were a major factor in the success of women who became published poets. Recognition by prominent men enabled some young writers to make their verse public. Others who shone in Parisian salon culture, such as Girardin and Colet, cultivated associations with established poets and publishers, while family ties opened doors for still others (Gautier, Houville). Independent wealth removed many obstacles for a privileged few (Vivien). If the achievements of some women relied on patronage as well as talent, the success of other poets was more extraordinary still: those who eschewed the spotlight (Ackermann), women obliged to support themselves and their families financially (Desbordes-Valmore, Michel), and autodidacts who rose from poverty (Mercœur, Blanchecotte). These fourteen poets represent all social classes and achieved distinction in a variety of ways. Similarly, the poems themselves illustrate diverse strategies for acceptance or recognition—among them, submission to preconceived notions of femininity, particularly among the Romantic poets; irony and pastiche

(e.g., Villard); and outright defiance of poetic norms (Kry-
sinska) or social conventions (Vivien).

To appreciate these strategies, we must reconsider lit-
erary history and read poetry in a way that recognizes
women's poetic production and the profound gendering
of aesthetic values.[8] The result is a narrative about poetic
creation that accounts for difference, one that analyzes
the evolving contexts and politics of the major poetic
moments of the century (Romanticism, Parnassianism,
symbolism) in their relation to sexual and social other-
ness. We can then see how Romantic ideology provided
a relatively hospitable environment for women poets,
since male poets of the period lauded and even assumed
the supposedly feminine qualities of sensitivity and
introspection. Consequently, women poets were widely
read during the first half of the century. Yet their critical
acceptance was often predicated on their conformity to
masculine parameters and obedience to gender norms.
When Delphine Gay de Girardin betrayed too much
(masculine) ambition, for example, Molènes chided her
for exhibiting "cette fatale prétention . . . [d]es idées ambi-
tieuses et exagérées" (71; "the fatal pretension . . . of ambi-
tious and exaggerated ideas").

But the sentimentality and effusion associated with
Romanticism lost favor. Emotion came to be disastrous
for poetry (see Collot), and, with the repudiation of sen-
timentality, femininity became anathema to the poetic
endeavor. Not only extremists such as Maurras equated
femininity with Romanticism. Beginning in the 1840s,
the popularity of Romanticism and, in particular, of
women's poetry rapidly declined. At mid-century, poets
of the movement that would come to be known as Par-

nassianism championed a particularly outspoken masculinist poetics, which privileged objective description and a return to formalism. In reaction to Romanticism, the Parnasse's most prominent poets railed against the softness or effeminacy of the Romantics. The poet and outspoken theoretician Charles Leconte de Lisle took aim at what he considered to be their emotional excesses, egotistical focus on the self, compositional slackness, and bleeding-heart political engagement. Parnassian poets assured the neutralization of femininity by unrelentingly representing women as static and statuesque in their poems. Such prevalent antifeminism made it more difficult for women poets to find an audience during the third quarter of the century, when Parnassianism flourished. Few women managed to break ranks during the Parnassian period, and fewer still achieved popular success, as Louisa Siefert did.

The symbolist aesthetic that followed seemingly created the conditions for welcoming women poets back into the fold. Its refusal of dogmatism, its cultivation of the new and unpredictable, and its exploration of otherness all set the scene for the inclusion of minority voices. After the Parnassian era of restricted inquiry, symbolist poets worked to surmount existing poetic boundaries and, in ways previously unimagined, placed subjectivity and difference at the heart of their thinking about the lyric. Arthur Rimbaud wrote famously, "Quand sera brisé l'infini servage de la femme, quand elle vivra pour elle et par elle, . . . elle sera poète, elle aussi! La femme trouvera de l'inconnu" (*Œuvres* 252; "When the endless servitude of woman is broken, when she lives for and by herself . . . she too will be a poet! Woman will find

some of the unknown" [*Complete Works* 379]). Yet femi-
nist theoretical and aesthetic positions such as Rimbaud's
did not translate into activist politics or even professional
acceptance and inclusion. Some of the most innova-
tive symbolist women were all but banished from male
poetic circles. Marie Krysinska was moved to write that
her male peers "[avait décrété qu'] une initiative émanant
d'une femme . . . peut être considérée comme ne venant
de nulle part" (*Intermèdes* xxi; "decreed that an initiative
coming from a woman could be considered to have come
from nowhere").[9] Even so, she and other women poets at
the century's end were bolder than their predecessors in
demanding that contemporary poetry live up to its prom-
ise of accommodating new voices.

In selecting the poems to be included in this anthol-
ogy, I have embraced symbolism's professed prefer-
ence for the unfamiliar, the multiple, the equivocal, the
ephemeral—in short, for the most modern poetic values
of the century. Without sacrificing representativeness, I
include poems that belie clichés of women's writing as
overly sentimental and necessarily domestic in concern.
In fact, this poetry is surprisingly invested in the public
sphere: it addresses such sociopolitical problems and
realities as slavery (Desbordes-Valmore), racial difference
(Girardin), nationalist movements (Colet), popular upris-
ings and worker rebellions (Michel), and class oppression
(Blanchecotte). These representations of outsiders and
other worlds often resonate with the poets' own strug-
gles, as sexual and social others, against discrimination.

Even poems having the anticipated domestic and inti-
mate themes of marriage, motherhood, children, and love

often challenge received ideas about women's poetry. Alongside Marceline Desbordes-Valmore's tableaux of maternal devotion and sacrifice, other women chose to write as daughters and represent mothers and maternity in complex and unpredictable ways. Malvina Blanche-cotte's "À ma mère" ("To My Mother"), for example, denounces a neglectful mother and, in so doing, contradicts the perception of women's poetry as idealistic and often saccharine (see other daughter poems by Nina de Villard and Gérard d'Houville). Contrary to this stereotype, Ackermann, Krysinska, and others manifest a profound cynicism toward the possibility of a true, idealized love. In "L'amour et la mort" ("Love and Death"), Ackermann depicts self-involved lovers as unwitting dupes of the reproductive imperative who are oblivious to the inevitability of death, and Krysinska's representation of young lovers is highly ironic ("Idylle" ["Idyll"]).

Moreover, a number of these poets express a sensuality that surpasses the bounds of conjugal reproductive heterosexuality. They explore the limits of physical passion, such as the intense sexual arousal that Desbordes-Valmore projects onto a rain-drenched garden in "La jeune fille et le ramier" ("The Young Girl and the Ring Dove"). Krysinska inventories the innumerable ways to touch in "Poème des caresses" ("The Poem of Caresses"), and Houville celebrates the sexual freedom of youth in "Vœu" ("Wish"). Likewise, the subjective lesbian poetry of Renée Vivien (and, more covertly, that of Gautier and Houville) places the objectifying lesbian poetry of Baudelaire and his contemporaries in a new light. Refusing the models of Baudelaire's "femmes damnées" (1: 113–14, 152–55;

"damned women") (in *Les fleurs du mal* [1857; *The Flowers of Evil*]), Paul Verlaine's naively titillating schoolgirls (486–89) (in *Les amies* [1867; *Girlfriends*]), or Pierre Louÿs's Sapphic women, these poets navigate the uncharted representational terrain of female homoeroticism.

Women authors examine the question of feminine beauty, the raison d'être of so much male-authored poetry, in startling, different ways. The figure of the mirror, no longer a clichéd symbol of female narcissism, takes on new and multiple meanings. For example, Krysinska writes of "cette grave entrevue" ("this grave meeting") with the mirror of self-scrutiny ("Devant le miroir" ["In Front of the Mirror"]), and Houville studies the mirror as a metaphor for solitary introspection in "L'ombre" ("The Shadow"). These poets analyze feminine appearance, finery, and adornment from a place of experience and in a manner fundamentally different from the Romantics' naturalized vision of ideal feminine beauty or the decadent tribute to the artificiality of makeup. Instead, they explore the relation between surface and interiority, turning a conventional poetic topos into an opportunity for subjective inquiry. While Girardin juxtaposes the happiness of beauty with the misfortunes of homeliness, Krysinska contrasts the pomp of feminine finery with the severe habit of a self-reflective nun ("La parure" ["Dressing Up"]). And Siefert rejects the accoutrements that do not fulfill their promise to procure love: "Rentrez dans vos cartons, robe, rubans, résille!" ("Back in your boxes, dress, lacework, ribbons!") ("Tristesse" ["Sadness"]). Aging is also a preoccupation, although one represented differently from such dehumanizing portraits as Baudelaire's "Les petites vieilles" ("Little Old Women"), which masculinizes and desexualizes the "êtres . . . décrépits" ("decrepit beings") and "monstres disloqués" ("dislocated monsters") who haunt the modern city (1: 89). Painfully aware of beauty's social capital, Louise Colet's speaking subject laments her whitening hair in "Mezza vita," and Amable Tastu's old woman looks back with regret on her disappointing life ("L'ange gardien" ["Guardian Angel"]).[10]

The poetry in this collection represents a variety of styles and chronicles important poetic innovations, thus placing into question the oft repeated assertion that women's poetry lacks originality. It took 170 years for Desbordes-Valmore to be credited with the inauguration of Romantic poetry, traditionally attributed to Alphonse de Lamartine (see Johnson). Feminist critics have only recently begun to study Krysinska's contribution to the invention of free verse. Similarly, topics such as Villard's revolt against poetic conformity, Mercœur's participation in the Romantic cult of the author, and Blanchecotte's urban poetry call for analysis.

Finally, the selections in this anthology illuminate the ways in which women poets reflect on the poetic enterprise and literary renown. Their precarious social positions frequently moved them to write about protection, whether in the form of a reimagined muse or a guardian angel (Tastu, Krysinska). Some used male pseudonyms, for a variety of reasons that merit further study (Gautier, Houville, Vivien). Some appeal to a powerful addressee, and their poems are often dedicated to prominent male writers. But they also address other women and engage in dialogues among themselves. Many of the poems included here show not only how these women interacted with and challenged the dominant tradition but also that they associated with and referenced one another (Desbordes-Valmore's "Roses de Saadi," to give one example, finds an echo in Vivien's "Roses du soir"). They were in frequent dialogue with one another: they dedicated to, borrowed from, responded to, honored, and occasionally ironized one another—just as they did the male poets whose works eclipsed theirs.

Women poets of the period frequently avoided Hugoesque displays of self-importance, which habitually accompany the quest for renown: Vivien predicted anonymity, while Desbordes-Valmore seemed to welcome it. This ostensible refusal to chase glory carried an implicit criticism of the traditional trope of virtuosic masculine genius. Yet others—Mercœur, Colet, Krysinska—openly displayed their ambitions and demanded recognition.

This collection therefore examines women's relations to lyric expression and to authorship, exemplifying their efforts to inhabit the canon, to contradict it, or to do away with it altogether. It reassesses literary history by going beyond an exclusively male-authored corpus; by reconsidering who or what determines poetic value; and, finally, by inviting readers to reevaluate what and how poetry means.[11]

Notes

[1]In keeping with the conventions of French literary history, the nineteenth century is here understood to extend from the French Revolution to the beginning of the Great War (1789–1914). The poems in this volume date from the 1820s, when Romanticism first took hold in France, to the first decade of the twentieth century.

[2]The French Renaissance was an exceptional era for poetry, from the "grands rhétoriqueurs" to the members of the Pléiade (notably Joachim du Bellay [1522?–60] and Pierre de Ronsard [1524–85]) and the École Lyonnaise. In addition to Maurice Scève (c. 1500–62), this last group included two prominent women poets, Pernette du Guillet (c. 1520–45) and Louise Labé (1524?–66).

[3]Christine Planté's *Femmes poètes du XIXe siècle* (1998), an excellent anthology and one to which this volume is indebted, is no longer in print.

[4]On the real and symbolic barriers to women becoming or being recognized as poets, see Paliyenko; Planté, "Quel compte"; Schultz, *Gendered Lyric*.

[5]The quotations that follow are from some of the most belligerently antifeminist critics of the period. Molènes attacked Desbordes-Valmore, Tastu, Girardin, and Colet (see Desbordes-Valmore's response in this volume, "Jeune homme irrité..."). Maurras and Gourmont both criticized Houville and Vivien. Barbey d'Aurevilly targeted Desbordes-Valmore, Girardin, Colet, and Ackermann (resp., in vols. 3, 5, and 11). But Crépet's volume contained praise for Desbordes-Valmore, Tastu, Girardin, and Ackermann; and Sainte-Beuve wrote approvingly of Desbordes-Valmore, Tastu, Girardin, and Blanchecotte (resp., in *Causeries* 3: 1–52, *Table* 1–21; *Causeries* 3: 384–406, and *Causeries* 15: 327–32).

[6]All translations are mine unless otherwise indicated.

[7]Many were multilingual. Krysinska's native language was Polish, but she made her career writing in French. Vivien negotiated between her native English and French, the language in which she wrote. It is perhaps not surprising, then, to find so many translators among the women poets represented in this volume. Fully half of them translated from a variety of sources—Romance and Germanic, but also Asian languages (Gautier) and Ancient Greek (Vivien).

[8]For an elaboration of this argument and analysis of the ideologies of sex and gender inherent in nineteenth-century French poetry, see Schultz, *Gendered Lyric*.

[9]The essay "On Rational Evolutions: Esthetics and Philology," published as the introduction to Krysinska's third and final collection of poetry, *Intermèdes* (1903), is her ars poetica. In it, Krysinska sets forth her poetic method, explains her part in the invention of free verse, and defends herself against her detractors (114).

[10]On representations of aging women in nineteenth-century poetry, see Schultz, "Through the Looking Glass."

[11]It is my hope that this compilation will move students and scholars to read further in source texts by the poets included as well as other poets who were not because of limitations of space and the editor's (undoubtedly partial) selection process. See, for example, Adélaïde Dufrénoy (1765–1825), Anaïs Ségalas (1814–93), Léocadie Penquer (1817–89), Marie Nizet (1859–1922), Marie Dauguet (1860–1942), Jane Catulle Mendès (1867–1965), Lucie Delarue-Mardrus (1874–1945), and Anna de Noailles (1876–1933). For a more exhaustive list of nineteenth- and early-twentieth-century women poets, see the "Répertoire" in

Planté 217–21. I refer the reader in search of broader historical selections to the collections edited by Séché; Moulin; Deforges; and to Shapiro's and Stanton's bilingual volumes.

Works Cited

Ackermann, Louise. *Pensées d'une solitaire*. Paris: Lemerre, 1882.

Barbey d'Aurevilly, Jules-Amédée *Les œuvres et les hommes*. 1860–1909. 26 vols. Geneva: Slatkine, 1968.

Baudelaire, Charles. *Œuvres complètes*. Ed. Claude Pichois. 2 vols. Paris: Gallimard, 1975–76.

Collot, Michel. *La matière-émotion*. Paris: PUF, 1997.

Crépet, M. Eugène, ed. *Les contemporains*. Paris: Quantin, 1887. Vol. 4 of *Les poètes français*.

Deforges, Régine, ed. *Poèmes de femmes des origines à nos jours*. Paris: Cherche Midi, 1993.

DeJean, Joan. *Tender Geographies: Women and the Origins of the Novel in France*. New York: Columbia UP, 1991.

Gourmont, Jean de. *Les muses d'aujourd'hui*. Paris: Mercure de France, 1910.

Hugo, Victor. *Poésie*. Ed. Bernard Leuilliot. 3 vols. Paris: Seuil, 1972.

Johnson, Barbara. "The Lady in the Lake." *A New History of French Literature*. Ed. Denis Hollier. Cambridge: Harvard UP, 1989. 627–32.

Krysinska, Marie. *Intermèdes: Nouveaux rythmes pittoresques*. Paris: Messein, 1903.

———. "On Rational Evolutions: Esthetics and Philology." Trans. Gretchen Schultz. *Nineteenth-Century Women Seeking Expression: Translations from the French*. Ed. Rosemary Lloyd. Liverpool Online Ser.: Critical Editions of French Texts 2. Liverpool: U of Liverpool, 2000. 113–23. 20 Nov. 2007 <http://www.liv.ac.uk/soclas/los/women.pdf>.

Leconte de Lisle, Charles. *Articles, préfaces, discours*. Paris: Belles Lettres, 1971.

Louÿs, Pierre. *Chansons de Bilitis*. 1894. Paris: Gallimard, 1990.

Maurras, Charles. "Le romantisme féminin: Allégorie du sentiment désordonné." 1904. *Romantisme et révolution*. Paris: Nouvelle Librairie Nationale, 1925. 131–203.

Molènes, Paul de. "Les femmes poètes." *La revue des deux mondes* July 1842: 48–76.

Moulin, Jeanine. *La poésie féminine du XIIᵉ au XIXᵉ siècles*. 2 vols. Paris: Seghers, 1966.

Paliyenko, Adrianna. "Re(placing) Women in French Poetic History: The Romantic Legacy." *Symposium* 53.4 (2000): 261–82.

Planté, Christine, ed. *Femmes poètes du XIXe siècle: Une anthologie.* Lyon: PU de Lyon, 1998.

————. "Quel compte donc fais-tu des femmes? Femmes et poésie en France au XIXe siècle." *Romantisme* 85 (1994): 67–78.

Pollack, Griselda. *Differencing the Canon.* London: Routledge, 1999.

Rimbaud, Arthur. *Complete Works, Selected Letters: A Bilingual Edition.* Trans. Wallace Fowlie. Ed. Seth Whidden. Chicago: U of Chicago P, 1966, 2005.

————. *Œuvres complètes.* Ed. Antoine Adam. Paris: Gallimard, 1972.

Sainte-Beuve, Charles. *Causeries du lundi.* 15 vols. Paris: Garnier, n.d.

————. *Table générale et analytique.* Paris: Garnier, n.d.

Schultz, Gretchen. *The Gendered Lyric: Subjectivity and Difference in Nineteenth-Century French Poetry.* West Lafayette: Purdue UP, 1999.

————. "Through the Looking Glass: Relections of Aging Women in the Poetry of Nineteenth-Century France." *Romance Studies* 26.3 (2008): 233–48.

Séché, Alphonse. *Les muses françaises: Anthologie des femmes poètes, 1200 à 1891.* Paris: Louis-Michaud, 1908.

Shapiro, Norman R., ed. and trans. *French Women Poets of Nine Centuries: The Distaff and the Pen.* Fwd. Rosanna Warren. Baltimore: Johns Hopkins UP, 2008.

Stanton, Domna, ed. *The Defiant Muse: French Feminist Poems from the Middle Ages to the Present: A Bilingual Anthology.* New York: Feminist, 1986.

Verlaine, Paul. *Œuvres poétiques complètes.* Ed. Y.-G. Dantec and Jacques Borel. Paris: Gallimard, 1962.

PRIMARY TEXTS

Where possible, the most recent editions of poems included in this volume have been consulted. Minor changes have been made to modernize spelling, regularize punctuation, and correct errors and omissions.

Ackermann, Louise. *Œuvres: Ma vie, Premières poésies, Poésies philosophiques*. 1874. Paris: L'Harmattan, 2005.

Blanchecotte, Malvina. *Les militantes: Poésies*. Paris: Lemerre, 1875.

——. *Rêves et réalités: Poésies*. Paris: Ledoyen, 1855.

Colet, Louise. "Absorption dans l'amour." *Le parnasse contemporain* 3 (1876): 78.

——. *Ce qu'on rêve en aimant*. Paris: Librairie nouvelle, 1854.

——. "Pæstum." *Le parnasse contemporain* 2 (1871): 135.

——. *Poésies complètes*. Paris: Gosselin, 1844.

Desbordes-Valmore, Marceline. *Œuvre poétique intégrale*. Ed. Marc Bertrand. Lyon: André, 2007.

Gautier, Judith. *Poésies: Les rites divins, Au gré du rêve, Badinages, Pour la lyre*. Paris: Charpentier, 1911.

Girardin, Madame Émile de (Delphine Gay). *Poésies complètes*. Paris: Charpentier, 1842.

Houville, Gérard d'. *Poésies*. Paris: Grasset, 1931.

Krysinska, Marie. *Intermèdes: Nouveaux rythmes pittoresques*. Paris: Messein, 1903.

————. *Joies errantes: Nouveaux rythmes pittoresques.* Paris: Lemerre, 1894.

————. *Rythmes pittoresques: Mirages, Symboles, Femmes, Contes, Résurrections.* 1890. Ed. and introd. Seth Whidden. U of Exeter P, 2003.

Mercœur, Élisa. *Œuvres complètes.* 3 vols. Paris: Pommeret, 1843.

Michel, Louise. *À travers la vie et la mort: Œuvre poétique.* Ed. Daniel Armogathe and Marion Piper. Paris: La Découverte, 2001.

Siefert, Louisa. *Rayons perdus.* Paris: Lemerre, 1868.

————. *Les saintes colères.* Paris: Lemerre, 1871.

————. *Les stoïques.* Paris: Lemerre, 1870.

Tastu, Amable. *Poésies complètes:* Premières poésies, Poésies nouvelles, Chroniques de France. Paris: Didier, 1858.

Villard, Nina de. *Feuillets parisiens, poésies.* Paris: Messager, 1885.

Vivien, Renée. *Poèmes.* 2 vols. Paris: Lemerre, 1923-24. New York: Arno, 1975 .

NOTE ON THE TRANSLATIONS

On French Versification

Because of significant dissimilarities between French and English versification, reading and translating French poetry can prove challenging for native Anglophones. While space prohibits a detailed exposition of French versification, this overview sets forth essential elements that might be unfamiliar to some readers.[1] The most notable difference between French- and English-language poetry is prosodic—that is, having to do with the kind of meter used to build poetic rhythm. Stress does not function the same in French and English. In English, the accent falls predictably within a word, usually on the penultimate (e.g., *eternal*) or antepenultimate (e.g., *forgetfulness*) syllable. In French, stress within a word is variable, falling instead on the final syllable of a word grouping (e.g., "une chaîne éter*nelle*," "l'éternel ou*bli*"). Hence French verse relies on a consistent number of syllables, rather than a consistent number of accents or beats, in a given line: it is syllabic rather than accentual.[2]

The twelve-syllable line is the most common in nineteenth-century French verse. Called the alexandrine, it is conventionally divided by a caesura (a pause within

the line) into two six-syllable hemistiches (half lines).[3]
Decasyllabic (ten-syllable) and octosyllabic (eight-syllable)
lines are also frequently employed. Shorter and uneven
lines are unusual in French, with the exception of the
heptasyllabic (seven-syllable) line, which is often used in
songs or lighthearted verse (in this volume, see Gautier's
"Bulle de savon" and Houville's "Vœu"). Desbordes-
Valmore presents an interesting case, since she employed
a wide variety of meters, both even and uneven, and
composed many heterometric poems built on recurring
patterns of different line types (e.g., see her "À Délie").

The pronunciation of French poetry differs markedly
from spoken French, thus affecting the determination of
line lengths. In particular, the mute *e* or *e caduc*, always
unstressed and often unpronounced in spoken French, is
pronounced in poetry and thus has the value of a syllable
when it precedes a consonant ("d'étoffe soyeuse"). When,
on the contrary, it precedes a vowel ("une oreille"), it is
elided and silent (and is equally silent in the end rhyme).[4]
As indicated in the following decasyllable from Colet, the
final *e* in "Vésuve" is not pronounced, since it is followed
by a vowel, whereas the preconsonantal *e* in "gronde"
and in "sourdement" is pronounced and therefore counts
as a syllable:

   1   2   3   4   5   6   7   8   9   10
   Le Vésuv[e] au loin gronde sourdement

French rhyme, moreover, conventionally relies on
stringent rules, in particular the requirement to alternate
masculine and feminine rhymes in a poem. The pres-
ence or absence of a final mute *e* determines rhyme gen-

der. Rhymes ending in an unpronounced *e* (or plural *es*) are considered to be feminine, whereas those ending in any other letter (including an accented *e*) are masculine. Grammatical gender has no bearing on rhyme gender. For example, "un homme" and "une pomme" form a feminine rhyme, while "la beauté" and "la difformité," both grammatically feminine, are masculine in rhyme. French poets traditionally paid attention to the richness of rhymes: the more sounds used to build a rhyme, the stronger or richer it is. A poor rhyme is made of words sharing a single vowel (*feu* and *jeu*: /ø/); a sufficient rhyme shares a consonant and a vowel (*difficile* and *asile*: /il/; *pleurer* and *soupirer*: /Re/); and a rich rhyme contains a vowel and two consonants (*larme* and *charme*: /aRm/; *mer* and *amer*: /mɛR/). A very rich rhyme involves additional phonemes (*respire* and *inspire*), and a leonine rhyme contains two or more syllables (*avenir* and *souvenir*).

Nearly all the rules governing rhyme and rhythm spelled out here, many dating to the sixteenth century,[5] were overthrown during the nineteenth century. The Romantic poets used enjambment to defy classical requirements for symmetrical lines of poetry.[6] For example, they attenuaed the midline caesura to create the trimeter alexandrine, composed of three measures of four syllables instead of two hemistiches of six: "Le prêtre est là, | marquant le prix | des funérailles" (in Desbordes-Valmore's "Dans la rue par un jour funèbre de Lyon") or "Voilà pourquoi | mon cœur vous aime | avec faiblesse" (in Colet's "Folles et saintes").

But such Romantic departures from classical prosody were minor compared with the symbolist poets' dismantling of traditional verse. The symbolists began to ignore the caesura and to use outrageous enjambments, thereby mocking the classical alexandrine (Verlaine's "vers libéré" ["liberated verse"]). They ceased to respect the regular alternation of masculine and feminine rhymes, replaced rhyme with assonance, or did away with rhyme altogether. They played with fixed forms, turning sonnets upside down (such sonnets were called inverted) or writing them in prose. Baudelaire and his followers explored the poetry of prose, thus inaugurating the prose poem, which became an integral part of twentieth-century poetry. When Krysinska and Rimbaud failed to account for the mute -*e* and stopped counting syllables, free verse was born. This response was about invention as much as destruction, a period of poetic liberation described by Mallarmé in his essay "Crise de vers" (1886).

Principles of Translation

Because, as Clive Scott has written, a translation cannot seek to reproduce but rather strives to reembody its source text (*Channel Crossings* 1), this volume approaches translation as a confrontation of two languages that optimally leads to two equally significant texts. As such, translation is an exchange between different linguistic and cultural structures. The translations in this volume aim first and foremost to respect both the source text and the poetic act; they illustrate a precarious balance between rendering a poet's work and making it new.

A selection of poetry by women, this collection pays particular attention to the work of gender in all aspects of the text, from prosodic to symbolic. Since women's poetry is rarely gender-neutral, the translators and editor have worked to illuminate features with which and moments in which the play of gender points to divergences from a dominant, or canonical, tradition. Most tangibly, gender can pose linguistic problems for the translator, particularly in a language, such as French, that is grammatically gendered. Desbordes-Valmore's "Son image" offers a fitting illustration of the exploitation of noun gender to create poetic ambiguity.

On the level of representation, the poems included here convey a culture and its points of reference, a variety of aesthetic outlooks, and diverse ideological viewpoints—all seen through the lens of gender difference. It is the translator's task to transmit this richness. The poems depict female figures in a variety of stances, from frozen statues to lovers in motion, from incendiaries prepared to throw bombs to musicians poised to play. They communicate the varying sentiments that intersubjective relationships can inspire: desire and tenderness, despair and rage, ambivalence and cynicism. They comment on the writing of poetry and its reception by both male and female readers. They draw from networks of mythological and symbolic references and in so doing resurrect ancient goddesses (Venus, Diana, the Fates) and reinvent cultural icons (Salomé). These translations therefore strive to convey poetic voices that speak about gendered experiences, voices that are at once both highly subjective and necessarily political. In order to render the subjectivities inscribed in these poems, translators have paid as much attention to precise phrasing as they have to something as elusive as mood. They have therefore translated and the editor has therefore edited with a mind to both personal and social contexts. These translations do the work of conveying a time and a place—a modernizing, expansionist nation rocked by revolutions and war—that sometimes seem far removed from twenty-first-century America and sometimes feel very close.

The translations strive, moreover, to illuminate and create a pathway to the aesthetic framework of the source texts. Because this volume is to a degree a pedagogical tool, I have encouraged contributing translators to stay fairly close structurally to the source texts in order to capture the variety of styles and evolution of forms in the nineteenth-century tradition. Because of the range of poetic techniques represented—from neoclassical to free verse and from intricate rhyme patterns to unrhymed poems—translators have negotiated a variety of confrontations between two disparate traditions. They have followed, as much as possible, the forms and visual presentation of the source texts and employed poetic structures that are equivalent or analogous to the French. Hence Rosanna Warren reflects Desbordes-Valmore's heterometric "À Délie" with a rhythmic structure and a typographic disposition that are analogous to the source text. Rosemary Lloyd's translations of Krysinska preserve the poet's ironic italics and proliferation of dashes and observe the syntax, marked by refrains, of the free-verse source texts. And Melanie Hawthorne has rendered Vivien's neoclassical French prosody by maintaining its syllabism, an unusual poetic strategy in the Anglo-American tradition (although famously employed by the twentieth-century American poet Marianne Moore). Some translators have reconciled the French syllabic and English accentual metric systems by using lines that are more or less cultural equivalents, such as substituting iambic pentameter for the French alexandrine—close in length, both carry the gravitas of tradition.

On a semantic level I have also encouraged the use of cognates where possible, although never at the expense of a poem's music. An overly literal translation runs the risk of sounding stilted, while linguistic flexibility expands the possibilities of achieving sound patterns that heighten the poetic value of the translation. The translations also heed the varying linguistic registers of the source texts, from the sometimes popular diction of Blanchecotte, Michel, and Villard to the more formal language of Tastu, Ackermann, and Siefert.

Given the array of contributing translators, strategies used and choices made are necessarily varied. Those who worked on this project are native speakers of American English, British English, and Australian English. Although most are scholars of French literature, and of French poetry in particular, some are poets from outside the academy. This diversity means different solutions for a given translation problem, differences that are illuminating to analyze. For example, the translator faces the question of how to render language that the passage of time has made archaic. Some strive for the freshness of the poem at the moment it was written and match nineteenth-century French colloquialisms with equally informal language in translation (see Lowe's contemporary Americanisms). Others mark the distance between the moment of composition and the moment of translation by tending toward greater formality in word choice and phrasing (as is Porter's and Bishop's tendency). The reader will note that approaches to rhyme and rhythm also vary according to the translator. For example, some have favored full rhymes (Porter, Hawthorne), while others have provided unrhymed translations (Caws and Terry, Bishop), and still others have opted for assonance or half rhymes.

With regard to these and other musical considerations in translation (alliteration and assonance, syntax and phrasing), I have felt it important to respect the diverse approaches and sensibilities that contributors bring to their work. The French poems' phonic structures perhaps cannot be translated so much as transposed through use of analogous sound patterns in English. Scott has called translation a "mode of linguistic exploration," but one in which the target language does all the work as it struggles with itself to render the source text (*Channel Crossings* 2). The very problems that confront the translator, from local word choices to marking echoes between different poems and poets, lead to solutions that allow poetry to happen a second time, in a different way.

Steven Yao has called translation "a complex cultural activity" that can "functio[n] as a strategy for negotiating issues of gender," among other differences (16, 18). We might then take translation as a figure for women's poetry: both live under the sign of difference and struggle with a prevailing discourse. Often marginalized as outsider language, women's poetry can function as rewriting, as the transposition of gendered cultures (see Simon). Just as the poets presented here confronted numerous obstacles to writing and publication, so must their poems cross various borders—geographic, linguistic, temporal—in order to reach a modern anglophone audience. The audience for which these translations are intended is varied: lay lovers of poetry both proficient in and unacquainted with the French language, students of French literature and gender studies, and specialists in these areas. The goal of this volume is to make these relatively unknown works available to all such readers, in the hope that the poets who wrote them, lost for so many years, will be found again—in translation.

Notes

[1] See the guides to French versification by Mazaleyrat; Scott, *Poetics*. On English versification, see Pinsky; Hollander.

[2] The rhythms of accentual-syllabic English-language poetry are determined instead by counting regular units or feet, which count each as a beat. The two-syllable iamb and three-syllable anapest, whose stresses fall on the final syllable, are the building blocks of English poetry (trochees and dactyls, dyads and triads respectively, place the stress on the first syllable). Iambic pentameter, the most prominent example, is a poetic line pattern constructed of five iambs. In practice, however, poets vary its rhythms by introducing other feet into the line.

[3] The caesura indicates fixed pauses in longer lines and so is found only in the alexandrine and the decasyllable (where there are two possible divisions: 4/6 or, less frequently, 5/5). In shorter poems and within a hemistich, unfixed pauses are called *coupes* ("breaks"), which divide the line into measures.

[4] French poetry traditionally avoids hiatus, the juxtaposition of two vowels. When two vowels are found together, a distinction is made between syneresis, in which they are pronounced as one syllable, and dieresis, in which they are separated into two. Compare, for example, Tastu's rhymes in "Ange gardien": "carrière-première" provides an example of syneresis, "mystérieuse-ambitieuse" of dieresis.

[5] Many of the rules and forms of modern French poetry date to innovations by sixteenth-century poets and to subsequent codifications by the classical poets of the seventeenth century. Du Bellay's influential *Défense et illustration de la langue française* (1549) rejected medieval fixed forms (such as the rondeau, virelay, and ballade), borrowed from antiquity (odes, elegies) and Italy (the sonnet), and called for the reinvention of a national poetic tradition.

Clément Marot's introduction and Ronsard and Du Bellay's subsequent popularization of the Petrarchan love sonnet (named for the fourteenth-century Italian poet) had a profound impact on the French, both formally and thematically.

Another important development during this time was the resurrection, by Ronsard, of the alexandrine, which gained such prominence that Mallarmé later called it the "national cadence"(362). The far less inventive seventeenth-century tradition, called classical for its rigorous attention to prosodic detail, avoidance of excess, emphasis on reason over imagination, and insistence on purity and symmetry, laid down rhythmic requirements that Romantic and, later, symbolist poets delighted in rejecting.

⁶Nicolas Boileau's *Art poétique* (1674) decried enjambment (literally, a "striding over"), which occurs when the syntactic unit (phrase or sentence) spills over beyond the limits of the metric unit (measure or line). Boileau demanded that caesuras be firmly marked and that the end of the line coincide with the end of a phrase.

Works Cited

Boileau-Despréaux, Nicolas. *L'art poétique*. 1674. Paris: Flammarion, 1998.

Du Bellay, Joachim. *La deffence, et illustration de la langue françoyse*. 1549. Ed. Jean-Charles Monferran. Geneva: Droz, 2001.

Hollander, John. *Rhyme's Reason: A Guide to English Verse*. New Haven: Yale UP, 1989.

Mallarmé, Stéphane. *Œuvres complètes*. Ed. Henri Mondor. Paris: Gallimard, 1945.

Mazaleyrat, Jean. *Éléments de métrique française*. Paris: Colin, 1974.

Pinsky, Robert. *The Sounds of Poetry: A Brief Guide*. New York: Farrar, 1998.

Scott, Clive. *Channel Crossings: French and English Poetry in Dialogue*. Oxford: Legenda, 2002.

———. *The Poetics of French Verse: Studies in Reading*. Oxford: Clarendon, 1998.

Simon, Sherry. *Gender in Translation*. London: Routledge, 1996.

Yao, Steven. *Translation and the Languages of Modernism: Gender, Politics, Language*. New York: Palgrave, 2002.

An Anthology
of Nineteenth-Century
Women's Poetry from France

Romanticism: Revolutions and Interiority

Broadly defined, the aesthetic of French Romanticism took shape during the period beginning with the Revolution of 1789 and the turbulent years that followed and endured to the middle of the nineteenth century. Politically, its adherents ranged from defenders of legitimism to idealistic social protesters and reformers. Germaine de Staël (1766–1817) supplied the movement's first theoretical elaboration in France, in her analysis of German Romantic poetry (*De l'Allemagne* [1813]). Contrasting the new sensibility with the classical quest for formal perfection, she pointed to emotionality, enthusiasm, and imagination as essential characteristics of Romantic expression. Nature, and its relation to introspection, became an important focus of the Romantic experience. Fueled by colonial expansion and travel literature, the exoticism of foreign cultures (particularly of Spain, the north and west African colonies, and the Persian empire) was also a privileged theme. Orientalism took hold of French literature, and its influence grew throughout the century.

As it developed in France, Romanticism's mood was sometimes heroic, often sorrowful (melancholia became known as "le mal du siècle" ["the malady of the century"]), and its writers consequently favored elegiac poetry. Its highly subjective voice, emotional effusion, and apparent spontaneity called for longer, narrative forms, rarely the short fixed genres, such as the sonnet, which would return later in the century (on the revival of long forms under French Romanticism, see Porter, *Renaissance*). Romantic prosody is typically associated with the repudiation of classicism and a loosening of the rigid requirements of French versification. In particular, the Romantics rendered the traditionally symmetrical alexandrine more supple with hardier use of enjambment and by deemphasizing the midline caesura.

The most prominent Romantics are Alphonse de Lamartine (1790–1869), Alfred de Vigny (1797–1863), Victor Hugo (1802–85), Gérard de Nerval (1808–55), and Alfred de Musset (1810–57). While seeing the poet as a prophet or interpreter of nature, they also emphasized qualities associated with femininity, such as sensitivity and emotionality: Hugo described the poet as an "homme [qui] est doux comme une femme" [1: 424; "a man who is soft like a woman"]. The tangible result was a proliferation of female poets. Nonetheless, the tragic grandeur of the solitary Romantic hero consolidated the identification of the poet with masculine genius. And despite success during their lifetime, women Romantic poets are mostly unknown today.

The harsh repression following the 1848 revolution, which put an end to the July Monarchy (1830–48), encouraged the decline of the idealism that fed the Romantic movement. When its poetry fell into disfavor, many once-successful women poets abandoned verse for more lucrative and traditionally feminine genres, such as children's literature (e.g., Desbordes-Valmore, Tastu, Colet). A number of Romantic poets, women in particular, fell into obscurity (Mercœur, Tastu). Some adopted other poetic styles (Colet).

For further reading, see Baale-Uittenbosch; Bénichou, *Mages* and *Temps*; Boutin, "Inventing"; Boutin and Paliyenko; Bowman; Jenson, *Trauma*; Planté, *Petite sœur*; Schultz, *Gendered Lyric*; Vincent.

MARCELINE DESBORDES-VALMORE

(1786–1859)

née Félicité Josèphe Marceline Desbordes

Translations by J. S. A. Lowe and Rosanna Warren

From an early age, Marceline Desbordes-Valmore led a turbulent, peripatetic life marked by financial want and personal loss. She was born in Douai to a working-class family ruined by the Revolution (her artisan father served primarily the aristocracy). In 1797, her mother, Catherine, left her husband and children for a lover, taking only the young Marceline with her. They traveled the country and worked on stage together and, when Marceline was fifteen, went to Guadeloupe to seek financial assistance from a cousin. They arrived to find the cousin dead. Catherine herself died during an epidemic of yellow fever soon thereafter. Marceline, returning to France alone, became an itinerant actress and singer and was continually on the move with her family around France and in Europe.

Desbordes-Valmore's self-determination, while attended by hardship, was extraordinary for a woman of her time. She sustained successful careers as an actress and writer, at times living in financial independence of men. Moreover, she was unencumbered by contemporary sexual mores: her domestic life was as unconventional and tumultuous—and at least as tragic—as that of her parents. She bore six children, two before her 1817 marriage to the actor Prosper Valmore, and continued to take lovers during her marriage. Of her offspring, two died in infancy, one as a child, and two as young adults. Only Hippolyte survived her.

Desbordes-Valmore wrote prolifically in numerous genres and maintained ties to prominent male poets of her time, such as Pierre-Jean de Béranger (1780–1857), Alphonse de Lamartine, Alfred de Vigny, Victor Hugo, and the influential critic Charles Sainte-Beuve (1804–69). Her many poems addressed to female friends and contemporaries (Juliette Récamier, Amable Tastu, Sophie Gay, Delphine de Girardin, and Élisa Mercœur, among others) bear witness to her close relationships with women. She published her first collection in 1819 and her last in 1843, and although she built her reputation as a poet, she was not able to support herself and her family by writing poetry. Additionally, she translated poetry from English; had a novel published; and wrote and sold short stories, lyrics, and, most lucratively, children's literature.

Desbordes-Valmore remains one of the most visible women poets of nineteenth-century France. She has been widely anthologized and her poetry praised by critics and poets from Hugo to Louis Aragon (1897–1982) to Yves Bonnefoy (1923–). Even Charles Baudelaire, notorious for his disdain of women writers, wrote an admiring essay on Desbordes-Valmore (2: 145–49). Her prevailing domestic preoccupations (motherhood, children) perhaps made her more palatable to critics and, as Anne Berger has argued, turned her into a sort of great mother to male poets. Yet her poetry conveys much more than normative femininity. Desbordes-Valmore is as interested in eroticism as she is in maternity, and her work, often politically progressive, is notably engaged in the social and political issues of her day.

Above all, the melodic qualities of her poems—fluid, urgent, affecting—ensure their continued readability today. Only recently has Desbordes-Valmore been credited with important formal innovations traditionally attributed to male poets: her first collection, *Élégies* (1819), predates Lamartine's *Méditations poétiques* (1820), long considered to have initiated elegiac Romanticism (see Johnson, "Lady"). And she sampled the prose poem well before Baudelaire's *Spleen de Paris* (1869), as with "Une plume de femme" ("A Woman's Pen"), included below, which prefaced *Bouquets et prières* (see Bertrand, Introd. 23). Like most Romantic poets, she avoided traditional fixed forms and furthermore explicitly rejected the sonnet as a masculine genre whose stringent regularity allowed for displays of technical brilliance but was ultimately confining. Desbordes-Valmore's frequent use of refrains (as in "A Woman's Pen," "Angry young man, slouched at your school desk . . . ," "The Slave") tells of her inherent musicality and predilection for the song. But the careful composition that her poems display belies the myth of simplicity and spontaneity that the author herself perpetuated (as in "A Woman's Pen"). Her metrical originality, including the use of uneven meters and revival of the eleven-syllable line (most notably in her long poem "Rêve intermittent d'une nuit triste" [*Poésies inédites*]), inspired Rimbaud and Verlaine to follow suit. Verlaine paid homage to Desbordes-Valmore by including her alongside Arthur Rimbaud and Stéphane Mallarmé in his collection of "poètes maudits" ("cursed poets"). Despite the acclaim she received during her lifetime, she was unable to find a publisher for her final—and arguably finest—collection of poetry (*Poésies inédites*). Poverty and illness marked her last years.

Her major poetic works are *Élégies, Marie et romances* (1819), *Poésies* (1830), *Les pleurs* (1833), *Pauvres fleurs* (1839), *Bouquets et prières* (1843), *Poésies inédites* (1860), and *Poésies en patois* (1896). Of the poems selected for this anthology, "Son image," "À Délie," and "L'étrangère" first appeared in *Poésies*; "Écrivez-moi" in *Les pleurs*; "Une plume de femme," "La page blanche," and "Jeune homme irrité sur un banc d'école…" in *Bouquets et prières*; and "Jour d'orient," "Les éclairs," "Les roses de Saadi," "La jeune fille et le ramier," and "L'eau douce" in *Poésies inédites*. "L'esclave" and "Dans la rue par un jour funèbre de Lyon" appeared in no collection during the poet's life.

Desbordes-Valmore has received an increasing amount of critical attention in both France and the United States during the last twenty years or so. She continues to gain in visibility, thanks in large part to Marc Bertrand, who twice reedited her complete poetry (in 1973 and 2007) and also published modern editions of some of her prose works; to Francis Ambrière's comprehensive biography (1987); and to Christine Planté, who has written over a dozen articles on Desbordes-Valmore. For further reading, see Bertrand, *Femme*; Boutin, *Maternal Echoes*; Danahy; Jasenas; Johnson, "Gender." Schultz (*Gendered Lyric*) includes readings of a number of the poems that follow. All texts refer to Bertrand's 2007 edition.

Son image

Elle avait fui de mon âme offensée ;

Bien loin de moi je crus l'avoir chassée :

Toute tremblante, un jour, elle arriva,

Sa douce image, et dans mon cœur rentra :

Point n'eus le temps de me mettre en colère ;

Point ne savais ce qu'elle voulait faire ;

Un peu trop tard mon cœur le devina.

Sans prévenir, elle dit : « Me voilà !

« Ce cœur m'attend. Par l'Amour, que j'implore,

« Comme autrefois j'y viens régner encore. »

Au nom d'amour ma raison se troubla :

Je voulus fuir, et tout mon corps trembla.

Je bégayai des plaintes au perfide ;

Pour me toucher il prit un air timide ;

Puis à mes pieds en pleurant, il tomba.

J'oubliai tout dès que l'Amour pleura.

Desbordes-Valmore renders the gender of the beloved ambiguous in this poem. In the first stanza, "elle" ("she") could refer either to a female lover or to "son image," which is grammatically feminine. Similarly, the "il" and masculine "perfide" of the second stanza point both to the personified "Amour," grammatically masculine, and to a male beloved.

The Image

Long since fled from my wounded soul,
Far, far from me I thought safely banished,
Until, all shivering, one day she arrived,
That sweet likeness—and reentered my heart.
I didn't have time to fly into a rage—
I had no idea what might happen to me—
A little too late, my heart guessed.

With no warning, she whispered: "I'm back!
And your heart's still here for me. I implore Love:
Just as before, let me come back to rule."
At the name of love, I fell all to pieces:
I wanted to run—my whole body trembled.
I stammered out in protest to the traitor
Who, to move me, adopted a timorous air
And fell at my feet, weeping and pleading.
But I forgot everything as soon as Love wept.

(trans. JSAL)

À Délie

Par un badinage enchanteur,

Vous aussi, vous m'avez trompée !

Vous m'avez fait embrasser une erreur ;

Légère comme vous, elle s'est échappée.

Pour me guérir du mal qu'Amour m'a fait,

Vous avez abusé de votre esprit aimable ;

Et je vous trouverais coupable,

Si je pouvais en vous trouver rien d'imparfait.

Je l'ai vu cet amant si discret et si tendre ;

J'ai suivi son maintien, son silence, sa voix.

Ai-je pu m'abuser sur l'objet de son choix ?

Ses regards vous parlaient, et j'ai su les entendre.

Mon cœur est éclairé, mais il n'est point jaloux.

J'ai lu ces vers charmants où son âme respire ;

C'est l'Amour qui l'inspire,

Et l'inspire pour vous.

Pour vous aussi je veux être la même ;

Non, vous n'inspirez pas un sentiment léger ;

Que ce soit d'amitié, d'amour, que l'on vous aime,

Le cœur qui vous aima ne peut jamais changer.

Laissez-moi ma mélancolie ;

Je la préfère à l'ivresse d'un jour :

To Delia

In your teasing game, so sweet,

You also, you led me astray!

You drove me to clasp a deceit;

Lightly as you, it breezed away.

To cure me from Love's wound

You indulged your affectionate wit;

And I would pronounce your guilt

If in you one fault I could find.

I've watched that lover, so tender, discreet;

I observed his bearing, his silence, his voice.

Could I be misled in the object of his choice?

His looks spoke to you, and I heard them right.

My heart is enlightened, but feels no jealous smart.

I've read those charming lines where his soul breathes through.

Love inspires his heart,

And inspires it for you.

For you, as well, I want to remain the same;

No, the feeling you inspire is nothing light or fey;

Whether in friendship or in passion one is drawn to you,

The heart that loved you once stays faithful to your name.

Leave me my melancholy;

I prefer it to a day's carouse:

One of four poems that Desbordes-Valmore wrote to Délie, the fictional love object addressed in the Lyonnais poet Maurice Scève's collection *Délie, objet de plus haute vertu* (1544)

On peut rire avec la Folie,

Mais il n'est pas prudent de rire avec l'Amour.

Laissez-moi fuir un danger plein de charmes ;

Ne m'offrez plus un cœur qui n'est qu'à vous :

Le badinage le plus doux

Finit quelquefois par les larmes.

Mais je n'ai rien perdu, la tranquille amitié

Redeviendra bientôt le charme de ma vie :

Je renonce à l'amant, et je garde une amie ;

C'est du bonheur la plus douce moitié.

One can laugh with Folly,

But to laugh with Love isn't wise.

Let me flee a danger full of charming fears;

Don't offer me a heart that is only yours:

Even the gentlest teasing

Sometimes ends in tears.

But I've lost nothing: friendship's peace

Will soon return and charm my life again.

I give up a lover and preserve a friend,

And keep the sweeter half of happiness.

(trans. RW)

L'étrangère

Ah ! que le monde est difficile !
Hélas ! il n'est pas fait pour moi.
Ma sœur, en ton obscur asile,
J'étais plus heureuse avec toi.
On m'appelle ici l'étrangère ;
C'est le nom de qui n'a point d'or.
Si je ris, je suis trop légère ;
Si je rêve... on en parle encor.

Si je mêle à ma chevelure
La fleur que j'aimais dans nos bois,
Je suis, dit-on, dans ma parure,
Timide et coquette à la fois ;
Puis-je ne pas la trouver belle ?
Le printemps en a fait mon bien :
Pour me parer je n'avais qu'elle ;
On l'effeuille, et je n'ai plus rien.

Je sors de cet âge paisible,
Où l'on joue avec le malheur :
Je m'éveille, je suis sensible,
Et je l'apprends par la douleur.
Un seul être à moi s'intéresse ;

The Stranger

Oh, how the world is hard!
Alas, it's not cut out for me.
Sister, far from the boulevard,
I was happier, hidden with you.
They call me the stranger here;
It's the name they give to the poor.
If I laugh, I'm thought insincere;
If I muse, they gossip still more.

And if I place in my hair
The blossom I loved from our youth,
They criticize my attire
As fear and flirtatiousness both.
Can't it simply be seen as sweet?
Springtime provided that style:
That bloom was my only conceit.
Once it fades, I've no trinket at all.

I've grown out of that tranquil age
When sorrowing feels like a sport:
I've woken up to the stage
Of learning to feel, through hurt.
One soul only attends to me.

Il n'a rien dit, mais je le voi ;[1]
Et je vois même à sa tristesse,
Qu'il est étranger comme moi.

Ah ! si son regard plein de charmes
Recèle un doux rayon d'espoir,
Quelle main essuîra les larmes
Qui m'empêchent de l'entrevoir ?
Soumise au monde qui m'observe,
Je dois mourir, jamais pleurer ;
Et je n'use qu'avec réserve
Du triste espoir de soupirer !

---

[1]"Voi" for "vois": an archaic spelling adopted here to maintain the "rime pour l'œil" ("visual rhyme") with "moi." See also footnote 5 on page 67.

He's said nothing, but I see it's true;

And in his sadness I see

That he is a stranger, too.

Ah! If his enchanting gaze

Conceals hope's gentle beam,

What hand will wipe dry the tears

That keep me from glimpsing him?

Thrall to the world of spies,

I'm to die, never to weep;

And I use with care my supplies

Of sighing in painful hope.

(trans. RW)

Écrivez-moi

Je volerais vite, vite, vite,
Si j'étais petit oiseau !
                    —Béranger

Pour Dieu ! mon amie,

Vivez-vous encor ?[2]

Ou, fleur endormie

Au jardin de mort,

Faites-vous un rêve

Doux comme vos yeux ?

Qu'un ange l'achève,

Et vous porte aux cieux !

Car cette vallée

Est sombre pour nous ;

Notre âme exilée

Y rampe à genoux ;

On coupe nos ailes,

Dans ce lieu d'effroi ;

Je pleure après elles,

Et l'on rit de moi !

---

[2]Poetic spelling of "encore," used here for the masculine rhyme, elsewhere
to maintain the meter

Write Me

> *I would fly so fast, so fast*
> *If I were a little bird!*
> —*Béranger*[3]

For God's sake, my darling,

Are you still alive?

Or, furled like a bud

In the garden of death,

Are you spinning dreams

As sweet as your eyes?

May an angel awake

And lift you to the skies!

Because this dark valley's

Steeped in shadow for us,

Our banished souls must

Crawl through on their knees.

In this place of terror,

Fear clips our wings.

I cry, longing for them:

Others laugh at my pain.

---

[3]Refrain from a song entitled "Si j'étais petit oiseau," by Pierre-Jean de Béranger (1780–1857), popular poet and songwriter. A Republican who opposed the monarchy, he was imprisoned twice during the Restoration for his writing.

Et vous ! si charmante,

Belle au triste accent,

Voyageuse amante

De quelque ange absent ;

Quand vos traits de femme

Dans l'ombre ont passé

« C'est, dis-je en mon âme,

 Un ange blessé ! »

Car votre auréole

Se montrait un peu ;

Dans votre parole

Languissait un feu ;

Vos grâces brûlantes

De divins amours,

Vous rendaient trop lentes

Les nuits de nos jours !

Si, frêle et chérie,

Vous quittez ce lieu,

De votre patrie,

Criez-nous adieu !

Pour moi, désolée

De l'oubli du temps,

Moi, l'autre exilée,

Je prie, et j'attends !

And you—so bewitching,

With your wistful voice—

Traveler, lover

Of some absent spirit;

When your feminine features

Have passed through the shade—

"I see," I say to my heart,

"Her bruised angel's face!"

I knew, because your halo

Glimmered, sometimes;

A little fire smoldered

In your every word.

Your elegance, burning

From celestial loves,

Surrendered too slowly

The nights of our days.

If, precious and frail,

You pass from this place,

From your fatherland,

Just bid us farewell.

For me, forgotten

By time, desolate—

Me, the other exile—

I wait. And I pray.

(trans. JSAL)

Une plume de femme

Courez, ma plume, courez : vous savez bien qui vous l'ordonne.

Je prie un génie indulgent de répandre sur votre travail le charme mystérieux de la fiction, afin que nul ne sache la source de vos efforts et de la fièvre qui vous conduit : on se détourne des sources tristes. Que mon âme soit ouverte seulement au regard du Créateur. Laissez-la seule dans ses nuits d'insomnie : elle ne raconte pas la cause de ses débats avec la terre. Dieu sait qu'à cette sainte cause est suspendu l'espoir de rentrer un jour dans son ciel, comme un enfant dans la maison de son père. L'enfant prodigue a souffert avant de voir la porte maternelle se rouvrir devant lui : sans ses larmes amères y serait-il jamais revenu ?

Courez donc, ma plume, courez : vous savez bien qui vous l'ordonne.

Je vous livre mes heures afin qu'elles laissent, par vous, une faible trace de leur passage dans cette vie. Quand elles traverseront la foule, sur les ailes de mon affliction, si l'on crie : « Elles n'ont pas d'haleine », dites que le grillon caché dans les blés forme une musique faible aussi ; mais qui n'est pas sans grâce au milieu du tumulte pompeux des merveilles de la nature ; répondez pour moi ce que Dieu a répondu pour le grillon :

« Laissez chanter mon grillon ; c'est moi qui l'ai mis où il chante. Ne lui contestez pas son imperceptible part de l'immense moisson que mon soleil jaunit et fait mûrir pour tous. »

Courez donc, ma plume, courez : vous savez bien qui vous l'ordonne.

A Woman's Pen

Run on, my pen, run on: you know who orders it.

I beseech an indulgent genie to spread the enchantment of fiction over your work, so no one will know the source of your struggles and of the fever that impels you; people are put off by springs of sorrow. Let my soul open only to the Creator's gaze. Leave her alone in her sleepless nights: she doesn't gossip about the cause of her quarrels with the earth. God knows that upon that hallowed cause hangs her hope of returning one day to His heaven, like a child returning to its father's house. The prodigal son suffered before seeing the maternal door opening before him: without his bitter tears, would he ever have come home?

So run on, my pen, run on: you know who orders it.

I grant you my hours, so that they may leave, through you, a frail trace of their passage in this life. When they float out through the crowd on the wings of my affliction, if people cry, "There's no power in their breath," reply that the cricket hidden in the wheat field also composes a frail music, but one which preserves its own grace in the midst of the pompous tumult of nature's marvels. Reply for me what God replied for the cricket:

"Let my cricket sing; it is I who have placed him where he sings. Don't begrudge him his imperceptible share of the vast harvest which my sun colors yellow and brings to ripeness for all."

So run on, my pen, run on: you know who orders it.

L'austère inconstant, le Sort, qui m'a dit : *Assez*, quand je lui demandais ma part des biens de l'existence ; le Sort qui m'a dit : *Non !* quand je levais mes yeux pleins de prières pour obtenir encore un de ses sourires, a laissé pourtant tomber dans ma consternation un bien dont l'apparence était de peu de valeur, mais qui deviendrait une palme de salut, si quelque fil de la Vierge l'enveloppait de divine pudeur : c'est vous, ma plume, détachée du vol d'un pauvre oiseau blessé comme mon âme, peut-être, c'est vous, que personne ne m'apprit à conduire ; c'est vous, que sans savoir tailler encore, j'ai fait errer sous ma pensée avec tant d'hésitation et de découragement ; c'est vous, tant de fois échappée à mes doigts ignorants, vous qui, par degrés plus rapide, trouvez parfois, à ma propre surprise, quelques paroles moins indignes des maîtres, qui vous ont d'abord regardée en pitié.

Ainsi, courez, ma plume, courez : vous savez bien qui vous l'ordonne.

Vous ne blesserez pas ; vous ne bégayerez pas un mot de haine, quand ce serait pour repousser l'injure : il vaudrait mieux tomber en poussière, afin que quand je serai poussière aussi, je ne tressaille encore que d'amour et jamais de honte ; afin que si j'attends au fond du purgatoire, décrit si triste, mais si doux, par Dante, qui l'a vu, toutes les âmes heureuses, en passant légères et sauvées devant moi, me disent avec un léger sourire : au revoir !

À ce prix donc, trempée d'encre ou de larmes, courez, ma plume, courez : vous savez bien qui vous l'ordonne.

The grim fickle one, Fate, who said to me, *Enough*, when I begged him for my share of life's goods; Fate, who said to me, *No!*, when I raised my eyes brimming with prayer to receive one of his smiles, still let fall upon my distress one gift of little apparent worth, but which could become a palm frond of salvation, if one of the Virgin's threads wrapped it in divine modesty. It's you, my pen, fallen from the flight of a poor bird as wounded as my soul, perhaps; it's you, whom no one taught me to guide; it's you, whom I—not yet knowing how to trim or cut—made to wander under my thought with so much hesitation and discouragement; it's you, so often a fugitive from my ignorant fingers; you who, bit by bit gaining speed, find sometimes, to my own surprise, a few words less unworthy of the masters who looked upon you at first with pity.

And so, run on, my pen, run on: you know who orders it.

You will not wound; you will not stammer out a word of hatred, even if it were to respond to insult. Better to fall to dust, so that, when I will be dust as well, I shiver only with love and never with shame; so that if I wait in the depths of the purgatory described as so sad but so tender by Dante, who saw it, all the happy souls, lightsome and saved as they pass before me, tell me smiling lightly, "Till we meet again!"

At this price, then, dripping with ink or tears, run on, my pen, run on: you know who orders it.

(trans. RW)

La page blanche

À ma fille

Ondine ? prends cette page,
Dans ton livre vierge encor ;
Ta plume éloquente et sage
Peut m'y verser un trésor.
Sur sa blancheur que j'envie
Ton âme se répandra,
Et du trouble de ma vie,
Un jour me consolera.

Seule en mon sentier mobile,
Au vaisseau navigateur,
Sous la lumière tranquille
D'un jeune astre protecteur,
J'écrirai de mon voyage,
Les écueils et les ennuis,
Et tu sauras, dans l'orage,
Quelle étoile je poursuis !

The White Page

To my daughter [4]

Ondine? Take this sheet
In your book, still virginal;
Eloquent, wise, your pen
Will pour out its treasure there.
Brimful, your soul will spill
Across its enviable white
And one day will comfort me
For my life's travail.

Alone on my shimmering course,
Captain, steering the ship,
Under the peaceful light
Of a young, guardian star,
I'll write you of my trip,
The reefs, the tedium,
And you'll know, in the storm,
What gleam I pursue so far.

The white page, for Desbordes-Valmore, is pure and full of the promise and comfort of writing, which creates a connection between mother and daughter that spans distance in both time and space. Later in the century, the "page blanche" became specifically associated with Mallarmé, for whom it signified poetic impotence, the writer's frustration and anguish. See, for example, his "Brise marine" ("le vide papier que la blancheur défend" [38]) and the frozen images of whiteness in *"Le vierge, le vivace et le bel aujourd'-hui..."* (67–68).

[4]Marceline-Junie-Hyacinthe (1821–53), called Ondine, was Desbordes-Valmore's fourth child and a poet also.

Chère ! adieu. Ce mot d'alarme,

Que vient d'essayer ma main,

Ce mot trempé d'une larme

Ouvre mon triste chemin !...

Mais ton regard qui m'écoute

Ne veut pas répondre adieu ;

Étends-le donc sur ma route,

Comme un doux rayon de feu !

Darling! Adieu. This fearful word
My hand has just set down,
This word steeped in a tear
Sets my sad course for me.
But your deep, listening eyes
Refuse to say "adieu";
Beam them along my way
Like a gentle glow of fire.

(trans. RW)

Jeune homme irrité sur un banc d'école,

Dont le cœur encor n'a chaud qu'au soleil,

Vous refusez donc l'encre et la parole

À celles qui font le foyer vermeil ?

Savant, mais aigri par vos lassitudes,

Un peu furieux de nos chants d'oiseaux,

Vous nous couronnez de railleurs roseaux !

Vous serez plus jeune après vos études :

　　　Quand vous sourirez,

　　　Vous nous comprendrez.

Vous portez si haut la férule altière,

Qu'un géant plierait sous son docte poids.

Vous faites baisser notre humble paupière,

Et nous flagellez à briser nos doigts.

Où prenez-vous donc de si dures armes ?

Qu'ils étaient méchants vos maîtres latins !

Mais l'amour viendra : roi de vos destins,

Il vous changera par beaucoup de larmes :

　　　Quand vous pleurerez,

　　　Vous nous comprendrez !

Angry young man, slouched at your school desk,

Whose heart only warms to the touch of the sun,

You'd deny the use of words and of ink

To those who make the home rosy and warm?

Well-read, but embittered by your weariness,

So irritated by our bright birdlike chirps,

You crown our heads with whippings and scorn.

You will be childlike once you have learned:

> When you can smile,

> You'll understand us.

You carry that arrogant ferule so proudly,

A giant would bend with its erudite weight.

You make our humble eyelids droop with shame,

Whip us so hard our small fingers will break.

Who taught you how to use such harsh weapons?

How brutal they were, your own Latin masters!

But love will come anyway, lord of your fate,

And soften your heart after so many tears:

> When you can weep,

> You'll understand us.

Desbordes-Valmore's response to the young Paul de Molènes's misogynist article, "Les femmes poètes" (1842)

Ce beau rêve à deux, vous voudrez l'écrire.

On est éloquent dès qu'on aime bien :

Mais si vous aimez qui ne sait pas lire,

L'amante à l'amant ne répondra rien.

Laissez donc grandir quelque jeune flamme,

Allumant pour vous ses vagues rayons ;

Laissez-lui toucher plumes et crayons ;

L'esprit, vous verrez, fait du jour à l'âme :

      Quand vous aimerez,

      Vous nous comprendrez !

Now you want to write down your intimate dream;

We're most fluent to lavish the one we love best.

But if she whom you love doesn't know how to read,

Your beloved will never make any response.

So let flare within you a tender new flame,

Lighting your heart with its vague, feeble rays.

Let it touch the tips of all pens with its glow:

You will see that the mind illumines the soul.

     When you can love,

     You'll understand us.

(trans. JSAL)

Jour d'orient

Ce fut un jour pareil à ce beau jour
Que, pour tout perdre, incendiait l'amour !

C'était un jour de charité divine
Où dans l'air bleu l'éternité chemine ;
Où dérobée à son poids étouffant
La terre joue et redevient enfant ;
C'était partout comme un baiser de mère,
Long rêve errant dans une heure éphémère ;
Heure d'oiseaux, de parfums, de soleil,
D'oubli de tout... hors du bien sans pareil.

Nous étions deux !... C'est trop d'un quand on aime
Pour se garder... Hélas ! nous étions deux.
Pas un témoin qui sauve de soi-même !
Jamais au monde on n'eut plus besoin d'eux
Que nous l'avions ! Lui, trop près de mon âme,
Avec son âme éblouissait mes yeux ;
J'étais aveugle à cette double flamme,
Et j'y vis trop quand je revis les cieux.

Pour me sauver, j'étais trop peu savante ;
Pour l'oublier... je suis encor vivante !

C'était un jour pareil à ce beau jour
Que, pour tout perdre, incendiait l'amour !

Eastern Day

It was a day as fine as this day here
Which — to ruin all — love set on fire.

It was a day of divine munificence
When eternity strolls in the sky's blue expanse;
When, escaping from her pressing chain,
The earth is free to play, a child again.
It was like a mother's kisses everywhere,
A long dream wandering in the fleeting hour,
Hours of birds, of scent, of the sun's blaze,
Forgetful of all except the one great prize.

Two of us! . . . One too many, when love's at play,
To save oneself . . . Alas! There were two of us.
To protect us from ourselves, no witnesses.
Never did we need others as that day
We needed them! He, leaning all too closely
Upon my soul, with his soul dazed my eyes;
That double flame dazzled and blinded me,
And I saw all too well, when I saw the skies.

To save myself, I was much too naive;
To forget him . . . Well, I'm still alive!

It was a day as fine as this day here
Which — to ruin all — love set on fire.

(trans. RW)

Les éclairs

Orages de l'amour, nobles et hauts orages,

Pleins de nids gémissants blessés sous les ombrages,

Pleins de fleurs, pleins d'oiseaux perdus, mais dans les cieux,

Qui vous perd ne voit plus, éclairs délicieux !

Les roses de Saadi

J'ai voulu ce matin te rapporter des roses ;

Mais j'en avais tant pris dans mes ceintures closes

Que les nœuds trop serrés n'ont pu les contenir.

Les nœuds ont éclaté. Les roses envolées

Dans le vent, à la mer s'en sont toutes allées.

Elles ont suivi l'eau pour ne plus revenir.

La vague en a paru rouge et comme enflammée.

Ce soir, ma robe encore en est toute embaumée...

Respires-en sur moi l'odorant souvenir.

Lightning

Dark tempests of love, strong, magnificent storms,
Full of groaning nests, wounded and tossed by the night,
Torn flowers, lost birds—but, wild in the skies,
To lose you is to go blind, stunning flashes of light!

(trans. JSAL)

Saadi's Roses

This morning, I wanted to bring you some roses;
But I'd tied up so many of them in my sashes
The straining knots just couldn't contain them—

They burst. And the roses—spun end over end,
They all blew down to the sea in the wind.
Lured by the water, they will never come home.

The waves blushed red with them, as if aflame.
Tonight, my gown is still soaked in their scent . . .
Breathe it here on my skin—their fragrance remains.

(trans. JSAL)

Saadi, a Persian poet (c. 1200–92?), is the author of the *Gulistan* or *The Rose Garden* (1258). Cf. Vivien's "Roses du soir" ("Evening Roses") on page 328.

La jeune fille et le ramier

Les rumeurs du jardin disent qu'il va pleuvoir ;
Tout tressaille, averti de la prochaine ondée ;
Et toi qui ne lis plus, sur ton livre accoudée,
Plains-tu l'absent aimé qui ne pourra te voir ?

Là-bas, pliant son aile et mouillé sous l'ombrage,
Banni de l'horizon qu'il n'atteint que des yeux,
Appelant sa compagne et regardant les cieux,
Un ramier, comme toi, soupire de l'orage.

Laissez pleuvoir, ô cœurs solitaires et doux !
Sous l'orage qui passe il renaît tant de choses.
Le soleil sans la pluie ouvrirait-il les roses ?
Amants, vous attendez, de quoi vous plaignez-vous ?

The Young Girl and the Ring Dove

Throughout the garden, murmurs promise rain.
Everything shivers, waiting for the shower;
And you, leaning by your book, not reading anymore,
Do you pity the lover who can't see you, who is gone?

Over there, damp, folding his wing among the leaves,
Exiled from the horizon he touches only with his eyes,
Calling his companion as he scans the skies,
A ring dove, like you, feels the storm and grieves.

Let it rain, o hearts, tender and alone!
Under the passing storm, many things are born again.
Would roses open in sunlight without rain?
Lovers, if you wait, why should you complain?

(trans. RW)

L'eau douce

L'eau qui a rencontré la mer
ne retrouve jamais sa première douceur.
                              —*Un poète persan*

Pitié de moi ! j'étais l'eau douce ;

Un jour j'ai rencontré la mer ;

À présent j'ai le goût amer,

Quelque part que le vent me pousse.

Ah ! qu'il en allait autrement

Quand, légère comme la gaze

Parmi mes bulles de topaze

Je m'agitais joyeusement.

Nul bruit n'accostait une oreille

D'un salut plus délicieux

Que mon cristal mélodieux

Dans sa ruisselante merveille.

L'oiseau du ciel, sur moi penché,

M'aimait plus que l'eau du nuage,

Quand mon flot, plein de son image,

Lavait son gosier desséché.

Le poète errant qui me loue

Disait un jour qu'il m'a parlé :

« Tu sembles le rire perlé

D'un enfant qui jase et qui joue.

Fresh Water

> *Water that has encountered the sea*
> *never again finds its first freshness.*
>   —A Persian poet

Have pity on me! I was fresh water once;

One day I met the sea;

Now my taste stings

Wherever the wind harries me.

Ah! It was otherwise

When, light as floating gauze,

I frolicked joyously

Among my bubbles, topaz-blue.

No sound greeted the ear

With more delicious grace

Than my crystal melodies

At play in rippling air.

Leaning over me, heaven's bird

Loved my water more than the cloud's,

When my stream, reflecting him,

Quenched his thirst to the brim.

A wandering poet, in praise,

Said of my water's purl,

"You seem the laughter of pearl

Of a child who babbles and plays.

Moi, je suis l'ardent voyageur,

Incliné sur la nappe humide,

Qui te jure, ô ruisseau limpide,

De bénir partout ta fraîcheur. »

Doux voyageur, si ta mémoire

S'abreuve de mon souvenir

Bénis Dieu d'avoir pu me boire,

Mais défends-moi de revenir.

Mon cristal limpide et sonore

Où s'étalait le cresson vert

Dans les cailloux ne coule encore

Que sourdement, comme l'hiver.

L'oiseau dont la soif est trompée

Au nuage a rendu son vol,

Et la plume du rossignol

Dans mon onde n'est plus trempée.

Cette onde qui filtrait du ciel

Roulait des clartés sous la mousse...

J'étais bien mieux, j'étais l'eau douce,

Et me voici traînant le sel.

I am the passionate traveler
Leaning over your murmuring gleam,
And I swear, clear-hearted stream,
I'll bless your freshness everywhere."

Gentle traveler, if in memory
You drink, and I quench your thirst,
Thank God that he let you taste me,
But let me not flow to the past.

My crystalline, ringing tones
Where the watercress floated clear
Mumble among the stones,
Dull, as if winter were here.

Disappointed, the thirsty bird
Has flown back to the cloud above;
The nightingale comes no more
To dip his wing in my wave.

This wave, filtering the sky,
Rolled glimmers beneath the foam . . .
I was happy once, fresh water, free;
Now I'm heavy with salt and gloom.

(trans. RW)

L'esclave

Pays des noirs ! berceau du pauvre Arsène,

Ton souvenir vient-il chercher mon cœur ?

Vent de Guinée, est-ce la douce haleine

Qui me caresse et charme ma douleur ?

M'apportes-tu les soupirs de ma mère,

Ou la chanson qui console mon père ?...

  Jouez, dansez, beaux petits blancs ;

  Pour être bons, restez enfants !

Nègre captif, couché sur le rivage,

Je te vois rire en rêvant à la mort ;

Ton âme libre ira sur un nuage,

The Slave

Country of the blacks! Where poor Arsène was born,

Is it your memory knocking at my heart?

Guinean wind, is it your tender breath

Caressing me, keeping my sorrow warm?

Do you bring back my mother's sighs again,

Or the melody which soothes my father's pain?

    Sweet white children, dance and play:

      To stay good, don't age a day.

Black man in chains, lying by the sea,

I see you laughing as you dream of death.

Your soul, released, will wing up to the sky

This poem first appeared in Desbordes-Valmore's novella "Sarah," collected in her *Veillées des Antilles* (1821). While watching two white children play, Arsène, a freed slave, sings of his homeland, Guinea: "Leurs jeux, leur âge, les éclats d'une innocente gaîté... étaient la seule récompense du nègre, qui, souvent absorbé par la fatigue et la chaleur, s'écartait de ses compagnons pour rêver un moment, pour oser penser à lui-même, à ses parents qu'il avait à peine connus, à son rivage aride, mais libre, dont, malgré ses cris et ses larmes, des blancs, des hommes, l'avaient arraché depuis plus de vingt ans.... Ses yeux erraient sur les bords de la mer, où quelque nègre, trainant un fardeau à l'ardeur du soleil, paraissait y succomber comme lui, et comme lui, peut-être, envoyer à sa patrie absente un soupir de regret et d'espoir. Il plaignait l'esclave, tous les esclaves" (99–100). See Paliyenko's critical edition of *Veillées*. *Engendering Race: Romantic-Era Women and French Colonial Memory*, a special issue of *L'Esprit Créateur* that Paliyenko edited, contains several articles on *Veillées* and on "Sarah" in particular.

Où ta naissance avait fixé ton sort :

Dieu te rendra les baisers de ta mère

Et la chanson que t'apprenait ton père !...

   Jouez, dansez, beaux petits blancs ;

   Pour être bons, restez enfants !

Pauvre et content, jamais le noir paisible,

Pour vous troubler, n'a traversé les flots ;

Et parmi vous, sous un maître inflexible,

Jamais d'un homme on n'entend les sanglots.

Pour vous ravir aux baisers d'une mère,

Qu'avons-nous fait au dieu de votre père ?...

   Jouez, dansez, beaux petits blancs ;

   Pour être bons, restez enfants !

Where your destiny was settled at your birth.

God will give back your mother's kiss again,

And the song your father taught you how to sing.

> Sweet white children, dance and play:
>
> To stay good, don't age a day.

Happy and poor, the peaceful black won't cross

The waves to threaten you at home.

And in your land, a heart-hardened boss

Never drives a man to sob and moan.

To snatch you from your mother's longing kiss,

What have we done to the god your fathers praise?

> Sweet white children, dance and play:
>
> To stay good, don't age a day.

(trans. RW)

Dans la rue

par un jour funèbre de Lyon

LA FEMME

Nous n'avons plus d'argent pour enterrer nos morts.
Le prêtre est là, marquant le prix des funérailles ;
Et les corps étendus, troués par les mitrailles,
Attendent un linceul, une croix, un remords.

Le meurtre se fait roi. Le vainqueur siffle et passe.
Où va-t-il ? Au Trésor, toucher le prix du sang.
Il en a bien versé... mais sa main n'est pas lasse ;
Elle a, sans le combattre, égorgé le passant.

Dieu l'a vu. Dieu cueillait comme des fleurs froissées
Les femmes, les enfants qui s'envolaient aux cieux.
Les hommes... les voilà dans le sang jusqu'aux yeux.
L'air n'a pu balayer tant d'âmes courroucées.

Elles ne veulent pas quitter leurs membres morts.
Le prêtre est là, marquant le prix des funérailles ;
Et les corps étendus, troués par les mitrailles,
Attendent un linceul, une croix, un remords.

In the Street

on a Funereal Day in Lyon

THE WOMAN

We don't even have money to bury our dead.

The priest wanders through, adding funeral costs;

And the bodies sprawl everywhere, riddled with grapeshot,

Awaiting a shroud, a cross, someone's remorse.

Murder's made king. The victor saunters offstage

To the treasury, well-paid for each drop of blood.

And so much blood was shed . . . but his hand isn't tired.

With scarcely a struggle, he slit innocent throats.

God saw. And he gathered them up, trampled petals:

The women, the babies, fluttered up to the skies.

But wind can't sweep away the most furious souls:

The men . . . they're still here, soaked in blood to their eyes.

Souls don't want to leave their corpses behind.

The priest wanders through, adding funeral costs;

And the bodies sprawl everywhere, riddled with grapeshot,

Awaiting a shroud, a cross, someone's remorse.

Provoked by insufficient wages and inhuman working conditions, the silk workers of Lyon (*les canuts*) rebelled in 1831 and 1834. The army violently repressed these uprisings. Desbordes-Valmore was unable to find a publisher for this poem during her lifetime, undoubtedly because of its politically explosive content (see *Œuvres* 2: 799–801).

Les vivants n'osent plus se hasarder à vivre.

Sentinelle soldée, au milieu du chemin,

La mort est un soldat qui vise et qui délivre

Le témoin révolté qui parlerait demain...

DES FEMMES

Prenons nos rubans noirs, pleurons toutes nos larmes ;

On nous a défendu d'emporter nos meurtris.

Ils n'ont fait qu'un monceau de leurs pâles débris :

Dieu ! bénissez-les tous ; ils étaient tous sans armes !

We left here alive don't dare live any longer.

Bought-off guard blocking the road: this soldier is death.

He takes aim and takes out the rebellious survivor,

In case later some witness should speak out the truth.

SOME WOMEN

Put on the black ribbons; let's cry and let's moan;

We have been forbidden to take home our slain.

All that's left is a pile of their pallid remains:

Oh God! Bless them all! Not a one had a gun!

(trans. JSAL)

Amable Tastu
(1795–1885)
née Sabine-Casimire-Amable Voïart

Translation by Gretchen Schultz

Born to a bourgeois family in Metz, then raised in Paris, Amable Tastu lost her mother while still a child. That same year, in 1801, her father remarried a woman closer in age to Amable than to himself. Èlise Voïart (1786–1866), who would become an accomplished translator (from German) and author in her own right, encouraged her stepdaughter Amable's literary aspirations and later collaborated with Amable on several children's books. In 1816, Amable married Joseph Tastu, a printer.

Widely published in numerous genres, Tastu wrote most of her works during the first half of her long life. She began publishing poetry in the early 1820s and during this decade was active in literary circles, including Juliette Récamier's salon and Charles Nodier's cenacle. Winner of the Jeux Floraux Prize on several occasions, she was highly praised by her contemporaries, including the poets Adélaïde Dufrénoy and Alphonse de Lamartine and the literary critic Charles Sainte-Beuve. She wrote both elegiac and historical poems; while perhaps more decorous than those of many of her peers, they were admired for their careful composition. "L'ange gardien" ("Guardian Angel"), in dialogue with a woman as she evolves across the seasons of her life, exemplifies her attention to poetic structuring. The poem's changing rhyme scheme, for example, evokes the speaking subject's various stages of development, from the simple forward-marching couplets of the child and young girl to the embraced rhymes enclosing the old woman. It is, moreover, one of Tastu's most notable poems for the ambivalence it betrays between conformity to normative femininity and the desire to pursue writerly ambitions and intellectual adventure.

Tastu enjoyed popular success during the 1820s and 1830s, but then her poetry was largely forgotten. She published her final collection in 1835. After the July Revolution (1830) and ensuing industrial crisis, Joseph lost his press. To support her family, Amable devoted herself to more lucrative nonfiction writing: educational treatises, scholastic manuals, literary histories, travel chronicles, and translations (e.g., of the English poet Felicia Hemans; on Tastu's translations, see Boutin, "Transnational Migrations"). Between 1847 and 1866 she traveled widely with her son Eugène, a diplomat, and lived with him in several foreign capitals and major cities, including Baghdad, Belgrade, and Alexandria. Shortly after the 1870–71 Franco-Prussian war (resulting in the annexation of her hometown, Metz) and the Paris Commune (in which her house was first occupied and then sacked), Tastu retired to Palaiseau, where she spent the remainder of her life.

Her poetic works are *Poésies* (1826), *Chroniques de France* (1829), *Poésies nouvelles* (1835), and *Poésies complètes* (1858). The poem selected for this anthology, "L'ange gardien," first appeared in *Poésies*. For further reading, see Finch; Marzouki; Poussard-Joly; Schapira.

L'ange gardien

Dieu a ordonné à ses anges de vous garder
pendant tout le temps de votre vie.
—*Psaume 91*

Oh ! qu'il est beau, cet esprit immortel,

Gardien sacré de notre destinée !

Des fleurs d'Éden sa tête est couronnée,

Il resplendit de l'éclat éternel.

Dès le berceau sa voix mystérieuse,

Des vœux confus d'une âme ambitieuse,

Sait réprimer l'impétueuse ardeur,

Et d'âge en âge il nous guide au bonheur.

L'enfant

Dans cette vie obscure, à mes regards voilée,

Quel destin m'est promis ? à quoi suis-je appelée ?

Avide d'un espoir qu'à peine j'entrevois,

Mon cœur voudrait franchir plus de jours à la fois !

Si la nuit règne aux cieux, une ardente insomnie

À ce cœur inquiet révèle son génie ;

Mes compagnes en vain m'appellent, et ma main

De la main qui l'attend s'éloigne avec dédain.

L'ange

Crains, jeune enfant, la tristesse sauvage

Dont ton orgueil subit la vaine loi.

Loin de les fuir, cours aux jeux de ton âge ;

Jouis des biens que le ciel fit pour toi :

Guardian Angel

God ordered his angels to watch over you
During every moment of your life.
　　　　　　　　—*Psalm 91*

Oh, how beautiful he is, this immortal spirit,

Sacred guardian of our destiny!

Upon his head a crown of Eden's flowers,

He radiates eternal clarity.

From the cradle, his mysterious voice

Restrains the impetuous fervor

Of an ambitious soul's confused desire;

From year to year, he guides us to happiness.

THE CHILD

In this obscure life, uncertain to my eyes,

What destiny awaits me? To what shall I be called?

Avid with a hope I can hardly discern,

My heart wants to leap across the days!

While night reigns in the skies, insomnia burns and

Reveals its genius to this apprehensive heart;

My friends call me in vain, and my hand

Withdraws from hands extended, in disregard.

THE ANGEL

Fear, small child, the solitary sadness

Whose futile law your pride endures.

Do not flee, but run to youthful games,

And prize the gifts by heaven granted:

Aux doux ébats de l'innocente joie

N'oppose plus un front triste et rêveur ;

Sous l'œil de Dieu suis ta riante voie,

Enfant, crois-moi, je conduis au bonheur.

LA JEUNE FILLE

Quel immense horizon devant moi se révèle !

À mes regards ravis que la nature est belle !

Tout ce que sent mon âme ou qu'embrassent mes yeux

S'exhale de ma bouche en sons mélodieux !

Où courent ces rivaux armés du luth sonore ?

Dans cette arène il est quelques places encore ;

Ne puis-je, à leurs côtés me frayant un chemin,

M'élancer seule, libre, et ma lyre à la main ?

L'ANGE

Seule couronne à ton front destinée,

Déjà blanchit la fleur de l'oranger ;

D'un saint devoir doucement enchaînée,

Que ferais-tu d'un espoir mensonger ?

Loin des sentiers dont ma main te repousse,

Ne pleure pas un dangereux honneur,

Suis une route et plus humble et plus douce.

Vierge, crois-moi, je conduis au bonheur.

LA FEMME

Oh ! laissez-moi charmer les heures solitaires ;

Sur ce luth ignoré laissez errer mes doigts,

No longer, with a gloomy, dreamy brow,

Resist pure joy's sweet frolics;

Under God's eye, follow your mirthful way;

My child, trust me, I lead to happiness.

THE YOUNG GIRL

How immense the horizon opening up to me!

To my enchanted eyes, how lovely nature!

All that my soul can sense or my gaze encounter

Flows from my mouth in soundful melody!

Where do they run, my lute-armed rivals?

In their realm, some places still remain;

Can't I, to their side, beat myself a trail,

Bounding, alone and free, my lyre in hand?

THE ANGEL

The orange blossom, unique crown

Destined for your brow, pales already;

Quietly enchained by a holy duty,

What would you with an illusory dream?

Far from pathways whence my hand restrains

You, do not regret a dangerous honor:

Follow a road more gentle, one that's humbler:

Maiden, trust me, I am leading you to happiness.

THE WOMAN

Oh, let me charm the solitary hours;

On this forgotten lute, let my fingers roam;

Laissez naître et mourir ses notes passagères

Comme les sons plaintifs d'un écho dans les bois.

Je ne demande rien aux brillantes demeures,

Des plaisirs fastueux inconstant univers ;

Loin du monde et du bruit, laissez couler mes heures

Avec ces doux accords à mon repos si chers.

L'ange

As-tu réglé, dans ton modeste empire,

Tous les travaux, les repas, les loisirs ?

Tu peux alors accorder à ta lyre

Quelques instants ravis à tes plaisirs.

Le rossignol élève sa voix pure,

Mais dans le nid du nocturne chanteur

Est le repos, l'abri, la nourriture...

Femme, crois-moi, je conduis au bonheur.

La mère

Revenez, revenez, songes de ma jeunesse ;

Éclatez, nobles chants ; lyre, réveillez-vous !

Je puis forcer la gloire à tenir sa promesse ;

Recueillis pour mon fils, ses lauriers seront doux.

Oui, je veux à ses pas aplanir la carrière,

À son nom, jeune encore, offrir l'appui du mien,

Pour le conduire au but y toucher la première,

Et tenter l'avenir pour assurer le sien.

Let live and die its fleeting tones

Like a plaintive echo resounding in the woods.

I give no heed to luminescent palaces,

Inconstant universe of sumptuous delight;

Far from the raucous world, let flow my hours

With these soft chords so dear to my repose.

The Angel

Have you, in your modest empire, tended to

The household tasks, the meals and recreations?

You may grant to your lyre, if so,

A few moments stolen from your diversions.

The nightingale raises its pure voice,

But the nest of the nocturnal singer

Offers rest, nourishment, and shelter . . .

Woman, trust me, I lead to happiness.

The Mother

Come back, come back, dreams of my youth;

Wake up, my lyre! Let shining songs flood forth!

I can force glory to keep its promise:

Gathered for my son, the laurels will be sweet.

Yes, I want to smooth the way before his feet,

And offer my name to hold up his, still young;

I'll reach the target first, and guide him to it,

And brave the future to ensure that his be sound.

L'ange

Vois ce berceau, ton enfant y repose ;

Tes chants hardis vont troubler son sommeil ;

T'éloignes-tu ? ton absence l'expose

À te chercher en vain à son réveil.

Si tu frémis pour son naissant voyage,

De sa jeune âme exerce la vigueur :

Voilà ton but, ton espoir, ton ouvrage.

Mère, crois-moi, je conduis au bonheur.

La vieille femme

L'hiver sur mes cheveux étend sa main glacée ;

Il est donc vrai ! mes vœux n'ont pu vous arrêter,

Jours rapides ! et vous, pourquoi donc me quitter,

Rêves harmonieux qu'enfantait ma pensée ?

Hélas ! sans la toucher, j'ai laissé se flétrir

La palme qui m'offrait un verdoyant feuillage,

Et ce feu qu'attendait le phare du rivage,

Dans un foyer obscur je l'ai laissé mourir.

L'ange

Ce feu sacré, renfermé dans ton âme,

S'y consumait loin des profanes yeux ;

Comme l'encens offert dans les saints lieux,

Quelques parfums ont seuls trahi sa flamme.

D'un art heureux tu connus la douceur,

Sans t'égarer sur les pas de la gloire ;

THE ANGEL

See this cradle in which your child slumbers?
Your spirited songs will trouble his repose.
You're leaving now? When he will waken
To your absence, he will cry out in vain.
If you should shudder for his nascent journey,
Foster strength in his embryonic soul;
This is your hope, your work, your goal;
I lead to happiness, Mother: trust me.

THE OLD WOMAN

Upon my head winter's icy hand is stealing;
So it's true! My longing could not hinder
Lightning days! And why, now, are you leaving,
Harmonious dreams, by my thoughts engendered?
Alas! Without even touching it, I let wither
The palm that offered me its lush foliage;
And in a dim home I let die this fire,
Awaited by the beacon on the shore.

THE ANGEL

This sacred fire, enclosed in your breast,
Consumed itself far from eyes that shame;
As in holy halls incense burns,
Only its scent betrayed its flame.
You sampled the charm of an art that pleases
Without straying on the pathway to glory.

Jouis en paix d'une telle mémoire ;

Femme, crois-moi, je conduis au bonheur.

LA MOURANTE

Je sens pâlir mon front, et ma voix presque éteinte

Salue en expirant l'approche du trépas.

D'une innocente vie on peut sortir sans crainte,

Et mon céleste ami ne m'abandonne pas.

Mais quoi ! ne rien laisser après moi de moi-même !

Briller, trembler, mourir comme un triste flambeau !

Ne pas léguer du moins mes chants à ceux que j'aime,

Un souvenir au monde, un nom à mon tombeau !

L'ANGE

Il luit pour toi, le jour de la promesse,

Au port sacré je te dépose enfin,

Et près des cieux ta coupable faiblesse

Pleure un vain nom dans un monde plus vain.

La tombe attend tes dépouilles mortelles,

L'oubli tes chants ; mais l'âme est au Seigneur.

L'heure est venue, entends frémir mes ailes ;

Viens, suis mon vol, je conduis au bonheur !

Rejoice peacefully in such a memory:

Woman, trust me, I lead to happiness.

THE DYING WOMAN

I feel my brow grow pale, and my voice,

While fading, welcomes death's approach.

One can depart from an innocent life fearlessly,

And my heavenly friend will not abandon me.

And yet . . . to leave nothing of myself when I am gone!

To sparkle, tremble, die a dismal flame!

Not even, to those I love, bequeath my songs,

Mementos for the world, for my tomb a name!

THE ANGEL

The promised day now shines for you at last:

I deliver you to the holy gate. Yet

Even now, so near to heaven, guilty still,

You mourn a name that's vain in a hollow world.

The tomb awaits your earthly remains,

Oblivion your songs; but to the Lord your soul belongs.

The hour is here: heed the quiver of my wings;

Come, follow my flight. I lead to happiness!

Delphine Gay de Girardin

(1804–55)

Translations by Christopher Rivers and Gretchen Schultz

Delphine Gay de Girardin was a product of Parisian salon culture. The daughter of the Directoire *salonnière* and writer Sophie Gay (1776–1852), she was named for the heroine of Germaine de Staël's novel *Delphine* (1802). Her mother encouraged her to write and introduced her to the notable contemporaries who frequented her salon.

Girardin was particularly prominent during the July monarchy (1830–48). In 1831 she married the influential journalist Émile de Girardin (who in 1836 founded *La presse*, the first mass-circulating daily, which was responsible for the rise of the *roman feuilleton* or serial novel). Girardin launched her own salon, whose habitués included many literary figures, such as Victor Hugo, Honoré de Balzac, Alphonse de Lamartine, Alfred de Musset, Alfred de Vigny, Théophile Gautier, and Juliette Récamier, as well as a number of politicians. She flourished in this privileged sphere and was so celebrated for her beauty, personality, and talents that she became known as the tenth muse.

A writer of many genres (poetry, journalism, novel, plays), Girardin composed most of her poetry early in life, winning the Académie Française's poetry contest at age nineteen. Her first two collections were published before her marriage and signed Mlle Delphine Gay. From 1836 until 1848, she wrote a weekly column in *La presse* entitled "La chronique de Paris" ("The Paris Column") under the transparent male pseudonym of Vicomte de Launay. She owes much of her lasting renown to these *Lettres parisiennes*. Later in life she wrote for the theater with great success and saw her plays broadly produced and translated.

Dorothy Kelly has called her poetry "feminocentric" for its many references to women writers and their work (190), a practice exemplified in "Ourika," a poem inspired by and dedicated to Claire de Duras, who wrote a short novel having the same name. That Girardin's poems are emotionally charged is signaled by the proliferation of exclamations at the end of "Le bonheur d'être belle" ("The Joy of Being Beautiful") and the self-doubting questions in "Ourika." Yet they are neither simple nor transparent. Kelly remarks that "veiling, irony, and reversal appear to be defenses against the penetrating gaze of the other" (192), an analysis particularly pertinent for the paired poems "Le bonheur d'être belle" and "Le malheur d'être laide" ("The Misfortune of Being Ugly"), the first of which is included here. In this first poem, it is interesting to note Girardin's throughgoing use of "rime pour l'œil,"[5] which emphasizes visual harmony. Girardin marks, moreover, the emotional climax at the poem's end with a series of rich rhymes.

Her poetic works are *Essais poétiques* (1824), *Nouveaux essais poétiques* (1825), *Le dernier jour de Pompéi, suivi de poésies diverses* (1828), and *Poésies complètes* (1842). "Le bonheur d'être belle" was first published in *Essais*; "Ourika" seems to have been first published by itself (1824). For further reading, see Braswell; Giacchetti; Lassère; Morgan; Nesci, Introd.; Schapira.

---

[5]Literally, "rhyme for the eye," a rhyme composed of sounds that share the same spelling. Such rhymes, in which visual uniformity underscores sound equivalence, were considered to be particularly elegant, and achieving them with the consistency shown in "Bonheur d'être belle" added an additional layer of difficulty to its composition.

Le bonheur d'être belle

Dédié à Madame Récamier

Quel bonheur d'être belle, alors qu'on est aimée !

Autrefois de mes yeux je n'étais pas charmée ;

Je les croyais sans feu, sans douceur, sans regard ;

Je me trouvais jolie un moment par hasard.

Maintenant ma beauté me paraît admirable.

Je m'aime de lui plaire, et je me crois aimable....

Il le dit si souvent ! Je l'aime, et quand je voi

Ses yeux, avec plaisir, se reposer sur moi,

Au sentiment d'orgueil je ne suis point rebelle,

Je bénis mes parents de m'avoir fait si belle !

Et je rends grâce à Dieu, dont l'insigne bonté

Me fit le cœur aimant pour sentir ma beauté.

Mais... pourquoi dans mon cœur ces subites alarmes ?...

Si notre amour tous deux nous trompait sur mes charmes ;

Si j'étais laide enfin ? Non..., il s'y connaît mieux !

D'ailleurs pour m'admirer je ne veux que ses yeux !

Ainsi de mon bonheur jouissons sans mélange ;

Oui, je veux lui paraître aussi belle qu'un ange.

Apprêtons mes bijoux, ma guirlande de fleurs,

Mes gazes, mes rubans, et, parmi ces couleurs,

Choisissons avec art celle dont la nuance

The Joy of Being Beautiful

Dedicated to Madame Récamier[6]

What joy to be beautiful when one is loved!

Before, no charm in my own eyes did I find;

I thought them without fire, expression, softness;

At times, by chance alone, I glimpsed my prettiness.

But now before my beauty do I marvel.

I love myself for pleasing him; I am lovable . . .

So often does he say it! I love him, and when I see

His eyes, with pleasure, fall on me,

I rebel not against the sentiment of pride,

And bless my parents for the beauty that they made!

And thank God, whose eminent bounty

Granted me a loving heart, to enjoy this beauty.

But . . . in my heart, whence come these alarms?

Has love deceived us both about my charms?

If I were ugly, what to do? No . . . *he* knows better!

Indeed, to love myself, his eyes are all I call for!

Thus let us celebrate my happiness, so pure,

That to the beauty of an angel I'll compare.

Prepare my jewels and my garland flowers,

My gauzes, ribbons, and, from all the colors,

Let us choose artfully the one whose nuance

---

[6]Juliette or Julie Récamier (1777–1849) was among the most prominent social figures of Paris during the first half of the century. Habitués of her salon included eminent literary and political figures of the time. All the Romantic poets who appear in this collection knew her. See Wagener.

Doit avec plus de goût, avec plus d'élégance,

Rehausser de mon front l'éclatante blancheur,

Sans pourtant de mon teint balancer la fraîcheur.

Mais je ne trouve plus la fleur qu'il m'a donnée ;

La voici : hâtons-nous, l'heure est déjà sonnée,

Bientôt il va venir ! bientôt il va me voir !

Comme, en me regardant, il sera beau ce soir !

Le voilà ! je l'entends, c'est sa voix amoureuse !

Quel bonheur d'être belle ! Oh ! que je suis heureuse !

Will most tastefully, and with elegance,

Enhance the radiant whiteness of my brow

But not sacrifice the freshness of my skin.

Oh dear! I cannot find the flower he brought;

Here it is: quickly now, for the clock has struck,

He will soon come! He will soon see me!

How handsome, as his gaze falls on me, will he be!

Hark! He's here! His loving voice is nigh!

What joy to be beautiful! How happy am I!

Ourika: Élégie

À Madame La Duchesse de Duras

Vous dont le cœur s'épuise en regrets superflus,
Oh ! ne vous plaignez pas, vous que l'on n'aime plus !
Du triomphe d'un jour votre douleur s'honore ;
Et celle qu'on aima peut être aimée encore.

     Moi, dont l'exil ne doit jamais finir,
Seule dans le passé, seule dans l'avenir,
     Traînant le poids de ma longue souffrance,
Pour m'aider à passer des jours sans espérance,
     Je n'ai pas même un souvenir.

     À mon pays dès le berceau ravie,
D'une mère jamais je n'ai chéri la loi ;
     La pitié seule a pris soin de ma vie,
Et nul regard d'amour ne s'est tourné vers moi.

     L'enfant qu'attire ma voix douce
Me fuit dès qu'il a vu la couleur de mon front ;
En vain mon cœur est pur, le monde me repousse,
     Et ma tendresse est un affront.

Ourika: Elegy

for Madame La Duchesse de Duras

You, whose hearts are weary with superfluous regrets,

If you are loved no longer, do not complain!

The triumph of a day your anguish honors,

And she who, once loved, can yet be loved again.

But my exile never ends:

Alone yesterday, I'll be alone tomorrow,

Bearing unwavering sorrow.

I have, to help me pass these hopeless days,

Not even memories.

Torn from my land while still a baby,

No mother's sympathy could I treasure;

Pity alone cared for me,

And no loving gaze embraced my features.

The child drawn near by my soft voice

Now flees when seeing the color of my face;

The world rejects me: my heart is pure in vain,

And my tenderness offends.

The best-selling novella *Ourika* (1824) was written by Claire de Duras (1777–1828), to whom this poem is dedicated. *Ourika* was inspired by the true story of a Senegalese woman raised from childhood among the Parisian aristocracy.

Une fois à l'espoir mon cœur osa prétendre ;

D'un bien commun à tous je rêvai la douceur ;

Mais celui que j'aimais ne voulut pas m'entendre ;

Et, si parfois mes maux troublaient son âme tendre,

L'ingrat ! il m'appelait sa sœur !

Une autre aussi l'aima ; je l'entendis près d'elle,

Même en voyant mes pleurs, bénir son heureux sort ;

Et celui dont la joie allait causer ma mort,

Hélas ! en me quittant ne fut point infidèle.

Je ne puis l'accuser ; dans son aveuglement,

S'il a de ma douleur méconnu le langage,

C'est qu'il croyait les cœurs promis à l'esclavage

Indignes de souffrir d'un si noble tourment !

Malgré le trait mortel dont mon âme est atteinte,

Auprès de ma rivale on me laissait sans crainte.

Elle avait vu mes pleurs et les avait compris ;

Mais, ô sort déplorable ! ô comble de mépris !

Charles, je t'adorais... et ton heureuse épouse

Connaissait mon amour et n'était point jalouse !

Que de fois j'enviai la beauté de ses traits !

En l'admirant mes yeux se remplissaient de larmes ;

Et triste humiliée, alors je comparais

Le deuil de mon visage à l'éclat de ses charmes !

To hope: my heart once dared;

I dreamt of riches sweet, desires all others shared;

But the one I loved chose not to hear me;

If ever my torment troubled his heart, so tender,

    The ingrate called me "sister"!

Another loved him, too. Though witness to my tears,

I heard him to her extol his happiness;

And he whose joy would cause my death,

Alas! In leaving me was not faithless.

I cannot blame him if, in his blindness,

He misconstrued the signs of my distress:

He thought hearts pledged to slavery

Unfit to suffer such a noble agony!

Despite the mortal blow my soul has borne,

No one feared that I'd outshine my rival.

She had seen my tears and understood them;

What deplorable fate! What ultimate scorn!

I adored you, Charles . . . and your happy spouse

Knew of my love and was not jealous!

How often I envied the beauty of her features!

Admiring her, my eyes would fill with tears;

And sad, humiliated, then would I compare

Her radiant charms to my face, so somber!

Pourquoi m'avoir ravie à nos sables brûlants ?

Pourquoi les insensés, dans leur pitié cruelle,

Ont-ils jusqu'en ces lieux conduit mes pas tremblants ?

Là-bas, sous mes palmiers, j'aurais paru si belle !

Je n'aurais pas connu de ce monde abhorré

Le dédain protecteur et l'ironie amère ;

Un enfant, sans effroi, m'appellerait sa mère,

Et sur ma tombe, au moins, quelqu'un aurait pleuré !

Mais, que dis-je ?... Ô mon Dieu ! le désespoir m'égare :

Devrais-je, quand aux cieux la palme se prépare,

Lorsque tu me promets un bonheur immortel,

Regretter la patrie où tu n'as point d'autel ?

Ah ! du moins qu'en mourant tout mon cœur t'appartienne !

La plainte, les regrets ne me sont plus permis :

Dans les champs paternels, à d'autres dieux soumis,

Je n'eusse été qu'heureuse !... ici je meurs chrétienne !

Why was I snatched away from burning sands?

Why did they, thoughtlessly benevolent,

Lead me from my home, trembling, to these lands?

Under palm trees, I would have been magnificent!

I would not have known, of this loathsome world,

The bitter irony and protective scorn;

I could have been a mother to a loving child,

And one would weep, at least, upon my tomb!

My God! What say I, drifting in despair?

As you prepare my heavenly seat of glory,

You who promise me eternal pleasure,

Why regret a homeland that's not holy?

At least in dying my heart's entirely yours!

Regrets and tears no longer are permitted:

In my father's fields, to other gods subjected,

I would perhaps be happy! . . . Here, I die converted!

ÉLISA MERCŒUR

(1809–35)

Translations by Michael Bishop

Born in Nantes, Élisa Mercœur was an illegitimate child raised by a single mother. She was self-schooled and, at the precocious age of sixteen, won regional fame for her poetry, thus gaining the epithet the Armoricain muse (for Brittany's ancient name). She pursued an advanced education, the first female in her school to do so, and supported herself by teaching while continuing to write. In 1827, Mercœur published her sole book of poetry, entitled *Poésies*, well-crafted verse indebted to Lamartinian elegiac Romanticism. Her work is expressive, in turns contemplative and exalting. It addresses the suffering of the disenfranchised but also strives for poetic glory. Indeed, eager for recognition in the capital, an ambition that her mother encouraged, Mercœur moved to Paris in 1828. Her poetry was praised by prominent writers, including François de Chateaubriand and Alphonse de Lamartine. Juliette Récamier, among others, welcomed her into their notable salons. Despite her fame and visibility, ongoing financial hardship obliged her to continue teaching and perhaps explains her abandonment of poetry for prose (essays, serial fiction, and theater).

Although Mercœur was wildly popular during her lifetime, her decline, in both health and reputation, was rapid. She lost many supporters following the July Revolution, fell ill, and, impoverished, died of tuberculosis at the age of twenty-six. This early death, and the renewed publicity it attracted, contributed to the construction of her Romantic persona as a consumptive young genius. Mercœur's mother cultivated this image with the lengthy eulogy that she wrote to preface her daughter's posthumously published complete works.

For further reading, see Geoffroy; Greenberg; Plötner.

Le réveil d'une vierge

La cloche matinale et résonne et t'appelle,
Vierge ; ne rêve plus un prestige effacé.
    Éveille-toi, l'airain de la chapelle,
Plaintive Nataly, déjà s'est balancé.

C'est l'heure où chaque jour, soulevant ta paupière,
    S'ouvrent tes yeux, cet asile des pleurs ;
Quand au pied des autels, près de tes jeunes sœurs,
    Ta douce voix soupire une prière ;

        Sur le marbre silencieux
        Incline-toi, vierge timide ;
Dans un calme sacré, fais méditer les cieux
        À ton âme pure et candide.
Oh ! ne rappelle pas un souvenir trompeur,
    En déchirant le voile des mensonges :
        Qu'échappée au séjour des songes,
Ton âme soit un ange au sein du Créateur !
Le monde te parut de loin comme un orage,
    Tu l'évitas, comme un craintif agneau ;
    Et de l'oubli sur sa funeste image
Le cloître qui t'enferme a posé le bandeau.

La cloche matinale et résonne et t'appelle,
Vierge ; ne rêve plus un prestige effacé.
    Éveille-toi, l'airain de la chapelle,
Plaintive Nataly, déjà s'est balancé.

Décembre 1825

A Maiden Awakes

The morning bell rings out, calling to your
Maidenhead; dream no more of faded glory.
    Awaken, the chapel bronze,
Plaintive Nataly, already has swung.

Each day at this hour, your eyelids open,
    Your gaze, refuge of tears, lifts up;
When, with your young sisters, below the altar,
    Your sweet voice sighs a prayer,

        Upon the silent marble
        Shy maiden, bend low;
In sacred serenity, let the heavens
        Contemplate your pure and candid soul.
Oh, let go all deceptive memory,
    Tearing asunder the veil of lies:
        May your soul, delivered of the realm
Of dream, be an angel in the Creator's bosom.
From afar the world appeared to you as a storm,
    You fled it, like a frightened lamb;
    And upon its fateful image the cloister
That shuts you in placed the blindfold of oblivion.

The morning bell rings out, calling to your
Maidenhead; dream no more of faded glory.
    Awaken, the chapel bronze,
Plaintive Nataly, already has swung.

December 1825

Le jeune mendiant

Je souffre, le besoin me contraint à le dire ;
Le malheur me retient sous sa méchante loi.
À ce monde bruyant, qui paraît vous sourire,
Dérobez un regard pour le jeter sur moi.

L'eau pure du Léman vient baigner ma patrie ;
Là, comme vous, jadis j'eus aussi mon bonheur.
Je suis pauvre à présent, je pleure, je mendie :
Près du beau lac Léman n'est resté que mon cœur.

Je serais sans désir, si vous viviez encore,
Bons parents, que vers lui rappela le Seigneur !
Mais je suis repoussé par la main que j'implore,
Et je n'obtiens jamais un mot consolateur.

Du pain, hélas ! voilà ce qu'il faut à ma vie,
Je ne sais point créer d'inutiles besoins ;
Ne fermez pas votre âme à la voix qui supplie :
Pour le pauvre le Ciel a réclamé des soins.

Vous n'osez m'approcher !... L'habit de la misère
De celui qu'il recouvre est-il le déshonneur ?
Quand votre œil dédaigneux (ou du moins je l'espère)
S'attache au vêtement, Dieu regarde le cœur.

The Young Beggar

I suffer, necessity forces me to speak;
Misfortune holds me in its spiteful law.
Steal your gaze from the noisy world that seems
To smile upon you; let it rest on me.

The pure waters of Leman bathe my homeland;
There, as you do, I too had my happiness.
Now am I poor, weeping, begging:
By lovely Leman my heart alone remains.

No desire would be mine, if you still lived,
Good parents, called back to him by the Lord!
But I am spurned by the hand I implore,
And never do I obtain a consoling word.

Bread, alas, is what my life requires,
My needs are not futile creations;
Do not close your heart to the supplicant voice:
For the poor, heaven demands ministrations.

You dare not draw near! . . . For him that wears it,
Is the coat of misery dishonor?
While your eye of disdain (or so I see it)
Clings to the garment, God gazes within.

Il lit au fond du mien ce qu'il a de souffrance,

Ah ! puisse-t-il au vôtre inspirer la pitié ;

Donnez ! bien peu suffit à ma frêle existence ;

Donnez ! j'ai faim ! j'attends !... aurai-je en vain prié ?

Février 1826

In the depths of my heart he reads suffering,

Ah, may he in yours inspire pity;

Please! So little my frail life is needing;

Please! I wait in hunger! . . . Have I begged in vain?

February 1826

LOUISE COLET

(1810–76)

née Révoil

Translations by Anne Atik

Louise Colet was born in Aix-en-Provence to a progressive and aristocratic, if fortuneless, mother and a prosperous but conformist and bourgeois father. Louise was educated by her mother, Henriette, and learned Italian from her father. She read widely from the family library and began to write poetry at an early age. On the death of her father, in 1825, and the loss of his income, the Révoils returned to the maternal family château to farm. Henriette died in 1834, a great loss for Louise, who cherished her mother. The following year, she married a musician, Hippolyte Colet, in part out of a desire to leave the intellectually and culturally stifling provinces for Paris. She did so against the wishes of her siblings, who had inherited the worldview of their traditionalist father, prompting a familial rupture that lasted her entire lifetime.

Moving to Paris with Hippolyte, Louise quickly made her way into Parisian literary society. A vivacious presence, she was ambitious and, reputedly, self-promoting. Although still poor, she succeeded in entering Charles Nodier's cenacle thanks to the success of her first collection, *Fleurs du Midi*. Once established, Colet occupied the center of the literary world. She established a salon in the 1840s and made friends (as well as some enemies) with many noted writers and personalities of her time, such as Victor Hugo, Juliette Récamier, François de Chateaubriand, Pierre-Jean de Béranger, Alfred de Vigny, and Charles Leconte de Lisle. Her numerous lovers included Alfred de Musset and, famously, the novelist Gustave Flaubert (1821–80). The philosopher Victor Cousin (1792–1867) allegedly fathered her daughter, born in 1838 and named Henriette, for Colet's mother. Two sons, born subsequently, died in infancy.

Colet was a prolific writer whose poetry was awarded several times by the Académie Française. She wrote in many other genres—theater, travel literature, short stories, and novels. A polyglot, she translated William Shakespeare as well as some Italian texts. In times of financial need, she turned to writing children's books (*Enfances célèbres* [1854]) and journalism (including fashion articles), more lucrative genres.

While her first collections bore all the marks of Romanticism, later in her career Colet adopted the Parnassian penchant for antiquity and descriptive formalism (as evidenced by "Paestum" and "Absorption in Love"; on her Parnassian poetry, see Schultz, *Gendered Lyric*). She was militantly to the left and vocal about her political beliefs: she supported the Paris Commune and the Italian Risorgimento (a lover of Italy, she lived there a while) and was a defender of workers and women. As Aimée Boutin has shown ("Inventing"), Colet defended these and other political and social movements in her work (see, e.g., her book-length *Poème de la femme*).

Her major poetic works are *Fleurs du Midi* (1836), *Penserosa* (1840), *Les chants des vaincus* (1846), *Ce qui est dans le cœur des femmes* (1852), *Ce qu'on rêve en aimant* (1854), *Quatre poëmes couronnés par l'Académie Française* (1855), *Le poème de la femme: La paysanne, la servante, la religieuse* (1853–56). Of the poems selected for this anthology, "Ma poésie" first appeared in *Fleurs du Midi*; "Sonnet" in *Penserosa*; "Mezza vita" and "Folles et saintes" in *Poésies complètes*; "À Monsieur Préault, statuaire" in *Ce qu'on rêve en aimant*; and "Paestum" and "Absorption dans l'amour" in the journal *Le parnasse contemporain*. For further reading, see Beizer; Bellet; Bood and Grand; Gray.

Ma poésie

Il est dans le Midi des fleurs d'un rose pâle
Dont le soleil d'hiver couronne l'amandier ;
On dirait des flocons de neige virginale
Rougis par les rayons d'un soleil printanier.

Mais pour flétrir les fleurs qui forment ce beau voile,
Si la rosée est froide, il suffit d'une nuit ;
L'arbre alors de son front voit tomber chaque étoile,
Et quand vient le printemps il n'a pas un seul fruit.

Ainsi mourront les chants qu'abandonne ma lyre
Au monde indifférent qui va les oublier ;
Heureuse, si parfois une âme triste aspire
Le parfum passager de ces fleurs d'amandier.

Paris, 1835

My Poetry

In the Midi pale-pink flowers grow,
Crowning the almond tree in the winter sun;
You could say flakes like virginal snow
Reddened by the springtime sun.

But to wither the flowers that form this fine veil,
If the dew is cold, you need but one night;
Then from its brow the tree sees each star fall,
And when spring comes not one fruit is left.

In an indifferent world, abandoned by my lyre,
My songs will thus die and be forgotten;
Happy if at times a despondent soul breathes in
The fleeting scent of the almond flower.

Paris, 1835

Sonnet

Le malheur m'a jeté son souffle desséchant :
De mes doux sentiments la source s'est tarie,
Et mon âme abattue, avant l'heure flétrie,
En perdant tout espoir perd tout penser touchant.

Mes yeux n'ont plus de pleurs, ma voix n'a plus de chant,
Mon cœur désenchanté n'a plus de rêverie ;
Pour tout ce que j'aimais avec idolâtrie
Il ne me reste plus d'amour ni de penchant.

Une aride douleur ronge et brûle mon âme,
Il n'est rien que j'envie et rien que je réclame ;
Mon avenir est mort, le vide est dans mon cœur.

J'offre un corps sans pensée à l'œil qui me contemple ;
Tel sans divinité reste quelque vieux temple,
Telle après le banquet la coupe est sans liqueur.

1834

Sonnet

Misfortune has cast its withering breath on me:
The source of my tender feelings is parched,
And my worn-out soul, shriveled before its time,
In losing hope, loses all kindly thought.

My eyes, drained of tears; my voice, of song bereft;
My disenchanted heart, devoid of reverie:
For everything I loved with idolatry,
There's no more love, no longing left.

An arid pain burns and gnaws at my soul,
There's nothing I desire or demand;
My future is dead, there's a void in my heart.

I offer my body indifferent to the gazing eye;
Like an old temple that's lost its deity,
Like a cup empty of liquor after the feast.

1834

Mezza vita

> *Nel mezzo del cammin di nostra vita,*
> *Mi ritrovai per una selva oscura.*

Le milieu de la vie, heure amère et néfaste,

Où des jours qu'on regrette arrive le déclin ;

Halte où nous ressentons le douloureux contraste

Que le sombre couchant fait au riant matin.

Alors tout s'obscurcit et tout se décolore :

Le temps marche amenant mille deuils après soi ;

Muettes sont les voix qui chantaient à l'aurore,

L'esprit n'a plus d'élan, l'âme n'a plus de foi.

Les beaux rêves s'en vont. – Illusions candides,

Ineffables amours, enthousiasmes saints,

Tout meurt : avec effroi l'homme compte les vides

Que laissent dans son cœur ses sentiments éteints.

On cherche vainement à ressaisir la vie,

À fixer le bonheur entre ses bras tremblants.

L'âme, comme autrefois, n'est plus épanouie,

Et déjà sur le front germent des cheveux blancs.

Mezza vita

Nel mezzo del cammin di nostra vita,
Mi ritrovai per una selva oscura.[7]

The middle of life, ill-omened and bitter hour,

When the close of regretted days comes on;

A pause when we feel the painful contrast

Between somber sundown and smiling morn.

It is then that all darkens and all colors fade:

Time marching leads a thousand griefs behind;

The voices that chanted at dawn are muted,

The soul has no faith, the spirit no bound.

Lovely dreams are past. —Guileless illusions,

Heavenly raptures, ineffable loves,

All dies: man feels the void—in fright—

That extinguished feelings have left in his heart.

One seeks to recapture life, in vain,

To hold happiness fast between trembling arms.

The soul blooms no longer as it did before,

And, on our brow, gray hairs already appear.

---

[7]The opening lines of Dante's *Inferno*: "Midway in the journey of our life /
I came to myself in a dark wood."

Si, détournant de soi l'importune pensée,

Sur ses enfants aimés on reporte ses vœux,

On voit dans l'avenir leur jeunesse éclipsée,

On pressent leurs douleurs et l'on souffre pour eux.

Et chaque jour en nous grandit la plaie ardente

D'un incurable ennui dont on se sent mourir ;

Et, comme la forêt où s'égara le Dante,

Lugubre est l'horizon qui reste à parcourir.

Août 1843

If we turn such intrusive thoughts from ourselves

And transfer our hopes to our children so loved,

We see in the future their youth dissolve;

Portending their pain, it's for their sake we grieve.

And each day we feel the burning sore spread

With an incurable ennui from which we feel we shall die;

And, like the forest in which Dante erred,

Grim is the landscape that we still must tread.

August 1843

Folles et saintes

Folles et saintes sœurs, écloses et formées

Dans les rêves divers que j'évoquais la nuit,

Visions que mon âme a tour à tour aimées,

       Au monde allez sans bruit.

Allez, vous n'êtes pas à briller appelées,

Et je n'attends de vous ni succès ni faveurs ;

Vous ne pouvez charmer, modestes et voilées,

       Que des esprits rêveurs !

Je vous aime et vous suis, mes filles idéales,

D'un cœur reconnaissant, d'un regard attendri.

Combien d'amers soucis, combien d'heures fatales

Vous m'avez épargné quand vous m'avez souri !

Vous avez, fruits légers de mon intelligence,

Distrait mon faible cœur de ses propres ennuis ;

Contre l'abattement et contre l'indigence

       Vous fûtes mes appuis.

Ces vers servent de préface à deux volumes de récits en prose publiés par le libraire Pétion. —Colet's note

Madwomen and Saints

Madwomen and saints, sisters born and formed
In sundry dreams, which I evoked nightly,
Visions my soul loved, each in turn,
      Worldward go, silently.

Go, now; you're not called on to shine,
And I don't ask you to succeed or be kind;
You can only charm, modest and veiled,
      A musing turn of mind.

I love and follow you, my ideal daughters,
With a grateful heart, with a tender regard.
How many bitter worries, fatal hours
      I was spared, when you smiled!

Lightsome fruit of my intelligence,
You drove away troubles from my fragile heart,
And against despair and indigence
      Gave me your support.

These lines serve as a preface to two volumes of stories in prose published by the bookseller Pétion. —Colet's note, referring to her *Folles et saintes* (Paris: Pétion, 1844)

Dans ce livre, il n'est pas un récit, une page,

Qui ne m'ait apporté l'obole du travail.

Mes veilles, mes douleurs, sont là dans chaque image

Et dans chaque détail.

Voilà pourquoi mon cœur vous aime avec faiblesse,

Frêles créations de mes plus mauvais jours ;

Pourquoi j'ai peur pour vous de ce monde qui blesse

Nos pleurs et nos amours.

Oh ! puissiez-vous, trompant ma crainte maternelle,

Ne trouver que des cœurs sympathiques et doux !

Allez, pauvres enfants, échappés de mon aile,

Dans la foule bruyante humblement glissez-vous !

Avril 1843

In this book there isn't a story or page

That didn't repay me with earnings or wage.

My vigils, my pains are in every detail

   And every image.

Hence this loving weakness for you in my heart,

Frail creatures of my least fortunate days;

Why I fear for you in this world that wounds

   Our loves and our tears.

Oh! May you belie my maternal dread,

And find only soft, sympathetic hearts!

Go now, poor children, flee from under my wings,

   Slip low through the noisy crowd!

        April 1843

À Monsieur Préault, statuaire :
Sur un masque funéraire

En flots tumultueux quand mon âme s'élance,
Impassible, il est là, ton grand sphinx du silence ;
Il est là, l'œil baissé, toujours muet et froid,
Et sur sa bouche close il allonge son doigt.

Son immobilité raille ma véhémence ;
Les douleurs du vivant pour le mort sont démence.
Le calme trépassé, dans son cercueil étroit,
Semble, en se soulevant, douter de ce qu'il voit.

« Encor, dit sans parler l'inflexible visage,
« Encor la passion et l'éternel orage !
« Le souffle qui t'abat comme toi m'a courbé ;

« Mais regarde : l'amour, qui ravit et qui navre,
« Sous le suaire blanc qui flotte à mon cadavre
« Avant moi dans la tombe en poussière est tombé ! »

To Monsieur Préault, Sculptor:
On a Funeral Mask

When my soul leaps up in a tumultuous wave,

He's there, your great silent sphinx, unmoved;

He's there, eyes lowered, always mute, without warmth,

Extending his finger upon his closed mouth.

His fixity ridicules my vehemence;

The pain of the quick for the dead is madness.

From his narrow coffin, the tranquil deceased,

Upon rising, seems to distrust what he sees.

"Again," the rigid face, without speaking, says;

"Again, the passion and eternal affray!

The blast that fells you, like you, bent me down.

But look: love, which saddens and entrances,

Under the shroud hanging loose on my corpse

Fell to dust—before I did—in the tomb."

Auguste Préault (1809–79), a Romantic sculptor known for violent subjects and extreme emotions, was the creator of *Vénus et le Sphinx* (1868) and *Jupiter et la Sphinge* (1868[?]).

Pæstum

La lascive Pæstum n'a pas laissé d'annales ;
L'oubli la châtia de son inanité ;
À peine si Tibulle en un vers a chanté
Les roses qui jonchaient ses molles saturnales.

Dans une plaine morne, où grincent les rafales,
Où la Mal'aria verse un souffle empesté,
Le néant la coucha de ses mains sépulcrales,
Et le passant se dit : « Elle n'a pas été. »

Mais voilà que, vibrant comme trois grandes lyres,
Surgissent lumineux d'un marécage noir
Ses trois temples, debout sur le pourpre du soir.

Clairs parvis, pleins jadis d'olympiens délires,
Les spectres de vos dieux errants sur les chemins
Sont-ils ces pâtres nus aux fiers profils romains ?

Paestum

No annals remain from Paestum the wanton;

Oblivion punished her vacuousness;

Tibullus sang hardly more thàn one verse

About the roses bestrewing her lewd abandon.[8]

Where gusts screech in a gloomy plain,

Where Malaria pours a poisonous breath,

Nothingness felled her with hands of death.

And the passerby thinks: "She has never been."

But, there, as vibrant as three great lyres,

Rise her three bright temples from a black quagmire

Upright on the evening's crimson sky.

Olympian frenzies once filled your bright squares;

Are these bare shepherds with proud Roman profiles

The ghosts of your gods on the roads, roving by?

Paestum, known for its three stunning Doric temples (6th cent. BCE), was an ancient city in the Gulf of Salerno, in southwest Italy. It was first founded as a colony by the Sybarites, reputed for their devotion to pleasure and luxury. The eruption of Mount Vesuvius in 79 AD partially destroyed the city. Its temples were rediscovered in the eighteenth century.

[8]Tibullus, a Latin elegiac poet (1st cent. BCE) translated into French by the revolutionary Comte de Mirabeau, was appreciated in France as an erotic poet.

Absorption dans l'amour

Comme si ses flancs renfermaient une âme,

Le Vésuve au loin gronde sourdement ;

Le ciel est zébré de langues de flamme,

La cendre jaillit du sommet fumant.

Au pied du volcan la mer fulgurante

Mugit sur ses bords et sur ses récifs ;

Dans les frais ravins où s'endort Sorrente,

Sous les orangers ils restent assis.

C'est le premier jour que la femme aimante

A revu celui qu'elle a tant pleuré ;

Qu'importe à son cœur la sombre tourmente,

Le gouffre béant, le ciel déchiré ?

Ivre de le voir, ivre de l'entendre,

Elle reste sourde aux bruits de l'alentour ;

La mort serait douce à cette âme tendre

En la foudroyant aux bras de l'amour.

1867

Absorption in Love

As though its flanks enclosed a soul,

Vesuvius, far off, emits a rumbling growl.

In the sky that tongues of flame have streaked,

Ash pours out of its smoky peak.

The flashing sea at the volcano's foot

Howls at its reefs and at its coast;

Where Sorrento slumbers in cool ravines,

They stay seated under orange trees.

For this loving woman, it's the first day

She sees again the man she'd not ceased to lament;

What does it matter, the lashing sky,

The yawning chasm, the grim torment?

Transported with seeing him, transported with hearing him,

She's deaf to sounds below, around, above;

To this tender soul death would be sweet if it came

And struck her down in the arms of love.

1867

Reaction and Rebellion:
Parnassianism, War, and the Fall of Empire

During the century's third quarter, which coincided with the rise and fall of the Second Empire (1852–70), poets associated with Parnassianism rebelled against what they considered to be the excesses of Romanticism. Although short-lived as a movement, it left a powerful imprint as a backlash in a century marked by inventive, farsighted poetry. The movement took its name from the review *Le Parnasse contemporain*, whose three volumes (1866, 1871, 1876) contained works by a hundred poets. In Greek mythology, the mountain Parnassus housed Apollo and the Muses; symbolically, it designates the home of poetry and poets. Albeit a diverse group, Parnassian poets shared an antiutilitarian aesthetic characterized by erudition and the quest for formal perfection. The movement's staunchest practitioners were Théophile Gautier (1811–72), Charles Leconte de Lisle (1818–94), Théodore de Banville (1823–91), Catulle Mendès (1841–1909), José-Maria de Heredia (1842–1905), and François Coppée (1842–1908).

Parnassian apoliticism derived, in part, from disenchantment following the 1848 revolution, which led to the proclamation of the Second Republic (1848–52). Progressive aspirations were dashed by Louis Napoléon's repressive presidency and, after his coup d'état in late 1851, by his emperorship, whose bourgeois mediocrity was execrated by the intelligentsia. In opposition to the Romantic propensity for political and social engagement, Parnassians refused to mix politics and literature and took the notion of art for art's sake to an extreme. Gautier, for example, in "Préface," describes shutting his windows to the noises of the revolution in order to write his poetry: "Sans prendre garde à l'ouragan / Qui fouettait mes vitres fermées / Moi, j'ai fait *Émaux et Camées*" (25; "Without giving heed to the storm / That whipped my closed windows / I wrote *Enamels and Cameos*"). Although continuing the Romantics' orientalist penchant, Parnassians, as their name suggests, also looked to antiquity, which provided a poetic model and thematic obsession. Neoclassical in its aesthetic, Parnassianism encouraged the rehabilitation of shorter fixed forms (in particular the sonnet,[9] but also the ballade and terza rima),[10] rich rhymes, and finely chiseled alexandrines. The objective poetry of the Parnassians shunned

---

[9]The sonnet originated in Italy and was introduced to France in the sixteenth century. The regular French sonnet contains five rhymes and is built on two quatrains (with the scheme *abba abba* or *abab abab*) followed by a sestet (normally disposed as two tercets with the scheme *ccd ede* or *ccd eed*). The Elizabethan or Shakespearean sonnet differs in rhyme scheme and stanza structure. It has seven rhymes, with three quatrains in crossed rhymes and a final couplet: *abab cdcd efef gg*.

[10]Terza rima (*aba bcb cdc* . . .) is a form introduced by Dante and later adopted in France by the poets of the Pléiade. See Siefert's "Orgueil!" for an example.

the first person and tended to be highly descriptive. Gautier's poem "L'art" (148–50) and Théodore de Banville's *Petit traité de poésie française* (1872) most aptly describe their poetic approach.

Parnassians turned to metaphors of hardness—statuary and stonework—while accusing their predecessors of softness. Leconte de Lisle suggested that poets such as Alphonse de Lamartine and his followers suffered from an excess of femininity: "il y a dans ce gémissement continu une telle absence de virilité..., cette langue est tellement molle, efféminée et incorrecte, le vers manque à ce point de muscles" (170; "this perpetual moaning betrays an incredible absence of virility, this language is exceedingly soft, effeminate and faulty; the poetry has no muscle").

More so than surrounding poetic movements of the nineteenth century, the Parnasse relegated woman to the role of object, a passive and impassive figure for idealized beauty. Its antifeminism reflected a poetic ideology and publishing practice that disadvantaged women poets. The *Parnasse contemporain* included no women in its first, most characteristic volume. Among the eight women who appear in the second and third volumes are the well-established Colet, who made made her first mark on literary history under Romanticism; Ackermann, her contemporary; Blanchecotte; and the younger poets Siefert and Villard. While this list of names is eclectic, female contributors explored either the sonnet form, the impersonal voice, or orientalist themes, all favored by the movement.

Although no women poets, with the significant exception of Villard, actively participated in Parnassian circles,

others wrote outside the confines of this apolitical move-
ment. Michel's poetry gave voice to the Paris Commune,
the popular uprising that was brutally repressed in May
1871. And the events leading up to and following the em-
pire's downfall inspired Siefert to chronicle the disastrous
Franco-Prussian war (1870–71).

For further reading, see Badesco; Denommé; Schaffer;
Schultz, *Gendered Lyric*; and Mortelette.

LOUISE ACKERMANN

(1813–90)

née Louise-Victorine Choquet

Translations by Laurence Porter

Born to bourgeois parents and raised in the Parisian countryside, Louise Ackermann describes her childhood as solitary, although marked by a love of nature and books. She was an avid reader from an early age, and her parents and teachers encouraged her at a time when it was uncommon to tend to the education of girls. Ackermann's father supported her freethinking and skepticism, and she rebuffed her mother's religious instruction and conventionally feminine socialization. She began writing poetry as an adolescent.

Although Louise "faisai[t] simplement un mariage de convenance morale" (xv; "simply married for moral convenience" ["My Life" 71]), she and Paul Ackermann formed a marriage of love and intellectual affinity. It nonetheless put an end to her creativity: she abandoned her writing to aid her husband in his. When he died two years after they married, Louise moved to the countryside near Nice and lived alone for the remainder of her life. She farmed, eventually returned to her books (with particular interest in literature, philosophy, and new scientific theories), and began to write again.

Both her life and poetic practice placed Ackermann at odds with cultural expectations for women: "Une femme artiste ou écrivain m'a toujours paru une anomalie . . . [C]'est son âme qu'elle met en circulation à ses risques et périls" (*Pensées* 18–19; "A woman artist or writer has always struck me as an anomaly. . . . She places her soul in circulation, at her own risk"). She was highly cerebral yet often divided between principles of intellectual honesty and moments of diffidence. Although critical of certain traits associated with normative femininity, such as piety and coquetry, at times she preached docility in women and was adamant about married women's duties to their husbands. Ultimately, she strikes the reader as a proud and private woman who wished to shield herself from ridicule. She retreated into voluntary obscurity at several points in her life, opting for tranquillity and a highly unusual independence.

Ackermann's poetry is among the least typical of work by women during the period. She distinguished herself by writing poems that defied stereotypes of women's poetry as sentimental, pious, and derivative. Even the notoriously misogynist critic Barbey d'Aurevilly recognized the originality of her "poésies . . . résolument athées . . . et superbes," written "avec une préméditation inouïe et l'intensité d'une rage froide" (II: 158; "superb, resolutely atheistic poetry written with incredible premeditation and the intensity of a cold passion"). And yet her very success unsexed her: "Madame Ackermann . . . est parvenue à tuer son sexe en elle et à le remplacer par quelque chose de neutre et d'horrible, mais de puissant" (165; "Mrs. Ackermann has managed to kill the woman in her and to replace it with something neuter and horrible, yet powerful"). Her *Poésies philosophiques*, in particular, place her among the most erudite of the poets in this anthology. Her poetry refers to philosophical and scientific concerns of her time. She is often placed in the tradition of positivist poets for her profound skepticism. Despite her contemporary characterization as a bluestocking, Ackermann had, in fact, a conflicted relation with feminism and struggled with her poetic aspirations—a struggle common among women writers living in a culture of masculine dominance. At times a model for feminism in her outspokenness and quest for intellectual liberty and material independence, at times a mouthpiece for feminine conformity, Ackermann demonstrated an ambivalence that collided with her unwavering devotion to critical thought.

Her poetic works are *Contes en vers* (1855), *Contes et poésies* (1863), *Poésies philosophiques* (1871), and *Œuvres* (1874). The poems selected for this anthology, "Mon livre," "L'amour et la mort," "Le positivisme," and "J'ignore!," first appeared in *Poésies philosophiques*. For further reading, see Charlton; Citoleux; Fontana; Jenson, "Gender" and "Louise Ackermann's Monstrous Nature"; Paliyenko, "Is a Woman Poet."

Mon livre

Je ne vous offre plus pour toutes mélodies
Que des cris de révolte et des rimes hardies.
Oui ! Mais en m'écoutant si vous alliez pâlir ?
Si, surpris des éclats de ma verve imprudente,
Vous maudissiez la voix énergique et stridente
        Qui vous aura fait tressaillir ?

Pourtant, quand je m'élève à des notes pareilles,
Je ne prétends blesser les cœurs ni les oreilles.
Même les plus craintifs n'ont point à s'alarmer ;
L'accent désespéré sans doute ici domine,
Mais je n'ai pas tiré ces sons de ma poitrine
        Pour le plaisir de blasphémer.

Comment ? la Liberté déchaîne ses colères ;
Partout, contre l'effort des erreurs séculaires,
La Vérité combat pour s'ouvrir un chemin ;
Et je ne prendrais pas parti dans ce grand drame ?
Quoi ! ce cœur qui bat là, pour être un cœur de femme,
        En est-il moins un cœur humain ?

Est-ce ma faute à moi si dans ces jours de fièvre
D'ardentes questions se pressent sur ma lèvre ?
Si votre Dieu surtout m'inspire des soupçons ?
Si la Nature aussi prend des teintes funèbres,

My Book

I can offer you only, in these times,

Shouts of rebellion set in daring rhymes.

Yes! What if hearing me made you turn pale?

If, startled by my bursts of reckless force,

You were to curse this voice, lusty and coarse,

      Which would have made you quail?

However, though I fashion such strong art,

I don't seek to shock your hearing or heart.

Even the most timid need feel no fear;

No doubt my despair dominates the rest,

But I have not torn these tones from my chest

      Only to wound God's ear.

Why then? I help Freedom unleash its rage;

Battling the errors of a bygone age,

Truth struggles in the dark to find its way;

In this drama, how could I not take part?

What? Is this woman's heart that beats today

      Less than a human heart?

Is it my fault in these times of unrest

If burning questions rush to fill my breast?

If your God above all inspires doubt?

If Nature, too, acquires funereal tones,

Et si j'ai de mon temps, le long de mes vertèbres,
    Senti courir tous les frissons ?

Jouet depuis longtemps des vents et de la houle,
Mon bâtiment fait eau de toutes parts ; il coule.
La foudre seule encore à ses signaux répond.
Le voyant en péril et loin de toute escale,
Au lieu de m'enfermer tremblante à fond de cale,
    J'ai voulu monter sur le pont.

À l'écart, mais debout, là, dans leur lit immense
J'ai contemplé le jeu des vagues en démence.
Puis, prévoyant bientôt le naufrage et la mort,
Au risque d'encourir l'anathème ou le blâme,
À deux mains j'ai saisi ce livre de mon âme,
    Et l'ai lancé par-dessus bord.

C'est mon trésor unique, amassé page à page.
À le laisser au fond d'une mer sans rivage
Disparaître avec moi je n'ai pu consentir.
En dépit du courant qui l'emporte ou l'entrave,
Qu'il se soutienne donc et surnage en épave
    Sur ces flots qui vont m'engloutir !

Paris, 7 janvier 1874

And if I feel this epoch in my bones,

      Quivering like a shout?

Long a plaything of the storm and the wave,

My ship has sprung too many leaks to save.

At all its distress flares, the lightning mocks.

I won't hide in the hold with a weak gasp

As my boat sinks so far from any docks:

      The helm I'll try to grasp.

Proudly aloof, above their angry bed,

I watched the churning waves the gale had sped.

Then, when shipwreck and death come to be lord,

Unafraid of anathema or blame,

I'll seize this book, the last trace of my name,

      And throw it overboard.

It is my only wealth, gleaned word by word.

I cannot let it find a fate absurd,

Whereby it would sink in a boundless sea.

Whether the spiteful tides carry or bind,

May it survive as flotsam after me,

      Whom none will ever find!

Paris, 7 January 1874

L'amour et la mort

À M. Louis de Ronchaud

I

Regardez-les passer, ces couples éphémères !

Dans les bras l'un de l'autre enlacés un moment,

Tous, avant de mêler à jamais leurs poussières,

      Font le même serment :

Toujours ! Un mot hardi que les cieux qui vieillissent

Avec étonnement entendent prononcer,

Et qu'osent répéter des lèvres qui pâlissent

      Et qui vont se glacer.

Vous qui vivrez si peu, pourquoi cette promesse

Qu'un élan d'espérance arrache à votre cœur,

Vain défi qu'au néant vous jetez, dans l'ivresse

      D'un instant de bonheur ?

Amants, autour de vous une voix inflexible

Crie à tout ce qui naît : « Aime et meurs ici-bas ! »

La mort est implacable et le ciel insensible ;

      Vous n'échapperez pas.

Love and Death

For M. Louis de Ronchaud[11]

I

See them passing, those lovers of a day!

Pressed in each other's arms an instant now,

All, before crumbling to primordial clay,

      Proffer the selfsame vow:

Forever! A bold word the aging skies

Hear with astonishment on humans' breath

Recklessly uttered by the lip that dies

      And soon stiffens in death.

Mortals whose life is brief, why promise this

Permanence with which hope deludes your heart,

Vainly defying the void, in your bliss

      Moments before you part?

Lovers, hear the inexorable voice

Shouting to all: "Love, then die here below!"

Implacable death will leave you no choice;

      None can escape the blow.

---

[11]A poet and, later, general secretary of fine arts, Ronchaud (1816–87) founded L'École du Louvre in 1882.

Eh bien ! puisqu'il le faut, sans trouble et sans murmure,

Forts de ce même amour dont vous vous enivrez

Et perdus dans le sein de l'immense Nature,

    Aimez donc, et mourez !

        II

Non, non, tout n'est pas dit, vers la beauté fragile

Quand un charme invincible emporte le désir,

Sous le feu d'un baiser quand notre pauvre argile

    A frémi de plaisir.

Notre serment sacré part d'une âme immortelle ;

C'est elle qui s'émeut quand frissonne le corps ;

Nous entendons sa voix et le bruit de son aile

    Jusque dans nos transports.

Nous le répétons donc, ce mot qui fait d'envie

Pâlir au firmament les astres radieux,

Ce mot qui joint les cœurs et devient, dès la vie,

    Leur lien pour les cieux.

Dans le ravissement d'une éternelle étreinte

Ils passent entraînés, ces couples amoureux,

Et ne s'arrêtent pas pour jeter avec crainte

    Un regard autour d'eux.

Ils demeurent sereins quand tout s'écroule et tombe ;

Leur espoir est leur joie et leur appui divin ;

Such is your fate, accept without lament,

Strong in the love that makes you throb and sigh

And lost in the breast of the firmament

      Love each other, and die!

    II

No! This is not the last word, when desire

Is drawn toward beauty with magical might;

When a kiss sears our frail bodies like fire,

      We tremble with delight.

It is from a deathless soul our vow springs;

The body fails, but spirit glides above;

It is her voice we hear, her rustling wings,

      In the transports of love.

So we'll repeat that word which, heard on high,

Makes the stars pale with envious surprise,

That word, which joins our hearts before we die,

      United for the skies.

Enraptured, in an eternal embrace,

Those devoted couples pass, borne along

Without pausing to turn a fearful face

      To see where they have gone.

Their calm defies the universal doom;

Their hope gives them joy, succor that God gave;

Ils ne trébuchent point lorsque contre une tombe
       Leur pied heurte en chemin.

Toi-même, quand tes bois abritent leur délire,
Quand tu couvres de fleurs et d'ombre leurs sentiers,
Nature, toi leur mère, aurais-tu ce sourire
       S'ils mouraient tout entiers ?

Sous le voile léger de la beauté mortelle
Trouver l'âme qu'on cherche et qui pour nous éclôt,
Le temps de l'entrevoir, de s'écrier : « C'est Elle ! »
       Et la perdre aussitôt,

Et la perdre à jamais ! Cette seule pensée
Change en spectre à nos yeux l'image de l'Amour.
Quoi ! ces vœux infinis, cette ardeur insensée
       Pour un être d'un jour !

Et toi, serais-tu donc à ce point sans entrailles,
Grand Dieu qui dois d'en haut tout entendre et tout voir,
Que tant d'adieux navrants et tant de funérailles
       Ne puissent t'émouvoir,

Qu'à cette tombe obscure où tu nous fais descendre
Tu dises : « Garde-les, leurs cris sont superflus.
Amèrement en vain l'on pleure sur leur cendre ;
       Tu ne les rendras plus ! »

They will not stumble, although in the gloom
      Their feet may strike a grave.

You whose woods shelter their joys for awhile,
Who strew their flowery path abundantly,
Nature, their mother, would you have that smile
      If they died utterly?

To find the kindred spirit born for me,
Beneath beauty's thin veil, beset by death
To glimpse her, and to exclaim, "It is She!"
      Then lose her in a breath,

And lose her forever! This single thought
Changes Love's image to a fleeting ghost.
Ah! Those unending vows, passion distraught
      Shared for a day at most!

And might you be so callous and unkind,
Great God who surely watches from on high,
That all our grievous losses leave you blind,
      And cannot mollify,

That you force loved ones into death's dark cave,
Telling it: "Keep them, for they wail in vain."
Futile our lamentations by their grave,
      Lost like tears in the rain.

Mais non ! Dieu qu'on dit bon, tu permets qu'on espère ;

Unir pour séparer, ce n'est point ton dessein.

Tout ce qui s'est aimé, fût-ce un jour, sur la terre,

Va s'aimer dans ton sein.

III

Éternité de l'homme, illusion ! chimère !

Mensonge de l'amour et de l'orgueil humain !

Il n'a point eu d'hier, ce fantôme éphémère,

Il lui faut un demain !

Pour cet éclair de vie et pour cette étincelle

Qui brûle une minute en vos cœurs étonnés,

Vous oubliez soudain la fange maternelle

Et vos destins bornés.

Vous échapperiez donc, ô rêveurs téméraires !

Seuls au pouvoir fatal qui détruit en créant ?

Quittez un tel espoir ; tous les limons sont frères

En face du néant.

Vous dites à la Nuit qui passe dans ses voiles :

« J'aime, et j'espère voir expirer tes flambeaux. »

La Nuit ne répond rien, mais demain ses étoiles

Luiront sur vos tombeaux.

Vous croyez que l'Amour dont l'âpre feu vous presse

A réservé pour vous sa flamme et ses rayons ;

No! God is merciful, or so they say;

To join, then separate, is not your plan.

All creatures that loved, were it for a day,

     Meet under Heaven's span.

    III

Oh vain delusion that we'll never die!

Love's chimerical hope where pride holds sway!

Give us a future! we brief phantoms cry

     Who had no yesterday!

When life and love gleam and flicker away

Quickly flaring in your astonished hearts,

You soon forget your original clay

     Whence your brief fate departs.

O rash dreamers! Would you alone evade

That fatal power that none can avoid?

Renounce your hopes, jests a cruel god made—

     Brothers facing the void.

To veiled Night you proclaim from afar:

"I love, and live till your lights yield to gloom."

Night answers nothing; tomorrow, her star

     Will shine upon your tomb.

You believe, driven by Love's acrid fires,

They have reserved all their bright rays for you;

La fleur que vous brisez soupire avec ivresse :
        « Nous aussi nous aimons ! »

Heureux, vous aspirez la grande âme invisible
Qui remplit tout, les bois, les champs de ses ardeurs ;
La Nature sourit, mais elle est insensible :
        Que lui font vos bonheurs ?

Elle n'a qu'un désir, la marâtre immortelle,
C'est d'enfanter toujours, sans fin, sans trêve, encor.
Mère avide, elle a pris l'éternité pour elle,
        Et vous laisse la mort.

Toute sa prévoyance est pour ce qui va naître ;
Le reste est confondu dans un suprême oubli.
Vous, vous avez aimé, vous pouvez disparaître :
        Son vœu s'est accompli.

Quand un souffle d'amour traverse vos poitrines,
Sur des flots de bonheur vous tenant suspendus,
Aux pieds de la Beauté lorsque des mains divines
        Vous jettent éperdus ;

Quand, pressant sur ce cœur qui va bientôt s'éteindre
Un autre objet souffrant, forme vaine ici-bas,
Il vous semble, mortels, que vous allez étreindre
        L'Infini dans vos bras ;

The flower you crush sighs as it expires:
      "We loved each other too!"

You joyously inhale the great world's soul
That fills fields and woods with its blazing kiss;
In Nature's smiles, your feelings play no role:
      She's heedless of your bliss.

This wicked stepmother who never dies
Wants forever and only to give birth.
For her alone, her maw engulfs the skies,
      Leaving you death and earth.

What will be born is all she has foreseen;
The rest, forgotten in a faceless mass.
You who have loved might well have never been:
      Her will has come to pass.

When you sense the inspiration of love
Fill you with tides of rapture unalloyed,
At Beauty's feet, when gods' hands from above
      Hurl you dazed, overjoyed;

When, pressing to your heart that soon must die
Another sufferer, an empty form,
Mortals, you feel you hold Infinity
      In your arms, safe and warm.

Ces délires sacrés, ces désirs sans mesure
Déchaînés dans vos flancs comme d'ardents essaims,
Ces transports, c'est déjà l'Humanité future
    Qui s'agite en vos seins.

Elle se dissoudra, cette argile légère
Qu'ont émue un instant la joie et la douleur ;
Les vents vont disperser cette noble poussière
    Qui fut jadis un cœur.

Mais d'autres cœurs naîtront qui renoueront la trame
De vos espoirs brisés, de vos amours éteints,
Perpétuant vos pleurs, vos rêves, votre flamme,
    Dans les âges lointains.

Tous les êtres, formant une chaîne éternelle,
Se passent, en courant, le flambeau de l'Amour.
Chacun rapidement prend la torche immortelle
    Et la rend à son tour.

Aveuglés par l'éclat de sa lumière errante,
Vous jurez, dans la nuit où le sort vous plongea,
De la tenir toujours : à votre main mourante
    Elle échappe déjà.

Du moins vous aurez vu luire un éclair sublime ;
Il aura sillonné votre vie un moment ;

Those sacred transports, limitless desires
Unleashed in burning swarms within your chest,
Are future humans; each to birth aspires,
   And quickens in your breast.

It will crumble, your insubstantial clay
Stirred by a momentary joy and pain;
The winds will cast your noble heart away
   To fall to dust again.

But hearts yet to be born reknit the frame
Of your broken hopes, your loves' meager sum,
Perpetuating your tears, dreams, and fame,
   Through ages yet to come.

All beings, forming an eternal chain,
Pass on Love's torch as in a relay race.
Each generation snatches that bright flame
   Without slowing the pace.

Blinded by the glare of its wandering light,
You swear to hold it till the break of day.
From your dying hand, in the fateful night,
   It slips, and falls away.

At least you will have glimpsed a sublime glow;
In your life, it may mark a swath of bliss;

En tombant vous pourrez emporter dans l'abîme

Votre éblouissement.

Et quand il régnerait au fond du ciel paisible
Un être sans pitié qui contemplât souffrir,
Si son œil éternel considère, impassible,

Le naître et le mourir,

Sur le bord de la tombe, et sous ce regard même,
Qu'un mouvement d'amour soit encor votre adieu !
Oui, faites voir combien l'homme est grand lorsqu'il aime,

Et pardonnez à Dieu !

You'll see that dazzlement yet as you go

       Down into the abyss.

And though in the depths of the peaceful sky

There reigned a being who enjoyed our pain,

If he looked down while his impassive eye

       Saw birth and death again,

Let a gesture of love be your farewell

Beneath that gaze, near your hole in the sod!

Yes, show how great are men when they love well,

       And grant pardon to God!

Le positivisme

Il s'ouvre par delà toute science humaine

Un vide dont la Foi fut prompte à s'emparer.

De cet abîme obscur elle a fait son domaine ;

En s'y précipitant elle a cru l'éclairer.

Eh bien ! nous t'expulsons de tes divins royaumes,

Dominatrice ardente, et l'instant est venu :

Tu ne vas plus savoir où loger tes fantômes ;

        Nous fermons l'Inconnu.

Mais ton triomphateur expiera ta défaite.

L'homme déjà se trouble, et, vainqueur éperdu,

Il se sent ruiné par sa propre conquête :

En te dépossédant nous avons tout perdu.

Nous restons sans espoir, sans recours, sans asile,

Tandis qu'obstinément le Désir qu'on exile

Revient errer autour du gouffre défendu.

Positivism

Beyond human knowledge, a void remains,

An abyss Faith was quick to occupy.

Those dark chasms have become her domains;

Rushing inside, she thought to clarify.

Now, ardent dominatrix, your end nears:

All of your holy kingdoms you must yield,

No dwelling is left for your ghostly fears;

     The Unknown we have sealed.

But your conqueror triumphs at great cost.

Victorious man soon is driven back;

Having vanquished, we learn that all is lost;

Besting you leaves us only with a lack.

We remain without shelter, hope, or home;

Although banished, stubborn Desires still roam

Near the forbidden gulf shrouded in black.

Positivism was a philosophy elaborated by Auguste Comte (1798–1857) around 1830. It rejects all phenomena that are not known or observable.

J'ignore !

J'ignore ! un mot, le seul par lequel je réponde

Aux questions sans fin de mon esprit déçu ;

Aussi quand je me plains en partant de ce monde,

C'est moins d'avoir souffert que de n'avoir rien su.

I Do Not Know!

I do not know! *is my only refrain*
To answer endless questions in my mind;
So as I leave this world, if I complain,
It's less of pain than of having been blind.

MALVINA BLANCHECOTTE
(1830–97)
née Augustine Alphonsine Malvina Souville

Translations by J. S. A. Lowe

Malvina Blanchecotte was born in Paris to a working-class family. Her early years remain obscure. An autodidact, she read poetry as a child and taught herself several languages (English, German, Latin). She married at twenty and raised her son alone after her husband's hospitalization due to mental illness. She worked as a seamstress until the success of her writing and ensuing literary associations freed her from working with her hands. But she never completely escaped financial hardship and was obliged to support herself as an instructor, a profession she despised. Her social transition to the middle class was not achieved without difficulty or ambivalence. Despite having signed her first work "Mme B, ouvrière et poète" ("Mme B, worker and poet"), she appeared to disassociate herself from her popular roots (tellingly, she wrote against the Commune). She nonetheless remained socially marginalized.

Blanchecotte did earn the respect of many contemporary writers, in particular Pierre-Jean de Béranger and Alphonse de Lamartine, with whom she developed a close friendship. Her first collection, *Rêves et réalités*, was awarded a prize by the Académie Française and earned the praise of the critic Charles Sainte-Beuve and a monetary prize from Napoléon III. She attended Colet's salon and collaborated on various reviews, where she met other writers. George Sand was among those who aided her.

Blanchecotte wrote three collections of poetry. While very much influenced by the Romantics, her poems are characterized by stoic bitterness and are often antisentimental. Some of her most interesting pieces are urban in inspiration. Pyotr Ilich Tchaikovsky and Reynaldo Hahn, among other composers, set her poems to music. Most of Blanchecotte's later writing was in prose, including two books of aphorisms (which she called "impressions d'une femme" ["a woman's impressions"]), essays, and a memoir of the Commune. Little is known of her final years.

Her poetic works are *Rêves et réalités* (1855), *Nouvelles poésies* (1861), and *Les militantes* (1875). Of the poems selected for this anthology, "À ma mère" and "Déshéritée" first appeared in *Rêves et réalités*; the remaining poems, in *Les militantes*, which is divided into three sections: "Combats," "Trêves," and "Paix." For further reading, see Coligny; Planté, Préface; Sainte-Beuve, "Rêves."

À ma mère : Sonnet

Ne me torturez plus, ô souvenirs d'enfance !
J'ai besoin d'oublier tout ce que j'ai souffert ;
J'ai sur mon cœur vieilli mis un sceau de silence,
Mon déchirant passé d'un linceul est couvert.

Cependant, ô ma mère ! oh ! malgré moi je pense
À ma vie isolée ainsi qu'en un désert ;
Je pense aux jours passés dans votre indifférence,
Au douloureux dédain à mon amour offert.

Oh ! vous n'avez pas lu dans mon âme embrasée !
Votre enfant près de vous dut gémir épuisée :
Vous n'avez jamais su combien je vous aimais !

Maintenant que tout dort sous la tombe profonde,
Dieu vous a dit sur moi ce qu'ignorait le monde :
Votre mot de retour je ne l'aurai jamais !

7 décembre 1853

To My Mother: Sonnet

O childhood memories, don't torture me now!
I need to forget everything, all the suffering;
I've sealed my wasted heart tightly with silence,
Covered my lacerated past with a shroud.

And yet, O my mother! against my own will
I think of my life, more alone than the desert;
I think of days spent, burnt by your indifference,
The contempt you returned for affection I spilled.

You never saw into my soul, incandescent!
The child at your bosom, worn out with weeping—
And you never knew how much I adored you.

Now that everything sleeps beneath the deepest tomb,
God finally told you what the world never knew:
But I never will hear what you say in return.

7 December 1853

Déshéritée

Comme on s'appelle Dorothée,
Léopoldine ou Maria,
Gabrielle ou Félicia,
On la nomme Déshéritée.

C'est elle : l'apercevez-vous ?
Distraite, elle vient en silence ;
Son ombre fine se balance,
Gracieuse, en venant vers nous.

Elle a de beaux cheveux d'ébène
Aux nombreux anneaux déroulés,
De grands yeux bleus toujours voilés,
Et puis une taille de reine.

Jamais on ne la voit aux jeux,
Jamais on ne la voit sourire ;
Bien fou près d'elle qui soupire
Et laisse échapper des aveux.

Jamais, jamais, à côté d'elle,
Ne prononcez le mot d'amour ;
Son cœur est fermé sans retour,
Ou peut-être il est trop fidèle.

The Outcast Girl

Everyone has a name, you know—
Like Dorothy, Aimée, or Pearl,
Gabrielle, Marie or Felicia—
So they call her the Outcast Girl.

That's her: see her over there?
In silence, unheeding, she comes.
Her slim shadow carefully balanced,
Graceful, she walks towards us.

Her hair is as black as fine ebony,
With a riot of loosening curls;
Her wide blue eyes are always veiled,
And she walks like she owns the world.

Never will you catch her playing;
Never will you see her smile.
Those who pine for her are mere fools
With their vows and their broken sighs.

Never, never waste time with her
Or swear that your heart is breaking:
Her heart's closed off for good now—
Or perhaps it's already taken.

Peut-être, en un lointain pays,

Il est une autre âme éplorée

Et d'elle à jamais séparée :

Ô temps, ô rêve évanouis !

Ce qui rend sa voix attristée,

Pâle son front, sombres ses yeux,

Est-ce un regret mystérieux ?

On la nomme Déshéritée.

Perhaps, in a faraway country,
There's another inconsolable one
From whom she's forever torn—
Oh time, oh vanishing vision!

Whatever darkens her voice,
Pales her cheek, shadows her eyes—
Is it regret, mysterious, furled?
They call her the Outcast Girl.

Combats (XXIII) : Représailles

Que viens-tu demander ? je ne te connais pas !
Que parles-tu d'un temps que ton rêve regrette ?
Nous ne sommes plus rien l'un à l'autre ici-bas :
Ton cœur m'a rejetée, et mon cœur te rejette !

Qu'oses-tu rappeler d'un outrage accompli ?
À ma hauteur d'amour tu ne pouvais atteindre ;
Le pardon est venu... peut-être ! non l'oubli :
Je ne te connais pas : tu n'as plus rien à craindre !

Dédaignée et roulée au gouffre en pleine mer,
Mon âme t'apparaît avec l'ancien prestige ;
Le bonheur méprisé t'est redevenu cher ;
Je ne te connais pas, ce n'est plus moi, te dis-je !

Reste au sein des plaisirs que tu m'as préférés !
Une chaîne d'or pur pèse à ta main légère ;
J'ai repris mes trésors et je les ai murés :
Je ne te connais pas : étranger, en arrière !

Battles (XXIII) : Payback

What do you want from me? I don't even know you!

What are you talking about, some time you regret?

We're no more to each other than targets for attack.

Your heart rejects me? Mine rejects you right back!

You'd dare to remind me of your perfect putdown?

My love arched so high, you never made it up here.

So maybe I forgave you (but I never forgot it);

Now I don't even know you—you've no more to fear.

Dumped and thrashing around in the bottomless sea,

Seems my soul starts to shine as it did once to you.

But the price has gone up on the fortune you blew;

I don't even know you; it's not my problem now.

Just stay with the pleasures you preferred over me!

A chain of pure gold's weighing down your light hand;

I've recaptured my treasure, and it's safe behind walls.

I don't even know you: so, stranger, back off!

Combats (LXX)

Bêtes de somme
Ont leurs grelots ;
Pour grelots l'homme
A ses sanglots.

Allons, pauvre machine humaine,
Cœur en tourmente, esprit fiévreux,
Tu n'es point libre de ta chaîne,
L'abîme n'est point assez creux.
La souffrance est insatiable ;
Après avoir souffert il faut,
Mourant, épuisé, misérable,
Souffrir encore de nouveau.

Bêtes de somme
Ont leurs grelots ;
Pour grelots l'homme
A ses sanglots.

Allons ! il faut marcher quand même !
« Je ne peux plus ! — Marche toujours ! »
L'effort est notre loi suprême
Du premier au dernier des jours !

Battles (LXX)

Beasts of burden
Wear jingling bells;
Men and women
Sob like hell.

Let's get going, poor human machine,
Heart in torment, spirit aflame,
Nowhere near being freed from this chain—
The abyss nowhere near empty enough.
Don't ever doubt suffering's insatiable;
And then after all you have suffered,
You must die—betrayed, miserable,
Just to suffer all over again.

Beasts of burden
Wear jingling bells;
Men and women
Sob like hell.

Let's go! Keep it up, no matter what!
"I can't, no more!"—"Move it along!"
Effort's the primary law to obey,
From the first to the last of your days!

Le cœur a toujours quelque goutte

De sang tout chaud pour s'épancher ;

Le pied doit fournir à la route,

Tout le voyage il faut marcher.

Bêtes de somme

Ont leurs grelots ;

Pour grelots l'homme

A ses sanglots.

The heart always has some drops left

Of hot blood to sputter and spout;

Our heels forever paving the road;

All the way, we must pick up our feet.

    Beasts of burden

    Wear jingling bells;

    Men and women

    Sob like hell.

Combats (LXXIV)

Elle est fière et sauvage et même un peu farouche.
—Sainte-Beuve

Oui, sauvage ! oui, fière ! oui, comme l'oiseau, libre !

Pour que ce large esprit ouvre son aile et vibre,

Il lui faut sans limite et par delà les yeux

Le tranquille silence et l'infini des cieux !

Nul collier, fût-il d'or, autour de sa pensée !

Nul joug lui courbant l'âme avilie, oppressée !

La pauvreté : C'est bien ! La solitude : Oh ! oui !

Mais le rêve éternel en son cœur ébloui !

Et bien loin au-dessus des vanités brutales

L'exquis et pur souci des choses idéales !

Battles (LXXIV)

She is proud and wild and even a little fierce.[12]
—Sainte-Beuve

Yes, wild! Yes, proud! Yes, like the bird—free!

For this broad spirit to spread trembling wings,

She needs—without limit, and far beyond sight—

The calm silence of infinite, wide-open skies!

No golden necklace chaining her thoughts!

No bruising yoke to cripple her soul!

Poverty—fine! Solitude—yes!

Just the dreaming eternal in her dazzled heart—

And far, far above all the brutal futilities,

The exquisite obsession with pure, perfect things!

This poem, replete with images of liberating ascension, is reminiscent of Baudelaire's "Élévation." While Blanchecotte's soaring spirit throws off the yokes of poverty and gender conformity, Baudelaire's flies freely "avec une indicible et mâle volupté" (1: 10).

[12]Cf. Phèdre's description of Thésée: "Mais fidèle, mais fier, et même un peu farouche" (Racine, *Phèdre* 2.5; "But she's faithful and proud, and even a little fierce").

Trêves (I)

Je suis partie ! Enfin, est-ce absolu ?
Suis-je partie à jamais pour moi-même ?
Est-ce un départ immuable et voulu ?
Détachement sans retour et suprême ?

Est-ce l'absence irrévocablement ?
Oh ! puisqu'il faut un jour plier bagage,
Comme il est bon de pauser un moment,
Et, sans un mot, d'affronter le voyage !

Sans regarder en arrière ! sans rien
Sur le passé : pièce close et finie !
Avant la mort, farce ou drame : c'est bien !
Fermer sur soi la porte de sa vie !

Truces (I)

I'm leaving! Can it really be true, at last?
Am I leaving forever, setting out for myself?
Am I ready for this? Is it what must be done?
Separation, no coming back, final, for good?

Will this absence be the irrevocable end?
Since I then need to pack up all of my things,
Perhaps it's okay if I pause for a moment
And then, without words, I'll be on my way!

Without going over it all one more time,
Without looking back: play's over, closed room.
Before death, farce or drama—everything's fine!
Just shut tight behind you the door of your life.

Trêves (XIII) : Impression

Un livre dans la main, qu'on ne lit pas, du reste,

Les yeux plongés au loin dans l'horizon de mer ;

De grands arbres ombreux, un paysage agreste,

Et mille tintements répercutés dans l'air ;

De rapides oiseaux fendant les cieux immenses,

Des musiques de brise et des rumeurs de flots ;

Nuage, azur, lueurs, brusques magnificences,

Soirs orageux, matins brillants, changeants tableaux ;

De bœufs insouciants le passage tranquille,

L'âne leste, paré de gais grelots au cou,

Oh ! quel rêve de paix pour qui sort de la ville,

Dans ce silence ami transporté tout à coup !

Oh ! quel rêve – prenant les chemins solitaires

Quand les flots sont bien sourds et les cieux sont bien noirs,—

De suivre dans la nuit les petites lumières

Qui tachent de clartés la profondeur des soirs !

Oh ! quel rêve surtout, aux heures matinales,

Laissant tomber le livre ou le journal d'hier,

De lire le vrai livre aux pages magistrales :

L'espace ! illuminé de voiles sur la mer !

Truces (XIII): Impression

Hand marking one's place in a book, unread,
Eyes plunged in all the way to the edge of the sea;
Rustic countryside, vast shady-leafed trees,
Countless shivering chimes echoing in the air;

Darting birds slicing through infinite skies,
Melodic breezes and murmuring streams;
Clouds azure, aglimmer, abruptly magnificent,
Stormy nights, sparkling mornings, such shifting scenes;

Calm cattle grazing along without fear,
Nimble donkey decked out in halters and bells,
Oh, leaving the city to find peaceful dreams,
Gentle silence sweeping us away easily.

Oh, to dream on—find the loneliest path
When streams all fall deaf and skies turn to black—
Follow in darkness the tiny faint lights
Whose clarity stains even duskier night!

Oh, to dream above all in the earliest hour,
Giving up on the book, or yesterday's news;
To read the true text, most majestic of pages:
Open space! and the sunlit sails on the sea!

Paix (VII) : Aux femmes

Où l'on souffre, que l'on nous voie !

Ayons cette sublime joie

—Aux heures de lâche abandon—

D'être la fierté, la vaillance,

La souveraine bienveillance,

Ô femmes ! d'être le pardon !

Restons ! ne quittons point la lice !

Qu'aucune de nous ne faiblisse !

Le calme, c'est l'autorité !

Restons ! quand gronde la colère

Soyons la douceur tutélaire,

Ô femmes ! soyons la bonté !

Cette vie est un champ de haine.

Chacun jette en la sombre arène

Ses passions, sinistre enjeu !

Femmes ! soyons le sacrifice,

Soyons le dévoûment propice !

Domptons l'homme, désarmons Dieu !

Peace (VII): To Women

Where there's suffering, let the world see our faces!

Let us feel this joy, sublime—

At the hour when cowards desert,

Let us become fierce pride and strength,

Let us be queens of sheer kindness—

O women! let us be forgiveness!

Endure! let us not leave the lists—

How not a one of us falters!

Calm equals the truest authority.

Endure! for when snarling, black anger

Faces our tender protectiveness—

O women! let us be compassion!

This life is a field rife with hatred.

Each throws down in the darkened arena

His passions—ominous gauntlet!

Women! let us be the sacrifice,

Let us be the consecrated offering—

Vanquish man, and disarm even God!

Paix (XIV) : En entendant un marteau de démolition

Prends ta pioche, démolisseur !

Mets à bas cette maison grise !

Frère du pâle fossoyeur

Sous tes coups que tout se détruise !

Frappe toujours des coups plus forts,

Fais crouler ces hautes murailles !

Ceux qui vivaient ici sont morts :

Rythme en chantant leurs funérailles !

Frappe ! ces vieux murs ébranlés

Ont enfermé plus d'une histoire !

Leurs hôtes qui s'en sont allés

Reviennent quand la nuit est noire,

Cherchant leurs souvenirs perdus,

Hanter le lieu de leurs misères :

Pour qu'ils ne s'y retrouvent plus,

Bouleverse toutes ces pierres !

Oh ! quels témoins de durs combats

Ces murs si longtemps insensibles !

Sous ta pioche ne sens-tu pas

Des résistances invincibles ?

Des cœurs brisés sont restés là,

Des désolations inouïes !

C'est rude à remuer, cela !

Ce tas d'épaves enfouies !

Peace (XIV): On Hearing a Demolition Hammer

Pick up your pickax, demolition man!

Bury this old gray house under rubble!

You, dirty brother of the pale gravedigger—

Beneath blows let all be destroyed!

Go on, strike again, even mightier strokes;

Crush these high walls into collapse!

Those who once lived here now are all dead:

Beat time for their funeral march!

Strike! for within these old tottering walls

More than one story's been locked up tight!

The dim, former tenants who long ago left

Return in the blackest of night—

Restless, seeking out lost memories—

To haunt the place of their dead miseries.

Make sure once and for all they never come back!

Overturn every one of these stones!

Oh! these walls, which witnessed hard combat

Have for so long, unconscious, endured!

How can your sledgehammer help but feel

Their callous, stubborn resistance?

They housed the broken hearts who lived here,

They sheltered unspeakable desolations.

How tactless and coarse, to disinter such things—

Stir up graves where wreckage is hid!

Frappe ! sans pitié hache tout !

Ces dépouilles-là sont ta proie !

Fais rouler jusque dans l'égout

Ces débris de cœurs que l'on broie !

Une nouvelle floraison

Réjouira le sol aride ;

Bientôt une jeune maison

Remplacera la maison vide !

Sur le sinistre emplacement

Où gisent des fleurs étouffées,

Quelque palais superbement

Dressera ses brillants trophées.

J'entends déjà les airs joyeux !

Sûrs d'eux-mêmes, raillant l'orage,

Les jeunes dansent sur les vieux :

Démolisseur, vite à l'ouvrage !

Go on, strike! without pity, chop everything up!

Think of these cast-off husks as your prey!

Tumble them down all the way to the sewer,

This debris of pulverized hearts.

A new blossoming now on its way

Will make dry ground rejoice;

And soon a young home will replace

This gutted house!

On this ominous, sinister site

Where overgrown flowers strangle each other,

Some brilliant palace is coming, and will

Raise up bright banners.

I can already hear cheerful songs!

So sure of themselves, scoffing at storms,

The youthful dance on the bones of the old:

Demolition man, hurry up with your work!

LOUISE MICHEL

(1830–1905)

Translations by Michael Bishop

The child of a young servant, Marianne Michel, and, reputedly, of the heir to the estate for which her mother worked, Louise Michel lived with and was schooled by her paternal grandparents at their château in the Haute-Marne region of northeastern France. Her schooling surpassed what her mother, who remained in the service of the chatelains, could have offered her. Louise received a liberal education, learned to write poetry, and benefited from the privileged environment in which she was raised. But in 1850, on the deaths of her grandparents, she was told to leave the château. She became a teacher and opened a progressive school in the area. In 1856 she moved to Paris, where she became increasingly active politically and eventually opened another school in Montmartre.

A lifelong militant who was known as the red virgin, Michel worked for a number of social protest movements in support of workers, women, and the disenfranchised. Fervently against the empire, she was a Republican in the 1860s, but her disgust with bourgeois Republicanism turned her into an anarchist after the Paris Commune. In 1871, as the Prussians laid siege to Paris and the Second Empire fell, revolutionary forces, including women who fought and died, refused the new Republican government's capitulation to the victors and established the Commune. Michel fought as a soldier during the Commune, whose tumultuous events are reflected in many of her poems, including "La danse des bombes" ("The Bomb Dance") and "Les œillets rouges" ("The Red Carnations"), both in this volume.

Charged for her role as a Communarde, she surrendered to the authorities in exchange for the freedom of her imprisoned mother. During her trial, she spoke forcefully against the men judging her:

J'appartiens tout entière à la révolution sociale... Vous êtes des hommes, vous allez me juger... et moi je ne suis qu'une femme, et pourtant je vous regarde en face... Prenez ma vie, si vous la voulez... Si vous me laissez vivre, je ne cesserai de crier vengeance. ("Louise Michel")

I belong entirely to the social revolution. You are men; you are going to judge me. I am but a woman, and yet I am facing you head-on. Take my life, if you want it. If you let me live, I will not cease to call for vengeance.

Michel was convicted and exiled to New Caledonia, the South Pacific archipelago colonized by the French. While there, she befriended and schooled the indigenous Kanaks and supported their unsuccessful revolt against the French in 1878. Following the amnesty of 1879, she returned to Paris to great acclaim and renewed political activity. She was jailed from 1883 to 1886 for her support of unemployed workers and survived an assassination attempt in 1888. She moved to London in 1890, although she remained politically active (notably during the Dreyfus Affair) and returned regularly to France until her death in 1905.

Michel wrote throughout her life: novels, plays, poetry, songs, memoirs, and political polemic. Her poems vary in topic but consistently oppose tyranny. In addition to her Commune poetry, she wrote in favor of the abolition of slavery at the outset of the United States Civil War, about her experience at the penal colony, about the New Caledonian Kanaks, about French peasants, and about disenfranchised women.

She published one collection of poetry during her lifetime (*À travers la vie* [1894]), and another was published posthumously (*Avant la Commune* in *Œuvres posthumes*, vol. 1 [1905]). For further reading, see Gauthier; Lejeune; Maclellan; Stivale; Thomas.

Paris

Toute l'ombre a versé ses ténébreuses urnes ;

Toute la sombre nuit, ses spectres taciturnes ;

L'eau dort sinistre et glauque, et dans son lit profond,

Gouffre toujours ouvert, dans l'horrible silence,

On entend tout à coup vers le mystère immense

      Quelque chose tomber d'un pont.

On dirait qu'à la fois les pâles réverbères,

Tous les souffles glacés de toutes les misères,

Les fantômes vivants et les froids trépassés,

Les bandits embusqués sous les portes dans l'ombre

S'en vont au même point, vers la morgue, où sans nombre,

      En entrant, ils sont effacés.

Procession hideuse ! où les hommes, les femmes,

Les enfants effarés, les uns, corps, d'autres, âmes,

En vain s'y refusant, s'en vont, s'en vont sans fin !

Tous y sont ! par les spectres ou bien par la pensée,

Oui, tous ont là leur place et la route est tracée

      Large et lugubre le matin.

Paris, 1861

Paris

Shadow has poured out its tenebrous urn;

All of somber night, its specters, taciturn;

Water sleeps, sinister, glaucous, and in its deep bed,

Ever gaping chasm, in the horrid silence,

Suddenly something is heard to drop

    From a bridge into mystery immense.

It seems as though the pale lamplights,

All the icy breath of every wretchedness,

Living ghosts and cold deaden,

Robbers lurking in shadowy doorways,

All flee together, to the morgue where, countless,

    Upon entering, they disappear.

Hideous procession! men and women,

Frightened children, now bodies, now souls,

Vainly resisting, disappearing without end!

All are there! as ghosts or pure thought,

Yes, a place awaits all and the way is traced out,

    Broad and gloomy, from first light.

Paris, 1861

La danse des bombes

Amis, il pleut de la mitraille.

En avant tous ! Volons, Volons !

Le tonnerre de la bataille

Gronde sur nous... Amis, chantons !

Versailles, Montmartre salue.

Garde à vous ! Voici les lions !

La mer des révolutions

Vous emportera dans sa crue.

En avant, en avant sous les rouges drapeaux !

Vie ou tombeaux !

Les horizons aujourd'hui sont tous beaux.

Frères, nous léguerons nos mères

À ceux qui nous suivront.

Sur nous point de larmes amères !

Tout en mourant nous chanterons.

Ainsi dans la lutte géante,

Montmartre j'aime tes enfants.

La flamme est dans leurs yeux ardents,

Ils sont à l'aise en la tourmente.

The Bomb Dance

Friends, it's raining gunfire.

Come! Let's fly! Let's fly!

All around the battle's thunder's

Rumbling . . . Friends, a song!

Versailles, Montmartre greets you.[13]

Attention! Here come the lions!

The high seas of revolution

Will sweep you clean away.

Come on, come on, raise the red flags!

Life or the grave!

All horizons today are beautiful.

Brothers, we'll bequeath our mothers

To those who follow us.

No bitter tears upon us!

Together in death we shall sing.

In the giant struggle, Montmartre,

Thus do I love your offspring.

The flame is in their burning eyes,

They are at ease with turmoil.

---

[13]Versailles, occupied by the Prussians during the war, became the seat of power for the government of Adolphe Thiers (1797–1877) during the Commune. The Communards called soldiers of the official army "les Versaillais." Montmartre was the site of the first conflict between the Versailles army and the revolutionary forces.

En avant, en avant sous les rouges drapeaux !

Vie ou tombeaux !

Les horizons aujourd'hui sont tous beaux.

C'est un brillant lever d'étoiles.

Oui, tout aujourd'hui dit : Espoir !

Le dix-huit mars gonfle les voiles,

Ô fleur, dis-lui bien : Au revoir !

Avril 1871

Come on, come on, raise the red flags!

> Life or the grave!

All horizons today are beautiful.

> Stars rise high and brilliant.

> All today proclaims Hope!

> March the eighteenth fills out the sails,[14]

> Give it, O flower, your final farewells.

April 1871

---

[14]The Communards' insurrection began 18 March 1871.

Les œillets rouges

À Th. Ferré

Si j'allais au noir cimetière,
Frères, jetez sur votre sœur,
Comme une espérance dernière,
De rouges œillets tout en fleur.

Dans les derniers temps de l'Empire,
Lorsque le peuple s'éveillait,
Rouge œillet, ce fut ton sourire
Qui nous dit que tout renaissait.

Aujourd'hui, va fleurir dans l'ombre
Des noires et tristes prisons.
Va fleurir près du captif sombre,
Et dis-lui bien que nous l'aimons.

Dis-lui que par le temps rapide
Tout appartient à l'avenir ;
Que le vainqueur au front livide
Plus que le vaincu peut mourir.

Maison d'arrêt de Versailles, 4 septembre 1871

The Red Carnations

To Th. Ferré[15]

If I go to the dark cemetery,
Brothers, upon your sister shower,
Like a lingering hope,
Red carnations in full flower.

In the Empire's last moments,
As the people awoke,
Your smile, red carnation,
Told us all was not just smoke.

Today, bloom, do, in the shadows
Of dark, sad prisons.
Bloom for the somber cellmate,
And tell him that we love him.

Tell him that in these fast times
All belongs to the future;
The dark-browed victor dies perhaps
More so than the vanquished.

Versailles Detention Center, 4 September 1871[16]

---

[15]Charles-Théophile Ferré (1845–71), a revolutionary and a member of the Commune, was executed by the Versaillais.

[16]Two days after Ferré was condemned to death and a year to the day following the collapse of the Second Empire

Chanson de cirque : *Corrida de muerte*

Les hauts barons blasonnés d'or,

Les duchesses de similor,

Les viveuses toutes hagardes,

Les crevés aux faces blafardes,

Vont s'égayer. Ah ! oui, vraiment,

Jacques Bonhomme est bon enfant.

C'est du sang vermeil qu'ils vont voir.

Jadis, comme un rouge abattoir,

Paris ne fut pour eux qu'un drame,

Et ce souvenir les affame ;

Ils en ont soif. Ah ! oui, vraiment,

Jacques Bonhomme est bon enfant.

Peut-être qu'ils visent plus haut.

Après le cirque, l'échafaud ;

La morgue corsera la fête.

Aujourd'hui seulement la bête,

Et demain l'homme. Ah ! oui, vraiment,

Jacques Bonhomme est bon enfant.

Circus Song: *Corrida de muerte*

High barons blazoned with gold,
Duchesses in similor,
Haggard pleasure seekers,
Those exhausted and white-faced,
All set on merriment. Oh, to be sure,
Jacques's a good lad.

It's red blood they're about to see.
Before, like a dripping slaughterhouse,
Paris was, for them, mere theater,
And, remembering this, they're hungry;
They're thirsty. Oh, to be sure,
Jacques's a good lad.

Perhaps they're aiming higher.
After the circus, the scaffold;
The morgue will liven the party.
Today, just an animal,
Tomorrow, man. Oh, to be sure,
Jacques's a good lad.

Daniel Armogathe notes that this poem was inspired by a bullfight that
Michel attended during a trip to Spain (Michel 242–43).

Les repus ont le rouge aux yeux.

Et cela fait songer les gueux,

Les gueux expirants de misère.

Tant mieux ! aux fainéants la guerre ;

Ils ne diront plus si longtemps :

Jacques Bonhomme est bon enfant.

The well-fed are red-eyed.

Which sets the beggars thinking,

The beggars dying in misery.

So much the better! war's for the idle;

They won't be saying much longer:

Jacques's a good lad.

V'là le choléra

Paraît qu'on attend le choléra
La chose est positive
On n'sait quand il arriv'ra
Mais on sait qu'il arrive

Les pharmaciens vont répétant
Il vient la chose est sûre
Ach'tez-nous du désinfectant
Du sulfat' de chlorure

Les sacristains et les abbés
Répètent des cantiques
Pour attirer les macchabées
Dans leurs sacrées boutiques

On rassemble des capitaux
Pour fabriquer des bières
On vendra des cercueils
À la port' des cimetières

The contractions in this poem—actually written to be sung—reflect the pronunciation typical of popular songs, in which the mute *e* is not pronounced. The song also employs the familiar diction of spoken French.

Cholera's upon Us

Seems cholera's expected
The matter's not in doubt
Don't know when for sure
But we know that it's about

The druggists keep repeating
It's coming it's for sure
Buy our disinfectant
Sodium chloride pure

Abbots and sextons
Chant away their hymns
Seducing dead men all
Into their blessed stall

Assets are gathered
Coffins for to make
Everything's on sale
At the cemetery gate

This unpublished, undated song was written after 1881, according to Armogathe. Although the great nineteenth-century cholera epidemics in France took place in 1832 (100,000 dead) and 1853–54 (150,000 dead), there were lesser outbreaks in 1884 and 1892. Epidemics of infectious diseases were a grim part of the nineteenth-century European landscape, and one of the most devastating coincided with the Franco-Prussian War and Paris Commune: as many as 400,000 died in 1870–71 of smallpox (see Delumeau and Lequin).

Tous les matins avant midi

Dans une immense fosse

On apport'ra les refroidis

Qu'on empil'ra par grosse

L'bon Dieu du haut du sacré cœur

Chant' avec tout' sa clique

Et les cagots reprennent en cœur

Crève la république

V'là l'choléra v'là l'choléra

V'là l'choléra qu'arrive

De l'une à l'autre riv'

Tout l'monde en crèv'ra

Every day by noon

They'll bring the frozen

To some huge tomb

Piled up by the dozen

The good Lord with all his clique

Sings out from on high

And the cretins echo in chorus

Death to the *République*

Cholera's upon us cholera alright

Cholera is coming

From left bank to the right

We'll all be gone or going

[Émilie Georgette] Louisa Siefert
(1845–77)
Translations by Michael Bishop

Born in Lyon to a Protestant family, Louisa Siefert led an intellectually active life despite the poor health she suffered during much of it. An independent child, she read avidly and pursued the study of music.

Siefert's first collection, *Rayons perdus*, was a critical success and went through several printings. Her poems speak with an introspective, often mournful voice and frequently reflect on such intimate themes as love lost and the passing years. Yet she maintains a proud stoicism in the face of offended dignity (see Czyba). Moreover, she writes of the prejudice that women poets suffered from hostile critics (e.g., "Préface"). While her poetry is sometimes Romantic in tone, her commitment to prosodic rigor betrays a rather Parnassian approach. Other collections leave behind the personal for the militantly political. *Les saintes colères*, excerpts of which are included here, voices outrage at the carnage of the Franco-Prussian War, for which Siefert lays withering blame on Napoléon III. Indeed, despite calls for moderation, the emperor launched the conflict in 1870. The Prussian army then swept into France and annexed its northeastern territories, leaving a high toll of military and civilian casualties and leading to the empire's rapid collapse. Siefert took part in the war by assisting the medical service.

In 1876 she married a journalist, Jocelyn Pène, with whom she collaborated professionally. She died the following year, of tuberculosis, at the age of thirty-two.

Her poetic works are *Rayons perdus* (1868), *L'année républicaine* (1869), *Les stoïques* (1870), *Les saintes colères* (1871), *Poésies inédites* (1881). Of the poems selected for this anthology, "Préface," "Orgueil!," and "Tristesse" first appeared in *Rayons perdus*; "Soupir" in *Les stoïques*; "Les saintes colères" in *Les saintes colères*. For further reading, see Greenberg; Marieton; Paliyenko, "Re-reading" and "Is a Woman Poet"; Siefert.

Préface

I

Quand, au bord du chemin, vient la biche craintive,

Elle hésite un instant avant de le passer ;

Elle voudrait cacher sa course fugitive,

Redoutant le chasseur qui la pourrait blesser.

Dans ses grands yeux scintille une larme captive,

Sur sa robe soyeuse un frisson vient glisser,

L'épouvante en son cœur comme un foyer s'active,

L'effroi de l'inconnu l'empêche d'avancer.

Mais de l'autre côté la forêt est plus verte,

Le gazon plus épais, le taillis plus fourré,

L'eau murmure plus fraîche en son lit plus serré.

Quelle arène splendide à son audace offerte !

Elle regarde encor, le courage la prend,

Et, relevant la tête, elle part en courant.

II

Je suis comme la biche indécise & tremblante

Devant le taillis vert au gazon savoureux ;

Un désir insensé prend mon cœur douloureux

D'échapper à tout prix à ma vie accablante.

Preface

I

When the fearful doe comes to the road,

She hesitates a moment before crossing;

Dreading the hunter who seeks to wound,

She'd hide from him her headlong fleeing.

In her great eyes glistening tears lie captive,

Over her silken robe a shivering glides,

Terror starts up in her heart like a blaze,

The fear of the unknown stops her advance.

But beyond the road the forest is greener,

Lusher the grass, denser the thicket,

Water whispers coolness in its narrow bed.

What a splendid arena tendered to her boldness!

She looks about once more, courage welling up,

And, head high, she races straight ahead.

II

I am like the uncertain and trembling doe

Before the green thicket's savory grass;

A wild desire seizes my paining heart

To escape come what may my life's morass.

Sous le lourd poids du sort je me sens chancelante ;
Mes rêves, succombant comme de vaillants preux,
Gisent là, devant moi, couchés en rangs nombreux,
Et l'espérance fuit, à revenir si lente !

Oh ! je veux m'en aller à la gloire, là-bas !...
Mais pour l'atteindre, il faut aussi franchir la route
Où tous les préjugés font le guet l'arme au bras.

Je les sais sans pitié, j'ai peur, je les redoute,
Le trouble où je me vois accroît encor mon doute,
Le danger est certain... Si je n'arrivais pas !...

Beneath fate's heavy weight I feel myself staggering;

My dreams, succumbing like valiant worthies,

Lie before me, laid low in numberless ranks,

And hope flees, so slow in returning!

Oh, to glory, yonder, I so want to go! . . .

But to reach it, the road too must be crossed

Where every prejudice lies in wait, weapons poised.

Each and all pitiless, frightened I am, full of dread,

The turmoil I feel heightens further my doubt,

Danger is certain . . . What if I did not succeed! . . .

Orgueil !

Non, non, je ne suis pas de ces femmes qui meurent
Et rendent ce dernier service à leurs bourreaux,
Pour qu'ils vivent en paix & sans soucis demeurent.

Vois-tu, ces dévoûments sont niais s'ils sont très-beaux.
Les hommes, je le sais, se complaisent trop vite,
Le pied sur ces cercueils, à poser en héros,

Et j'ai dégoût d'ouïr la manière hypocrite
Dont ils disent toujours de ces doux êtres morts :
« Un ange prie au ciel pour moi. Pauvre petite ! »

Tu m'as trop bien appris que l'empire est aux forts.
Mourir, c'est oublier. J'aime mieux ma misère.
Tu ne me verras pas succomber sans efforts.

Aux affres du tombeau, moi, que l'angoisse enserre,
Je ne réponds encor que par un fier refus ;
Car je veux qu'à défaut d'un repentir sincère,
Tu te dises un jour : « Quel aveugle je fus ! »

Pride!

No, no, I am not a woman to die
And provide this last service to her executioner,
So he may live in peace and quite carefree.

You see, such devotion is silly, were it most fine.
Men, I know, find too quick a satisfaction,
Their foot upon such graves, playing the hero,

And it disgusts me to hear the hypocritical way,
Of those creatures that sweetly die, they ever say:
"Poor little thing! An angel prays for me in heaven."

Well have you shown me power is just might.
To die is to forget. My wretchedness I prefer.
Me you will not see succumb without a fight.

Hemmed in by anguish, to the horrors of the tomb
I still reply but with refusal's pride;
For, one day, though true repentance aside,
I want you to say: "What a blind man I was!"

Tristesse

Rentrez dans vos cartons, robe, rubans, résille !

Rentrez, je ne suis plus l'heureuse jeune fille

Que vous avez connue en de plus anciens jours.

Je ne suis plus coquette, ô mes pauvres atours !

Laissez-moi ma cornette & ma robe de chambre,

Laissez-moi les porter jusqu'au mois de décembre ;

Leur timide couleur n'offense point mes yeux :

C'est comme un deuil bien humble & bien silencieux,

Qui m'adoucit un peu les réalités dures.

Allez-vous-en au loin, allez-vous-en, parures !

Avec vous je sens trop qu'il ne reviendra plus,

Celui pour qui j'ai pris tant de soins superflus !

Quand vous & mon miroir voulez me rendre fière,

Retenant mal les pleurs qui mouillent ma paupière,

Sentant mon cœur mourir & l'appeler tout bas,

Je répète : « À quoi bon, Il ne me verra pas ! »

Je pouvais autrefois, avant de le connaître,

Au temps où je rêvais en me disant : « Peut-être ! »

Je pouvais écouter votre frivolité,

Placer dans mes cheveux les roses de l'été,

Nouer un ruban bleu sur une robe blanche,

Et, comme un arbrisseau qui sur l'onde se penche,

Contempler mollement mes quinze ans ingénus.

(Songes, songes charmants, qu'êtes-vous devenus ?)

Je le cherchais alors & j'attendais la vie.

Sadness

Back in your boxes, dress, lacework, ribbons!

Back, I am no more the happy young woman

You knew in days long, long gone.

Gone my coquetry, oh my poor attractions!

Leave me my coif and my nightgown,

Let me wear them to December still;

Their timid color offends not my eyes:

It is a mourning most humble, most tranquil,

Softening slightly the harshest realities.

Away with you, adornments, away!

With you I feel keenly he will not return,

He for whom futile was my caring!

When you and my mirror seek to make me proud,

Half-restraining tears that wet my gaze,

Feeling my heart die, calling low to him,

I repeat: "To what avail, me he will not see!"

I could before, before knowing him,

When I would dream and say: "Perhaps!"

I could listen to your frivolity,

Place summer roses in my hair,

Tie a blue ribbon on a dress of white,

And, like a low tree bending over water,

Softly gaze upon my pure fifteenth year.

(Dreams, magical dreams, where are you now?)

So I sought after him and awaited life.

Mais aujourd'hui, comment me feriez-vous envie ?

Le soleil n'a pour moi ni chaleur ni clarté.

Tout venait de lui seul dans ce temps enchanté,

L'amour comme l'espoir, l'air comme la lumière...

J'ai perdu, j'ai perdu mon aurore première ;

Celle qui rit pour rire & chante pour chanter,

Un souffle d'épouvante est venu l'emporter.

Tout est noir, tout est mort & je me sens glacée.

Oh ! ne m'arrachez plus à ma sombre pensée,

Rien sur ce flot amer ne peut me retenir,

Et l'ombre du passé s'étend sur l'avenir !

But today, how might you stir my desire?

The sun, for me, is neither warm nor bright.

All came from him alone in that enchanted time,

Love as well as hope, air like light . . .

I have lost, lost, my dawning prime;

She who laughs to laugh and sings to sing,

A breath of terror has carried her off.

All is black, all is dead, and I am of ice.

Oh! do not tear me from my thoughts so somber.

Nothing on these bitter waters can keep me longer,

The shadow of the past stretches o'er the future!

Soupir

I

Sans le soupir, le monde étoufferait.
—Ampère

Rêves, anxiétés, soupirs, sanglots, murmures,

Vœux toujours renaissants & toujours contenus,

Instinct des cœurs naïfs, espoir des têtes mûres,

Ô désirs infinis, qui ne vous a connus ?

Les vents sont en éveil, les hautaines ramures

Demandent le secret aux brins d'herbe ingénus,

Et la ronce épineuse, où noircissent les mûres,

Sur les sentiers de l'homme étend ses grands bras nus.

« Où donc la vérité ? » dit l'oiseau de passage.

Le roseau chancelant répète : « Où donc le sage ? »

Le bœuf à l'horizon jette un regard distrait,

Et chaque flot que roule au loin le fleuve immense

S'élève, puis retombe & soudain reparaît

Comme une question que chacun recommence.

Sighing

I

Without sighing, the world would choke.
—Ampère[17]

Dreams, worries, sighs, sobbings, whispers,

Wanting ever reborn and ever contained,

Instinct of naive hearts, hope of minds mature,

O, infinite desires, who has not known you?

The winds are awake; the high boughs

Seek the secret of simple blades of grass,

And the thorny bramble, blackened with berries,

Stretches out, along the paths of man, its great bare arms.

"Where then is truth?" asks the bird in flight.

The tottering reed echoes: "Where the wise man?"

The ox stares absently into the distance,

And every wave rolling by in the vast river

Rears up, falls back, and suddenly reappears

Like a question each begins over and over.

---

[17]Jean-Jacques Ampère (1800–64), a professor of literature at the Collège de France, was elected to the Académie Française in 1847. He was born in Lyon, like Siefert.

II

À vingt ans, quand on a devant soi l'avenir,

Parfois le front pâlit. On va, mais on est triste ;

Un pressentiment sourd qu'on ne peut définir

Accable, un trouble vague à tout effort résiste.

Les yeux brillants hier demain vont se ternir.

Les sourires perdront leurs clartés. On existe

Encor, mais on languit. On dit qu'il faut bénir,

On le veut, mais le doute au fond du cœur subsiste.

On se plaint, & partout on se heurte. Navré,

On a la lèvre en feu, le regard enfiévré.

Tout blesse, & pour souffrir on se fait plus sensible.

Chimère ou souvenir, temps futur, temps passé,

C'est comme un idéal qu'on n'a pas embrassé,

Et c'est la grande soif : celle de l'impossible !

II

At twenty, when before us lies the future,

Sometimes we turn pale. Going on, but sadly,

A dull foreboding we cannot define takes

Over, a vague worry resisting every effort.

Yesterday's shining eyes tomorrow are dulled.

Smiles will lose their brilliance. We still

Exist, but languish. Give blessings we should,

We know, we want to, but doubt runs deep in the heart.

We complain, and everywhere we clash. Heart-

Broken, our lips are on fire, our eyes fevered.

Everything hurts, and to suffer we grow touchier.

Chimera or memory, future or past,

All is an ideal we have not embraced,

And we thirst, and thirst after the impossible!

Les saintes colères (II)

C'est horrible. La terre crie,
Ainsi qu'un pressoir trop chargé ;
Le cellier devient boucherie,
Et le vin en sang est changé.

Par les âmes des morts qui passent,
On dirait le ciel obscurci ;
Ces vents qui d'un frisson nous glacent,
Ont apporté leur râle ici.

Partout les villes bombardées
Fument dans la rougeur des soirs ;
Plaines, forêts sont débordées
De soldats blonds, de chasseurs noirs.

La cuve est pleine, elle est immense.
Le ferment bout avec fureur.
— Ne viendras-tu pas voir, ô France,
Les vendanges de l'empereur ?

20 août 1870

Holy Wrath (II)

It's horrible. The earth screams,
Like an overloaded winepress;
The storeroom, a place of butchery,
And wine is changed to blood.

From the souls of the dead departed
The sky seems black and darkened;
The winds that chilled us to the marrow
Have brought us their death rattle.

All about, the bombed towns
Smoke in the evening's redness;
Forests and plains are brimming
With soldiers fair and infantry black.

The vat is full and immense,
Bubbling and stewing furor.
—Won't you come and see, O France,
The grape harvest of the Emperor?

20 August 1870

Siefert borrows a metaphor from the Book of Revelations to describe the bloody battlefield, for which she attributes blame to Napoléon III: " . . . the angel who has power over fire . . . called with a loud voice to him who had the sharp sickle, 'Put in your sickle, and gather the clusters of the vine of the earth, for its grapes are ripe.' So the angel swung his sickle on the earth and gathered the vintage of the earth, and threw it into the great wine press of the wrath of God; and the wine press was trodden outside the city, and blood flowed from the wine press . . . " (Rev. 14.18–20 [Rev. Standard Ed.]).

Les saintes colères (III)

Vivat et Te Deum ! c'est le couronnement
    De cet admirable édifice.
Le rapt a commencé, puis vient l'égorgement :
    — « Il faut qu'on en finisse ? »

L'esclave, après vingt ans, s'éveillait et vivait ;
    Pensive, elle disait : — « Je souffre ! »
Pour en avoir raison, cette fois on devait
    La jeter dans le gouffre.

Avec un peu de gloire on tenait le moyen,
    (Gloire ou gloriole, n'importe !)
Et l'on se promettait de l'en griser si bien,
    Qu'elle en fût ivre-morte.

Alors en la berçant de sonores discours,
    Comme cette folle en écoute,
On la lierait de nœuds souples, fermes et courts,
    Qui la livreraient toute.

Holy Wrath (III)

Vivat et Te Deum! Now is the crowning
    Of this admirable edifice.
The rape has begun, next the throat-slitting:
    —"Shall we finish things off?"

The slave, after twenty years, awoke to life,
    Saying, pensively: "Suffering and disgust!"
To deal with her, this time cast her
    Into the abyss they must.

With a touch of glory they had the means to,
    (Glory or vainglory, of no matter!)
And the promise was to intoxicate so,
    As to blind drunk have her.

Thus lulling her with sonorous speech,
    To which the madwoman hearkens,
They would bind her with knots firm and supple
    Offering her whole and entire.

The female slave in the poem is a metaphor for France, lulled and rendered powerless by the Emperor Napoléon III during the nearly twenty years of his reign. In the final stanza, Siefert exhorts France and its people to rise up against their war-mongering ruler, who is already weakened by the war he launched, and to demand the liberty they passively took for granted during peacetime.

On l'enterrerait vive, et pendant qu'elle dort
    On rebâtirait sur sa tombe
L'édifice ébranlé par le dernier effort
    Auquel elle succombe.

— Mais le pied du bandit a glissé ; mais sa main
    Tâtonne ; mais sa voix s'enroue ;
Mais devant lui le sang qui remplit le chemin
    En a fait de la boue.

Mais derrière lui, sombre et fatal, son passé
    Le repousse dans cette lutte,
Et son dernier exploit tant de fois annoncé,
    Précipite sa chute.

Et la France regarde avec un œil d'effroi
    Ce charnier aux terreurs funèbres,
Dont il voulait lui faire à jamais sous sa loi
    Un lit dans les ténèbres.

— Oh ! n'est-ce pas qu'enfin tu te rebelleras,
    Fière, superbe et si meurtrie,
Et qu'à la liberté tu vas rouvrir tes bras,
    Ô ma mère, ô Patrie !

25 août 1870

Bury her alive they would, and in her sleep
    Rebuild upon her tomb
The edifice shaken by the deep
    Effort to which she will succumb.

—But the bandit's foot has slipped; his hand
    Gropes about; his voice grows hoarse;
Before him blood fills the road and
    Turns it to a muddy mess.

But behind him, dark and fatal, his past
    Pushes him again into the fray,
And his final deed so often forecast
    Hastens his downfall today.

And France gazes in frightened horror
    Upon the charnel house of funeral terror,
From which he sought to make forever for her,
    Beneath his rule, a bed of darkness.

—Oh, tell us please at last you will rebel,
    Proud country, high-minded, so bruised,
And freedom you will welcome open-armed,
    O my mother, O land I love so well!

25 August 1870

NINA DE VILLARD

(1843–84)

née Anne-Marie Gaillard,
also known as Nina de Callias

Translations by Mary Ann Caws and Patricia Terry

An influential and flamboyant bohemian figure, Nina de Villard is remembered among literary historians for the salon she held from 1863 to 1882. With her eccentric mother, Ursule Villard (the owner of a pet monkey—see "À Maman" ["To Mother"]), Villard, who adopted Ursule's name after a short-lived marriage, provided an animated meeting place for artists, musicians, political figures, and writers. Édouard Manet left an image of her as "La dame aux éventails" (1873; "Woman with Fans") and the portrait *Nina do Villiard* (1873–74), which is reproduced in the cover of this anthology. An acclaimed pianist, she also composed and was among the first to champion the music of Richard Wagner. Villard welcomed Republicans during the final years of the Second Empire, which prompted her temporary exile. Literary habitués of her salon included François Coppée, Charles Cros, Judith Gautier, Stéphane Mallarmé, Catulle Mendès, and Paul Verlaine.

One of the few women included in the *Parnasse contemporain*, Villard also collaborated with poets ("la bande à Nina" ["Nina's crowd"]) who frequented her salon during the heyday of Parnassianism and the dawning of symbolism. Her only collection of poems, *Feuillets parisiens* (1885; "Parisian Pages"), was published posthumously. Much of what is known about her must be gleaned from the memoirs, fiction, poetry, and biographies of the male figures who surrounded her. She is consequently figured, in most cases, as an eccentric *salonnière* rather than a writer. But her *Feuillets parisiens* show her to be a sharp satirist of Parnassian neoclassical poetry (and in particular of Théophile Gautier's orientalist fascination with Egypt), whose preferred metaphor for poetic perfection was feminine statuary. Moreover, her *dixains* (exemplified below by "À Maman" and "L'employé" ["The Clerk"]) offer witty pastiches of the ten-line form popularized by Coppée, a widely read if banal poet (in similar spirit, Villard collaborated with Cros and Germain Nouveau on a collection entitled *Dixains réalistes* [1876]).

Although largely unknown today, Villard held an important place among both the Parnassians and the presymbolist *zutistes* (young poets, including Verlaine and Arthur Rimbaud, who wrote salty poetry laced with slang). She was one of the few women to integrate, influence, and finally to satirize these circles in her poetry and collaborations. In both her life and her work, she refused the petrified image of femininity so cherished by the Parnassians: she was more like a "Déesse fuyant de son piédestal" ("Impromptu"; "a goddess fleeing her pedestal").

For further reading, see Abélès; Baude de Maurceley; Bersaucourt; Harismendy-Lony; Zayed; and Harismendy-Lony.

Jalousie du jeune dieu

Un savant visitait l'Égypte ; ayant osé
Pénétrer dans l'horreur des chambres violettes,
Où les vieux rois Thébains, en de saintes toilettes,
Se couchaient sous le roc, profondément creusé,

Il vit un pied de femme, et le trouva brisé
Par des Bédouins voleurs de riches amulettes.
Le baume avait saigné le long des bandelettes,
Le henné ravivait les doigts d'un ton rosé.

Pur, ce pied conservait dans ses nuits infernales
Le charme doux & froid des choses virginales :
L'amour d'un jeune dieu l'avait pris enfantin.

Ayant baisé ce pied posé dans l'autre monde,
Le savant fut saisi d'une terreur profonde
Et mourut furieux, le lendemain matin.

Jealousy of a Young God

A scholar went to Egypt; daring
Those horrendous violet chambers
Where Theban kings of old, in holy garb,
Rested under the rock so deeply dug,

There he saw a tiny lady's foot, broken
By Bedouins thieving rich trophies.
Balm had bled along the wrappings,
Henna brought a blush of life to the toes.

This foot, pure in its infernal nights,
Kept the sweet cool charm of virginal things:
A young god's love had possessed it first.

When he kissed this foot, there in the other world,
Overwhelming terror struck the scholar;
The next morning he died mad.

This poem is undoubtedly inspired by and, in turn, satirizes Théophile
Gautier's works, in particular the short story "Le pied de momie" (1840) and
novel *Le roman de la momie* (1858). See Schultz, "Loathsome Movement."

L'enterrement d'un arbre

L'arbre déraciné, grand cadavre verdi,

Sur un chariot lourd est traîné par les rues.

Les oiseaux sont partis d'un coup d'aile hardi,

Les nids sont renversés, les chansons disparues.

Les branchages souillés dans le faubourg malsain

Traînent lugubrement leur chevelure verte.

Ainsi sous le couteau cruel d'un assassin

S'échevèle une femme à la blessure ouverte.

Impromptu

Vénus aujourd'hui met un bas d'azur

Et chez Marcelin conte des histoires ;

Elle garde au fond, dans le vert si pur

De ses grands yeux clairs sous leurs franges noires,

Le reflet du flot son pays natal.

Quand au Boulevard on la voit qui passe,

Déesse fuyant de son piédestal,

Et venant chez nous promener sa grâce,

On lui voudrait bien dresser des autels,

Mais elle répond que cela l'ennuie

Et qu'elle permet aux pauvres mortels

De parler argot en sa compagnie.

The Burial of a Tree

The uprooted tree, tall green-colored corpse,
Is pulled through the streets on a heavy cart.
The birds have bravely taken flight,
Their nests overturned, their songs fled.
Through that insalubrious neighborhood,
Their branches drag along, green locks in the dust.
Just so, under a murderer's cruel knife,
A woman's hair flies back from her open throat.

Impromptu

Venus today pulls on her azure hose
And tells her stories at Marcelin's;
In the pure green of her bright
Eyes, under their black bangs,
She reflects her native land.
When we see her pass on the Boulevard
Like a goddess fleeing her pedestal,
Approaching us with all her grace,
We'd like to raise altars to her;
But she says that bores her
And prefers to let the simplest mortals
Speak to her in slang.

Vers à peindre

Elle a posé sur son front pâle
    Un bandeau blanc
Tout semé de perles — opale
    Et diamant.

Sa robe est longue et très galbeuse.
    On aperçoit
Dans des flots d'étoffe soyeuse
    Son pied chinois.

La main blanche, aristocratique,
Nerveuse, dompte un instrument,
Et des arômes de musique
Rôdent dans l'air languissamment.

Plus bas, on sent vibrer la foule ;
Et son sourire est infernal,
Tandis qu'à ses pieds tombe et roule
Un chaste bouquet lilial.

Hautaine, l'œil plein de menace,
Sein de lys et cœur indompté,
Blagueuse, rouée et tenace,
Mais pure par férocité.

Lines to Paint

On her pale forehead
  She's put a white ribbon
All strewn with pearls—opal
  And diamond.

Her dress is long and well-fitting.
  You can see
In the fabric's silky sweep
  Her Chinese foot.

Aristocratic, her white hand,
So nervous, strokes an instrument,
And aromas of melody lurk
Languidly in the air.

Further down, you feel the crowd quiver,
And her smile is infernal,
While at her feet a chaste lily
Falls and rolls about.

Haughty, her eye full of threat,
Her bosom of lilies and her heart free,
Teasing, clever, tenacious,
Yet ferociously pure.

À Maman

Va, n'espère jamais ressembler à ces mères

Qui font verser à l'Ambigu larmes amères ;

Tu n'es pas solennelle et tu ne saurais pas

Maudire, avec un geste altier de l'avant-bras ;

Tu n'as jamais cousu, jamais soigné mon linge,

Tu t'occupes bien moins de moi que de ton singe ;

Mais, malgré tout cela, les soirs de bonne humeur,

C'est avec toi que je rirai de meilleur cœur ;

Ensemble nous courrons premières promenades,

Car je te trouve le plus chic des camarades.

L'employé

Le petit employé de la poste restante

Vient tard à son bureau, son allure est très lente.

Il s'assied renfrogné sur son fauteuil en cuir,

Car il sait qu'aux clients il lui faudra servir

Les lettres, les journaux à timbre coloriste

Et même les mandats ! — Cet homme obscur est triste.

Il se dit, en flairant un billet parfumé,

Qu'il ne voyage pas, et qu'il n'est pas aimé,

Que son nom composé de syllabes comiques

N'est jamais imprimé dans les feuilles publiques.

To Mother

Oh go on, you'll never be like those mothers

Who make Ambiguity weep those bitter tears;

You aren't solemn and wouldn't know how

To malign, with a haughty gesture of your arm;

You've never sewn, never done my wash,

You pay me less heed than your monkey;

Despite that, good-tempered in the evenings,

Whole-hearted I can laugh with you;

Together we'll rush to scores of adventures,

For you're the best companion of all.

The Clerk

The little clerk at general delivery

Comes to his desk late, his gait slow.

He sits brooding on his leather chair,

Knows he'll have to give the clients

Letters, papers with colorful stamps,

And even postal orders! This unknown man is sad.

He tells himself as he sniffs a perfumed note

That he doesn't travel, isn't loved,

That his name, composed of funny syllables,

Is never printed in scandal sheets.

The Promises of Symbolism

In his essay "Crise de vers" (1886; "Crisis in Poetry"), Sté-
phane Mallarmé (1842–98) described the aesthetic mo-
tivating a new generation of poets whose work tended
toward rhythmic fluidity and musicality and away from
the austere precision of Parnassianism. Instead of objec-
tive description, the young poets described by Mallarmé
privileged suggestion and nuance. Charles Baudelaire
(1821–67), predeceasing symbolism as a movement, none-
theless was one of the greatest influences on that genera-
tion thanks to the throughgoing symbolism of some of his
poems (such as "Correspondances"). In addition to Mal-
larmé, these symbolist poets figured prominently: Paul
Verlaine (1844–96) and Arthur Rimbaud (1854–91) (also
considered to be precursors), Rémy de Gourmont (1858–
1915), Gustave Kahn (1859–1936), Jules Laforgue (1860–87),
Pierre Louÿs (1870–1925), and Paul Valéry (1871–1945). A
variegated movement, symbolism was characterized by
numerous splinter groups and offshoots.

During the period coinciding with the Third Republic (1871–1914), symbolist poets overturned many long-standing rules of French verse in favor of a poetics of mobility, leading first to "liberated verse" (traditional meters freed of end stops and required pauses) and then to the advent of free verse. They experimented with new forms, notably the prose poem, and did away with the traditional alternation of masculine and feminine rhymes and then with rhyme altogether.

Innovation in language and form coincided with a reappraisal of what constituted appropriately poetic subject matter. During this period of urban development and industrial growth, poets wrote of cities and sidewalks, of new loves and new sexualities, of change and the ephemeral. Rejecting the impersonality of Parnassianism, they returned to lyrical perspectives forgotten since Romanticism and forged new subjectivities. But the symbolists chose irony in exchange for Romantic sentimentality and candor, linguistic and referential obscurity in exchange for the apparent transparency of Romanticism.

The poetic project suggested by Rimbaud's aphorism "je est un autre" (*Œuvres* 249; "I is someone else" [*Complete Works* 371]) completely transformed the lyric representation of subjectivity. Rhetorically, at least, symbolism opened the door to otherness and so to women. Laforgue called for gender equality in a manner remarkable for the 1880s: "Ô jeunes filles, quand serez-vous nos frères, nos frères intimes sans arrière-pensée d'exploitation!" (48; "Young women, when will you be our brothers, our intimate brothers, with no fear of exploitation?"). In this heady time for feminist activism, women gained access to free primary education and the right to divorce, and there were other important changes in their legal and social status. Laforgue went so far as to associate femininity with modernity: "Ô fémini-culture, pôle moderne!" (50; "O feminiculture, modern pole!"). In addition to women's cultures, gay and lesbian frames of reference contributed to the making of symbolist modernity. Renée Vivien and others in her circle addressed lesbian readers in search of poetry that spoke to rather than disdained or excluded them.

That women are generally accorded only a footnote in the history of symbolism indicates less a paucity of women poets before the turn of the century than the problem of writing literary histories in terms of manifes-tos and cenacles, which tend to overlook the production of women writers. Yet, defined broadly, the symbolist era witnessed the participation of a number of exceptional women poets from its earliest manifestations in the 1870s to the years before World War I.

For further reading, see Barre; Billy; Finch; Porter, *Cri-sis*; Schultz, *Gendered Lyric*; Scott.

Judith Gautier

(1845–1917)

Translations by Rosemary Lloyd

Judith Gautier was born in Paris, the daughter of the singer Ernesta Grisi and the writer Théophile Gautier. She was surrounded from childhood by the most prominent authors of her day, including Charles Baudelaire, Charles Leconte de Lisle, and Gustave Flaubert. Encouraged to write by her father and his literary friends, Judith enjoyed the freedom and independence of her bohemian upbringing. Brilliant and talented, like Girardin and Houville she also benefited from her celebrated beauty and family connections.

Her talents and interests were broad-ranging. She had a life-long passion for Far Eastern cultures and spoke Chinese, Japanese, and Persian. She also sculpted and painted and was an admirer of contemporary music. Gautier had a close friendship with Richard Wagner, whose *Parsifal* she inspired and subsequently translated. In later years she was linked with writers such as Victor Hugo, Stéphane Mallarmé, Robert de Montesquiou, Pierre Louÿs, and Jean Lorrain. She married Catulle Mendès at twenty one. Their unhappy union led to a separation in 1874. Gautier later entered into a romance with Suzanne Meyer-Zundel (1882–1971), which lasted from 1904 until Gautier's death.

Gautier wrote prolifically as a poet, novelist, playwright, journalist, and memoirist (*Le collier des jours*). She succeeded in earning her living with her pen, sometimes doing so using a pseudonym (she wrote for the press as Judith Walter, Judith Mendès, or Ferdinand Chaulnes). Her collected poetry was published in 1911 (*Poésies*). Although she honored her father Théophile's work, her poetry branched out in new, more fluid directions. It bears an unlikely combination of traces: Parnassian for its formalism but also modern and classical, decadent and orientalist, sensual and descriptive.

In addition to her literary production, Gautier broke ground for women of letters in several ways. In 1904 she participated in the inauguration of the Prix Femina by serving on its jury with Anna de Noailles and Rachilde, among others. In 1910 she was the first woman elected to the Académie Goncourt (followed by Colette in 1945 and Françoise Mallet-Joris in 1970). In 1911 she was named chevalière de la Légion d'Honneur.

For further reading, see Brahimi; Caws; Knapp; Mihram; Noblet; Richardson.

Tigre et gazelle

Dans les temps, je me le rappelle,
Quand j'étais tigre, ivre de faim,
C'était toi, la tendre gazelle
Qui fuyais au désert sans fin...

Pour vivre il me fallait ta vie.
Un désir fou creusait mes flancs,
Et je t'ai longtemps poursuivie
Sous le feu des midis brûlants.

Par monts et vals, bois et clairières,
Sur tes pas j'allais sans répit,
Et près des haltes familières
Je guettais, dans l'ombre tapi.

Auprès de la source où, furtive,
Pour boire tu penchais le front
Vers le frais cristal de l'eau vive,
Enfin, je t'ai prise d'un bond !...

J'ai saisi ta chair pantelante,
Pour la dévorer au soleil...
Tu râlais sous l'étreinte lente
Et je buvais ton sang vermeil.

Tiger and Gazelle

In the past, as I remember,

When I was a tiger, wild with hunger,

You were the tender little gazelle

Fleeing into the infinite desert.

If I were to live, you had to die.

A mad desire dug out my flanks,

And I pursued you long and far

Beneath the fire of burning noons.

Through hills and vales, through woods and clearings,

I followed your tracks relentlessly,

And near the old familiar haunts,

I crouched in the shade and watched for you.

Besides the spring where furtively

You bent your head down low to drink

Cool running water, crystal clear,

At last I seized you with a bound! . . .

There I grasped your heaving flesh,

To devour it in the sun's bright light.

In my slow embrace you groaned your last,

And there I drank your crimson blood.

Le goût m'est resté sur les lèvres ;
C'est pourquoi, lorsque je te vois,
J'éprouve en d'inquiétantes fièvres
La faim farouche d'autrefois,

Une très âpre convoitise,
Un si poignant et fol amour,
Que d'un rêve j'ai la hantise :
C'est d'être la proie à mon tour.

Mais je lis dans tes yeux étranges
Le trouble de l'ancien effroi...
Tu te souviens, car tu te venges
Et je fus moins cruel que toi !...

The taste still lingers on my lips

And that is why each time I see you,

I feel in disconcerting fevers

The savage hunger of days long gone.

A very bitter longing fills me,

So poignant and so wild a love,

That I am haunted by this daydream:

I long to be hunted by you in my turn.

But I can read in your strange eyes

The panic of that ancient terror . . .

You remember, and take your revenge

And I was less cruel than you are!

La vestale

La neige des hauteurs, ironique, consent
Au baiser du soleil qui ne peut la dissoudre.
Le volcan livre au ciel son cœur incandescent
Et reçoit, impassible, ou l'ondée ou la foudre.

L'oiseau n'a nulle peur de se précipiter
En folâtrant tout près d'un insondable abîme,
Sans risque même il peut un moment s'y jeter,
En un joyeux coup d'aile il regagne la cime.

Le sphinx pensif, les yeux ouverts sur l'inconnu,
Laisse l'audacieux, que son sourire charme,
S'efforcer de graver un nom sur son sein nu :
Contre le granit rude il va briser son arme.

En défiant l'ivresse et les troubles du cœur,
La vestale un instant s'assied près des bacchantes,
Elle mouille sa lèvre à la rouge liqueur,
Elle essaye en riant la couronne d'acanthes,

Puis, tranquille, revient vers le divin autel
Où luit sans s'obscurcir l'inextinguible flamme,
Bûcher dévorateur de tout rêve mortel,
L'amour pur et sacré sur qui veille son âme.

The Vestal Virgin

Mockingly, the snow on the heights accepts

The sunlight's kiss that cannot melt it.

The volcano gives the heavens its burning heart,

Impassively receiving both downpours and lightning.

The bird feels no fear in plummeting down

And playing on the brink of a measureless abyss,

It can safely risk plunging in for a moment,

A joyous wing beat restores it to the sky.

The brooding sphinx, eyes open on the unknown,

Allows the bold man, charmed by her smile,

To try carving a name on her naked breast:

On the harsh granite surface his knife will shatter.

Defying the frenzy of wine and of the heart,

The vestal for a moment sits down with the bacchantes,

She moistens her lips on the ruby-red liquor,

And laughingly tries on the crown of acanthus.

Then tranquilly she returns to her holy temple,

Where ever bright the unquenchable flame gleams,

That fire that devours all earthly dreams,

That pure, sacred love, watched over by her soul.

In ancient Rome, priestesses, chosen as young girls and vowed to chastity, ministered to the temple of Vesta and watched over its eternal flame.

D'après Saadi

Je suis tout près de toi, mais ne peux te saisir...

La coupe du baiser se refuse à ma bouche,

Et, près du puits scellé, pour mourir je me couche,

L'âme et le corps brûlés au feu de mon désir.

Ainsi, dans le désert, à la peine succombe

Le chameau, cheminant sous un trop lourd fardeau,

La lèvre desséchée, il tombe sur sa tombe,

Et meurt de soif, lui qui portait la charge d'eau !

Inspired by Saadi

I am close by you and yet I may not touch you . . .
My mouth may not share the cup of the kiss,
And beside a sealed well I lie down to die,
Burning body and soul in the fire of my longing.

Thus in the desert the camel succumbs
To suffering, as it carries its heavy burden,
Its lips have grown dry and it falls on its tomb
And dies of thirst though fraught with water!

Vénus chez Diane

À la Comtesse Greffulhe

Diane a convié Vénus en la forêt...
Et la reine d'amour, toute pâle d'ivresse,
Les bras noués au cou de Tannhæuser, paraît...
Sa turbulente cour autour d'elle se presse.

Le faune, la bacchante et la nymphe aux beaux yeux,
Le satyre velu, bondissent sur ses traces ;
Et les couples d'amants, languides ou joyeux,
Entourent en dansant le groupe des Trois Grâces.

Un dieu prête sa voix aux cris de volupté,
Un glorieux fracas gouverne le tumulte...
Et l'impudique ardeur se revêt de beauté ;
La folle bacchanale est le rite d'un culte.

Venus Visits Diana

For the Countess Greffulhe[18]

Diana has invited Venus to the forest . . .

And love's queen, now colorless with wine,

Her arms wreathing Tannhäuser's[19] neck, appears . . .

Around her throngs her turbulent court.

The faun, the bacchante, and the lovely-eyed nymph,

The hairy satyr all leap on her traces;

And the pairs of lovers, languid or joyful,

Dance in a circle around the three Graces.[20]

A god lends his voice to the cries of deep pleasure,

A glorious din swells over the tumult . . .

And all this brazen passion is adorned with beauty;

The mad bacchanal is the rite of a cult.

---

[18]Élisabeth de Riquet de Caraman-Chimay, comtesse Greffulhe (1860–1952), was an influential *salonnière* and patron of the arts. She is thought to be a model for Marcel Proust's duchesse de Guermantes in *À la recherche du temps perdu.*

[19]A thirteenth-century German minnesinger or troubadour, Tannhäuser was established as a legendary figure in the fifteenth century. In legend, the wandering Tannhäuser arrives at Venusberg, the supernatural home of Venus. Based on and named after Tannhäuser, Wagner's 1845 opera was performed in Paris in 1861. Although the opera failed miserably, Wagner gained the acclaim of the French literati.

[20]In Greek and Roman mythology, the Graces were the goddesses of splendor, mirth, and rejoicing. In painting and sculpture, they were sometimes accompanied by Venus.

Et c'est pourquoi Diane écoute et voit ce jeu

Sans déplaisir, sourit même, à l'ivresse brève.

Mais aux amours où l'âme est mêlée, elle rêve,

Sous son nimbe lunaire idéalement bleu.

Sonnet décadent

Outremer, ambre, rubis : c'est le jour.

Joyaux, prisme, sur la dalle il frissonne.

Aux froides stalactites, rien ne sonne ;

Le silence ogival fuit au détour.

Les mains jointes, les pieds droits, l'ombre autour

Effaçant ce que l'albâtre emprisonne.

Gerbes d'élans mystiques, mais personne.

Lointains sonores, lys, tremblant amour,

Muet, le grillage embaumé d'aveux.

Hors des paumes, l'or jaillit en cheveux.

L'aiguille d'un rayon vient compter l'heure.

Sur le mort d'ivoire, s'éteint le sang.

L'écrin meurt, aux plis imprégnés d'encens,

Et, dans l'invisible, la nuit demeure...

And that's why Diana can observe this game
Undismayed, even smiling at this brief intoxication,
But she dreams of a love that enmeshes all the soul,
Beneath her moonlight halo of perfect azure.

Decadent Sonnet

Lapis lazuli, amber, and ruby: that's daylight.
Jewels, a prism, it trembles on the flagstone.
The cold stalactites are utterly silent;
The ogival silence flies off at a tangent.

Hands joined, feet aligned, surrounding shadow
Effacing what the alabaster imprisons.
Sprays of mystical surges, but no one there,
Sonorous distances, lilies, trembling love.

Silent, the grille with its perfume of confessions.
Far from palms, gold bursts forth in plumes of hair.
A clock hand of sunshine comes to count the hour.

On the ivory deadpan, blood lies dying.
The screen expires, its folds redolent of incense,
And in the invisible, night lingers on . . .

Bulle de savon

D'un souffle la bulle est née,
Et la frêle éclosion
S'élance en la vision
D'une longue destinée.

Beau globe de cristal clair,
Comme un astre par l'espace,
Elle oscille, roule, passe,
Silencieuse dans l'air.

Et des prismes, des féeries
S'ébauchent dans sa clarté.
C'est un palais enchanté,
Un écrin de pierreries,

Un monde artificiel,
Où l'on voit d'exquises choses :
Des lacs, des jardins, des roses,
Et même on y voit le ciel.

Mais un choc brise le charme,
Azur, prisme, taillis verts,
Tout l'adorable univers
Se résout en une larme.

Soap Bubble

From a breath the bubble's born:
Its fragile blossoming
Bursts forth in the vision
Of a long destiny.

Lovely globe of clear crystal,
Like a star in outer space
It trembles, rolls, and passes,
Silent in the air.

And prisms and fairylands
Appear briefly in its brightness.
It's a palace that's enchanted,
It's a jewelry case.

It's an artificial world,
Where you see exquisite things:
You see gardens, lakes, and roses,
And you even see the sky.

But a blow can break the spell.
Azure, prism, and green thickets,
All the lovely universe
Disappears in a tear.

Légende arabe

À Clermont-Ganneau

Il y avait dans Ecbatane
Une très hautaine sultane,
Plus belle que le plus beau jour,
Qui pourtant dédaignait l'amour.

Elle était sévère et cruelle
À ceux qui se mouraient pour elle,
Jurant qu'aucun n'aurait son cœur.
Mais toujours l'amour est vainqueur.

Il arriva, pour sa défaite,
Que, dans la ville, un jour de fête,
L'Hébreu Joseph entra le soir,
Et sous un figuier vint s'asseoir.

Or, la sultane à l'âme altière
Le vit du fond de sa litière.
Soudain son orgueil fut dompté,
L'amour brisa sa volonté.

Arabic Legend

For Clermont-Ganneau[21]

In Ecbatana[22] there dwelled
A very haughty sultana,
Fairer than the fairest day,
And yet she cared nothing for love.

She was harsh and she was cruel
To those who were dying for her,
Swearing none would have her heart,
But love is ever the victor.

It happened, it was her undoing,
That one feast day in the town,
Joseph the Hebrew came one evening
And beneath a fig tree sat him down.

The proud-hearted sultana
Saw him from her palanquin's depths.
Her pride was suddenly conquered,
Love broke her will in two.

---

[21]Charles Simon Clermont-Ganneau (1846–1923) was an archaeologist, diplomat, and professor of Eastern languages at the Collège de France.

[22]Ancient name for Hamadan, in western Iran, one of the capitals of the Persian Empire

Toutes les femmes d'Ecbatane
Se moquèrent de la sultane
Qui s'était éprise à son tour ;
Surtout les dames de la cour.

Ah ! ne me gardez pas rancune,
Dit la reine. Il n'en est aucune
Qui n'aimerait un tel amant.
— Voyons s'il est si beau, vraiment ?

Et les odalisques narquoises,
Les cheveux ornés de turquoises,
S'assemblèrent à petit bruit,
Rieuses, en pelant un fruit.

Mais quand parut le beau jeune homme
Au front d'albâtre, au regard froid,
Toutes, croyant peler la pomme,
Se coupèrent le bout du doigt.

All the women of Ecbatana
Ridiculed the poor sultana,
Whose turn it was to fall in love,
Especially the ladies of the court.

"Oh, don't be unkind,"
Said the queen. "Not one of you
Would fail to love such a lover."
"Shall we see if he's truly handsome?"

And the mocking odalisques,
Their hair adorned with turquoise,
Gathered with barely a sound,
Laughing and peeling fruit.

But when the fair young man appeared
With his alabaster brow and cold eye,
Each in peeling her apple
Cut the tip of her finger.

Marie Krysinska

(1857–1908)

née Maria Anastazja Wincentyna Krysinska

Translations by Rosemary Lloyd

Marie Krysinska was born in Warsaw and reportedly moved to Paris as a young woman to pursue studies in music. She began to publish poems in the early 1880s and was one of the few women to become actively involved in the poetic circles of her time, an involvement that often met with hostility from male writers. She established her own literary salon and was a fixture at the cabaret the Chat Noir, where she played piano, both her own songs and poems by contemporaries that she set to music. In 1885 she married the artist and illustrator Georges Bellenger. The couple spent the following two years in the United States, where Krysinska gathered observations and material included in some of her prose works.

In addition to three collections of poems, the first published in 1890, Krysinska wrote novels, short stories, numerous essays, and musical compositions. But it was with her poetry and among poets that she made her mark as one of the first to write in free verse in France. Indeed, since she was the first to publish a free-verse poem (in 1883), she must be recognized as one of the great innovators of modern French poetry, along with Arthur Rimbaud, whose free-verse compositions were written earlier but published after hers. Yet poets and critics from Krysinska's day to our own often discounted her claim to having inaugurated free verse. Gustave Kahn waged a campaign to be recognized as its inventor, casting Krysinska as an interloper. She readily defended herself in print: it was perhaps this refusal to be compliant that animated the invective of some of her contemporaries. Despite the volume and importance of her work, she is only beginning to attract the attention of scholars.

Her poetic works are: *Rythmes pittoresques* (1890), *Joies errantes* (1894), *Intermèdes* (1903). Of the poems selected for this anthology, "Symphonie en gris," "Berceuse macabre," "Nature morte," and "L'ange gardien" first appeared in *Rythmes pittoresques*; "La parure," "Devant le miroir," "Idylle," "Le poème des caresses," and "Marines" in *Joies errantes*; and "Les lampes" in *Intermèdes*. For further reading, see Brogniez; Goulesque; Paliyenko, "In the Shadow"; Schultz, *Gendered Lyric*; Whidden, Introd. and "Marie Krysinska."

Symphonie en gris

À Rodolphe Salis

Plus d'ardentes lueurs sur le ciel alourdi,

Qui semble tristement rêver.

Les arbres, sans mouvement,

Mettent dans le loin une dentelle grise. —

Sur le ciel qui semble tristement rêver,

Plus d'ardentes lueurs. —

Dans l'air gris flottent les apaisements,

Les résignations et les inquiétudes.

Du sol consterné monte une rumeur étrange, surhumaine.

Cabalistique langage entendu seulement

Des âmes attentives. —

Les apaisements, les résignations, et les inquiétudes

Flottent dans l'air gris. —

Les silhouettes vagues ont le geste de la folie.

Les maisons sont assises disgracieusement

Comme de vieilles femmes —

Les silhouettes vagues ont le geste de la folie. —

Symphony in Gray

For Rodolphe Salis[23]

No more glowing lights on the heavy sky,

Which seems lost in sad dreams.

The motionless trees

Trace on the distance their gray lace.—

On the sky that seems lost in sad dreams,

No more glowing lights.—

In the gray air float calm,

And resignation, and disquiet.

From the dismayed earth rises a strange, superhuman murmuring.

A cabalistic language heard only

By attentive souls.—

Calm, resignation, and disquiet

Float in the gray air.—

The vague silhouettes gesture like madmen.

The houses squat as awkwardly

As old women.—

The vague silhouettes gesture like madmen.—

This poem can be read as a response to Théophile Gautier's "Symphonie en blanc" (*Emaux et camées*), a meditation on whiteness, transparency, and purity.

[23]An artist, Salis (1851–97) established the famous Montmartre cabaret the Chat Noir, in 1881.

C'est l'heure cruelle et stupéfiante,

Où la chauve-souris déploie ses ailes grises,

Et s'en va rôdant comme un malfaiteur. —

Les silhouettes vagues ont le geste de la folie. —

Près de l'étang endormi

Le grillon fredonne d'exquises romances.

Et doucement ressuscitent dans l'air gris

Les choses enfuies.

Près de l'étang endormi

Le grillon fredonne d'exquises romances.

Sous le ciel qui semble tristement rêver.

4 novembre 1882

It is the cruel and astounding hour,

When the bat unfolds its gray wings,

And takes off, prowling like a criminal.—

The vague silhouettes gesture like madmen.—

By the sleeping lake

The cricket sings exquisite romances.

And gently brings back to life in the gray air

Things fled away.

By the sleeping lake

The cricket sings exquisite romances.

Under the sky that seems lost in sad dreams.

4 November 1882

Berceuse macabre

À Maurice Vaucaire

— Qu'elles sont cruelles et lentes, les heures !

Et qu'il est lourd — l'ennui de la mort !

Qu'elles sont cruelles et lentes, les heures.

Les heures silencieuses et froides, qui tombent dans l'Éternité, comme des gouttes de pluie dans la mer.

Donne-moi la main, ô ma sœur, et viens sous la Lune calmante, parler de *ceux* que nous avons laissés seuls quand nous sommes descendues dans la tombe.

— Un sommeil très lourd m'engourdit, et je fais un rêve qui durera toujours ; — rendors-toi, ma sœur, — nos aimés nous ont oubliées,

— J'ai mis mon cœur dans son cœur et je suis sienne à travers la Mort.

— Ces murs sont hauts, et la terre des vivants est loin ; — rendors toi, ma sœur.

— J'ai senti des diamants humides tomber sur ma bouche desséchée, — c'est mon ami qui pleurait.

— Rendors-toi, pauvre sœur ; — c'est la pluie qui violait ton cercueil.

Macabre Lullaby

For Maurice Vaucaire[24]

—How cruel and slow the hours are!

How heavy weighs death's tedium!

How cruel and slow the hours are.

The silent chilly hours that fall into Eternity, as drops of rain into
the sea.

My sister, now give me your hand, and come beneath the
calming Moon, where we can speak of *those* we left alone when we
went down into the grave.

—A very heavy slumber makes me numb, and I dream a dream
that will last forever; —go back to sleep, my sister, —our loved
ones have forgotten us.

—I set my heart in his heart, and I am his beyond the Grave.

—These walls are high and the living live far away. —Go back
to sleep, my sister, do.

—I have felt wet diamonds fall upon my withered mouth, —it is
my friend who mourned for me.

—Go back to sleep, poor sister; —it was the rain that violated
your coffin.

---

[24]A writer, lyricist, and librettist (1863?–1918)

— Ô souvent j'entends des sanglots lointains ; — c'est mon aimé qui gémit, hanté par nos chers souvenirs.

— Non, c'est le hibou qui jette un cri dans la nuit profonde ; — profonde comme nos tombeaux, et comme l'oubli de ceux qui nous avaient aimées ; — rendors-toi, ma sœur.

2 décembre 1882

—Often I hear some distant sobs; —it's my beloved who moans, my beloved who's haunted by sad memories.

—No, it's the owl that sends his cry far into the depths of night, —deep as our tombs, deep as the oblivion of those who loved us; —go back to sleep, my sister.

2 December 1882

Nature morte

À Louis Forain

Un boudoir cossu :

Les meubles, les tentures et les *œuvres d'art,* ont la banalité requise.

Et la lampe — soleil à gage — éclaire les deux amants.

Elle est teinte en blonde, car *Il* n'aime que les blondes.

Lui, a les cheveux de la même nuance que son complet très à la
mode.

★

Par la fenêtre ouverte on voit un ciel bleu comme une flamme de
soufre.

Et la lune, radieuse en ces voiles, flotte vers de fulgurants hymens.

★

Ayant achevé de lire le cours authentique de la Bourse, *Il* allume un
cigare cher — et songe :

« C'est une heure agréable de la journée, celle où l'on SACRIFIE À
L'AMOUR. »

Ils se sont rapprochés et causent

DE L'ÉGOÏSME À DEUX, DES ÂMES SŒURS...

Lui, bâillant un peu

Elle tâchant à éviter la cendre du cigare.

★

Still Life

For Louis Forain[25]

An opulent boudoir:
Furniture, hangings, and *works of art* all have the requisite banality.
And the lamp—a sun paid by the hour—illuminates the two lovers.

Her hair is tinted blonde, for *He* prefers blondes.

His hair is the same shade as his suit, and the suit's the height of
    fashion.

             ★

Through the open window can be seen a sky as blue as a sulfur
    flame.
And the moon, radiant in these veils, floats towards dazzling nuptials.

             ★

After reading the authentic Stock Exchange figures, *He* lights up an
    expensive cigar—and dreams:
"It's that pleasant hour of the day in which one SACRIFICES TO
    LOVE."
They have drawn closer to each other and talk
OF DUAL EGOISM AND SISTER SOULS . . .
He yawning slightly
She trying to avoid the ash from his cigar.

             ★

---

[25]An impressionist painter and illustrator (1852–1931)

Par la fenêtre ouverte on voit un ciel bleu comme une flamme de
   soufre
Et les arbres bercés de nuptiales caresses.

⋆

Lui, ayant fini son cigare, se penche pour donner un baiser à celle
Qu'au club il appelle « sa maîtresse ».
Il se penche pour lui donner un baiser — tout en rêvant :
« Pourvu que la Banque Ottomane ne baisse pas ! »
Elle, offre ses lèvres pensant à ses fournisseurs

Et leur baiser sonne comme le choc de deux verres vides.

⋆

Par la fenêtre ouverte on voit un ciel bleu comme une flamme de
   soufre
Et les oiseaux veilleurs chantent l'immortel Amour
Tandis que de la terre monte une vapeur d'encens
Et des parfums d'Extase.

⋆

— Si nous fermions — disent-ils — cette fenêtre qui gêne NOTRE
   EXTASE ?

Through the open window can be seen a sky as blue as a sulfur
   flame
And the trees rocked with nuptial caresses.

★

He, his cigar finished, leans over to give a kiss to the woman
Whom, at the club, he calls his "mistress."
He leans over to give her a kiss—while all the time dreaming:
"Let's hope the Ottoman Bank doesn't drop!"
She offers her lips while she thinks of her suppliers

And their kiss rings out like the clash of two empty glasses.

★

Through the open window can be seen a sky as blue as a sulfur
   flame
And the watching birds sing of deathless Love
While from the earth rises the smoke of incense
And perfumes of Ecstasy.

★

"How about," they say, "we close that window, which thwarts our
   ECSTASY?"

L'ange gardien

À Xavier Krysinski

L'Être blanc au pur regard, à la lumineuse chevelure, suit nos pas
   tout le long de la vie.

★

L'enfant le voit, tendre et doux, se pencher sur son sommeil,
Et notre premier sourire est pour l'Être blanc
Au pur regard.

★

Plus tard, ainsi qu'un frère aîné, il nous conduit par la main ;
Indulgent et joyeux,
Il pleure seulement s'il voit notre visage déshonoré
Par une grimace laide, —
Car il veut qu'on soit beau et qu'on lui ressemble
L'Être blanc au pur regard.

★

Et quand est disparue la fraîche ronde des insoucieuses années ;
Quand le dernier clair rire et la dernière petite robe s'envolent au
   ciel des souvenirs,

Guardian Angel

For Xavier Krysinski[26]

The white Being with unsullied gaze and luminous hair follows our
    steps our whole life long.

★

The child sees it, tender and gentle, leaning over its sleep,
And our first smile is for the white Being
With unsullied gaze.

★

Later, like an older brother, it leads us by the hand;
Indulgent and joyous,
Weeping only if it sees our face dishonored
By an ugly scowl, —
For it wants us to be lovely and to be like it,
The white Being with unsullied gaze.

★

And when that fresh circle of careless years has gone from sight;
When the last bright laugh and the last little dress fly off to the sky
    of memories,

---

[26]Krysinska's father. See Seth Whidden's notes to *Rythmes pittoresques*
(Krysinska).

Quand nos âmes, encore virginales, frissonnent au vent d'indicibles
  angoisses ;

Et que nos yeux extasiés versent des pleurs dans la solitude des
  nuits ;

C'est l'Être blanc au pur regard

Qui, de son aile diaprée,

Essuie nos larmes.

                    ⋆

Puis vient l'heure des luttes héroïques :

L'Indifférence aveugle et sourde qui fait nos cœurs desséchés et
  pareils à du bois mort,

L'Hypocrisie au sourire fardé,

La Bêtise lâche et féroce,

Rendent nos bras lassés et nos âmes sans courage ;

Alors, douloureusement, il voile sa face, l'Être blanc au pur regard ;

Car il veut que, semblables à lui,

Nous gardions notre splendeur et notre beauté premières.

                    ⋆

Dans les murmures des bois, par les matins ensoleillés :

Dans la grondante voix de la mer,

Dans le silence mélancolique des soirs,

Dans la douleur et dans la joie,

When our souls, virginal still, tremble in the wind of unspeakable
   anguish;
And when our ecstatic eyes shed tears in the solitude of the
   night;
It's the white Being with unsullied gaze
Who with many-colored wing
Wipes our tears away.

*

Then comes the hour of heroic struggles:
The blind and deaf Indifference that dries our heart until it's like
   dead wood,
Hypocrisy with its lipstick smile,
Cowardly and ferocious Stupidity,
Weary our arms and strip our hearts of courage;
Then in grief it veils its face, the white Being with unsullied gaze;
For it wants us, like itself,
To keep our first splendor and our first beauty.

*

In the murmuring woods, on sunlit mornings:
In the roaring voice of the sea,
In the melancholy silence of evenings,
In grief and in joy,

Au milieu du saint émoi dont nous vibrons quand l'aile prodigieuse
   de l'Art nous effleure ; —
Et au milieu des hymnes de flamme que chantent nos cœurs à
   l'Amour victorieux et sublime ;
Notre oreille entend la voix de l'Être blanc
Qui, consolant et radieux,
Suit nos pas tout le long de la vie.

*

Et lorsque notre tête lasse s'endort dans la fraîcheur paisible du
   tombeau,
Encore bercée par la chanson lointaine et douce des souvenirs,
   — comme l'enfant sur les genoux de sa mère,
Il accompagne notre âme, par delà les bleus éthers et par delà les
   étoiles, jusqu'au Portique du Ciel grand ouvert ;
Portant, dans sa tunique de lin immaculé, les belles fleurs aux
   parfums ineffables — qui sont nos belles actions ;
Tandis qu'avec des rythmes de harpes triomphales, flotte sa
   lumineuse chevelure.

9 février 1884

In the midst of a holy emotion that sets us quivering when the
  prodigious wing of Art touches us; —
And in the midst of hymns of flame that our hearts sing to
  victorious and sublime Love;
We hear the voice of the white Being
Who, consoling and radiant,
Follows our steps our whole life long.

*

And when our weary head falls asleep in the cool peace of the
  tomb,
Still rocked by the sweet distant song of memory, —like a child on
  its mother's lap,
It goes with our soul, through the blue ether and beyond the stars,
  to the wide open Portico of the Sky;
Bearing, in its tunic of immaculate linen, the lovely flowers with
  ineffable perfumes—that are our good deeds;
While its luminous hair floats out to the rhythms of triumphant
  harps.

                                        9 February 1884

La parure

À Antoine Périvier·

Un peu de l'âme somptueuse et barbare
De nos primitifs aïeux
Passe en nous avec les feux des pierres rares
Et l'éclat du métal précieux.

L'or ciselé en bagues alliantes[27]
Et en bracelets nous enchaîne
D'une fidèle tendresse où s'enchante
La tendresse de nos grand'mères lointaines.

Les perles rient en colliers
Sur notre cou qu'elles caressent
Licencieuses comme au beau temps
　　　Des mouches, des paniers
Et des galantes paresses.

Les mousselines légères
　　　Nous font
Un cœur de papillon,
Et les fraîches toiles à fleurettes suggèrent
Un cœur de bergère.

---

[27]Neologism built on the verb *allier* ("to ally or unite by marriage"), to form a synonym for *alliance* ("wedding ring")

Dressing Up

For Antonin Périvier[28]

A hint of the sumptuous, barbarian soul
Of our primitive ancestors
Passes into us with the fire of rare stones
And the gleam of precious metal.

Gold, chiseled into betrothal rings
And bracelets, chains us
With a faithful tenderness where
The tenderness of our far-off grandmothers finds delight.

Pearls laugh in necklaces
On our neck that they caress
As licentiously as in the good old days
        Of beauty spots and hoop skirts,
And idle gallantries.

Light muslins
        Make us
Butterflies' hearts,
And cool sprigged fabrics suggest
A shepherdess's heart.

---

[28]Antonin Périvier (1847–1924), a journalist, from 1879 to 1901 was co-publisher of *Figaro*, of which he founded the literary supplement. He was the editor of *Gil Blas* from 1903 to 1909.

Dans la soie murmurante et câline
C'est l'amoureuse qui veut qu'on devine
Ses abandons et ses langueurs, toutes.

Les plis souples de la dentelle
Sont d'aimables routes
Fleuries, vers la fantaisie fière qui s'y recèle.

Le riche apparat des velours
  Nous fait un peu reine,
Un peu châtelaine aux fastueuses amours.

Mais en l'asile discret des sombres laines
Une âme de nonnain
  Nous vient ;

Tant l'Art et le Rêve sont les vrais vainqueurs
  De nos faibles cœurs.

In the murmurous, affectionate silk

Is the loving girl who wants her beau to guess

Her yielding and her languor, all of it.

The supple folds of lace

Are lovely flower-strewn roads

Toward the proud fantasy that hides there.

The rich pomp of velvet

    Gives us a hint of queenliness

A hint of the chatelaine with her luxurious loves.

But in the discreet shelter of dark wool

The soul of a nun

    Comes to us;

Thus Art and Dream are the true conquerors

    Of our frail hearts.

Devant le miroir

Cette grave entrevue

Est fertile en émois,

L'image, pourtant connue,

Surprend toujours ; — est-ce bien soi

Cette soudaine apparue ?

Et les petites mines d'aller

Pour calmer l'inquiétude qui vient

De n'être pas — il se peut — aussi bien

Que l'on voudrait ;

Mais, bientôt, une distribution de récompenses

Généreuses, commence.

Les cheveux ? ah ! les cheveux, parfait !

Surtout de profil ; on dirait

De telle peinture d'artiste admiré ;

Puis on retrouve à des détails menus,

Le souvenir du même visage des jours révolus

Des jours enfantins si vite — en somme — disparus.

Et l'on songe à cet autre miroir enchanté

Si impressionnant pour nos jeunes cœurs :

L'eau de l'étang que l'on croyait

Un morceau de ciel tombé

Où poussaient aussi des herbes et des fleurs.

In Front of the Mirror

This grave meeting

Is rich in turmoil:

The image, although well known,

Always surprises; —is it really me,

This sudden apparition?

And the little feints at leaving,

To calm the anxiety that comes

From not being—it can happen—as attractive

As we would like.

But soon, a shower of rewards,

Generous rewards, begins.

The hair? ah! the hair is perfect!

The profile especially; it's like

A certain painting by an admired artist;

Then you rediscover through little details,

The memory of the same face as in days gone by,

Days of childhood so swiftly—in short—fled away.

And you think of that other enchanted mirror

That so impressed our young hearts:

The water of the pond that we thought

Was a piece of sky that had fallen to earth,

And where grass and flowers also grew.

The first of three poems collected under the heading "Notes féminines" and dedicated to the writer Edmond de Goncourt (1822–96). Edmond, with his younger brother Jules (1830–70), wrote *La femme au XVIIIe siècle*.

Idylle

À Rachilde

Sur la route bordée de vertes haies
Où le chèvrefeuille chevrote, bercé
Par le tiède vent d'été,
Comme de vieux airs atténués ;

Ils vont épris ; lui et elle —
L'éternel *lui* et l'*elle* éternelle —
Qui pensent être premiers
À tant s'aimer.

C'est tout le ciel pour lui — *ses* yeux,
C'est pour elle un cher paradis
Que le bras fort de l'amoureux,
Où la main de l'aimée se blottit —
Comme un frêle oiseau dans un nid.

Tout le sang de leur cœur s'est fait vin de tendresse
Et tous leurs rêves sont à deux ;

Cependant viennent au devant d'eux
— Sur la route bordée de vertes haies —
Leurs inconjurables destinées

Qui sont : — La Mort
Et l'Oubli — cette pire des Morts.

Idyll

For Rachilde[29]

On the road bordered with green hedges
Where the honeysuckle suckles, rocked
By the warm summer wind,
As if by old and faded songs;

They walk, in love; he and she—
The eternal *he* and the *she* eternal—
Who think themselves the first ever
To love so deeply.

They're all the sky for him—*her* eyes;
For her it's a dear paradise,
The strong arm of the lover,
In which the beloved's hand can snuggle—
Like a fragile bird in a nest.

All the blood of their heart has become a wine of tenderness
And all their dreams are dreams for two;

And yet toward them come,
On the road bordered with green hedges—
Their implacable destinies

Which are: —Death
And Oblivion—the worst of Deaths.

---

[29]Rachilde gained celebrity with her decadent novel *Monsieur Vénus* (1884).

Le poème des caresses

Inoubliables baisers qui rayonnez
Sur le ciel pâle des souvenirs premiers !
Baisers silencieux sur nos berceaux penchés !

— Caresses enjouées sur la joue ;
Tremblantes mains des vieux parents, —
Pauvres chères caresses d'antan,

Vous êtes les grandes sœurs sages
Des folles qui nous affolent
Dans les amoureux mirages.

Baisers ingénus en riant dérobés,
Moins à cause de leur douceur souhaités,
Que pour s'enivrer de témérité.

Premières caresses, vacillantes —
Comme, dans le vent âpre,
Des lumières aux lampes ;

Caresses des yeux, caresses de la voix,
Serrements de mains éperdues
Et longs baisers où la raison se noie !

The Poem of Caresses

Unforgettable kisses that glow
In the pale sky of early memories!
Silent kisses leaning over our cradles!

—Playful caresses on the cheek;
Trembling hands of old relatives, —
Poor dear caresses of days gone by,

You are the wise older sisters
Of the crazy ones that drive us mad
In ardent mirages.

Naive kisses stolen in laughter,
Longed for less for their sweetness
Than to grow drunk with boldness.

First caresses, wavering—
As, in the bitter wind,
The lamp light wavers;

Caresses of the eyes, caresses of the voice,
Wild handshakes
And long kisses in which reason drowns!

Puis, belles flammes épanouies,

Sacrilèges hosties

Où tout le Dieu vainqueur avec nous communie !

Caresses sonores comme des clochettes d'or,

Caresses muettes comme la Mort,

Caresse meurtrière qui brûle et qui mord !...

Baisers presque chastes de l'Amour heureux,

Caresses frôleuses comme des brises,

Toute-puissance des paroles qui grisent !

Mélancolique volupté des bonheurs précaires,

Pervers aiguillon du mystère,

Éternel leurre ! ironique chimère !

Puis, enfin, dans la terre —

Lit dernier, où viennent finir nos rêves superbes, —

Sur notre sommeil, la calmante caresse des hautes herbes.

Then, lovely flames in full flower,

Sacrilegious hosts,

Where the conquering God, entire, takes communion with us!

Caresses as sonorous as golden bells,

Caresses as silent as Death,

Murderous caress that burns and bites! . . .

Kisses of happy Love, almost chaste,

Caresses that fondle like breezes,

All-powerful words that intoxicate!

Melancholy pleasure of precarious joys,

Perverse spur of mystery,

Eternal lure! ironic chimera!

Then, finally, in the earth—

That final bed, where our superb dreams come to an end, —

Over our sleep, the calming caress of long grasses.

Marines

I: Marine sombre

À Joseph Caraguel

La plaine marine s'est attristée

Comme d'un deuil infiniment morne ;

Sous les cieux, noirs de funèbres nuées ;

Gronde, en sanglots sourds, sa mélancolie sans bornes.

Les vagues sont de lourdes étoffes sombres

Frangées d'argent funéraire ;

Et les brises du large — véhémentes pleureuses — vocifèrent

Comme sur des Morts gisants aux liquides décombres.

Des Morts glorieux — chers aussi —

Dont les regards se fussent éteints

Comme s'éteignent les claires étoiles au gris matin,

Des Morts emblématiques dont les noms seraient :

Espoir, Courage, Amour, Fierté,

Et que la mer sinistre aurait engloutis.

Seascapes

I: Dark Seascape

For Joseph Caraguel[30]

The plain of the sea is sunk in sorrow
As if in an infinitely mournful mourning;
Under the heavens, black with funereal clouds,
Rumbles, in stifled sobs, its boundless melancholy.

The waves are made of a heavy dark fabric
Fringed with the silver of funerals;
And the winds from the open sea—vehement mourners—
    vociferate
As if over Dead ones lying in the liquid debris.

As if the gaze of the glorious Dead—dear Dead, too—
Had gone out
As bright stars go out in the gray of morning,
Emblematic Dead whose names could be:
Hope, Courage, Love, Pride,
And whom the sinister sea might have engulfed.

Although it is unknown whether Krysinska read Rimbaud before composing
this poem, it is interesting to compare the prominent ocean imagery in their
free-verse pieces. See Rimbaud, "Marine" and "Mouvement" (*Illuminations*,
written c. 1872 and published 1886).

[30]Caraguel was a playwright (1855–?).

II: Marine claire

À Stuart Merrill

Le bleu marin, doré de ciel, déroule ses soies lentes
Comme pour un manteau de Vierge byzantine.
Puis ce sont de gracieux rubans, irisés d'eau câline,
Que nulle âpre respiration du vent ne tourmente.

Les crêtes saphirines des vagues sont fondues
De tendresse, au sein de la brillante étendue
Soulevée à peine en paresseux mouvements
D'ailes frissonnantes — comme d'un ramier dormant.

C'est le Pardon joyeux et l'oubli des orages,
Le baiser unissant les éléments candides
Si intimement que — vertigineux mirage —
La mer semble un ciel doux, onduleux et liquide,
Où — telles des nuées — les navires oscillent
— Et le vrai ciel paraît une mer immobile.

II: Bright Seascape

For Stuart Merrill[31]

The blue of the sea, washed gold by the sky, unfolds its slow silk
As if for a Byzantine Virgin's cloak.
Then there are gracious ribbons, turned all the colors of the
   rainbow by the caressing water,
And no harsh wind torments it.

The sapphire crests of the waves melt
In tenderness, in the heart of the glittering expanse
Scarcely raised in lazy movements
Of trembling wings—like those of a sleeping dove.

It's the joyful Pardon, all storms forgotten,
The kiss uniting the candid elements
So intimately that—vertiginous mirage—
The sea seems a gentle, undulating, liquid sky,
Where ships bob up and down—like clouds—
And the real sky seems a motionless sea.

---

[31]Merrill, an American-born symbolist poet, was educated and lived most
of his life in France. He wrote primarily in French (1863–1915).

III: Soir en mer

À Georges Rodenbach

La mer et le ciel se sont parés

De lueurs rouges, de lueurs roses,

De lueurs pourpres — en chantante gamme

— C'est — comme des linges éclaboussés de sang, parmi des roses,

Ce qui resterait

De quelque galant drame.

Puis, des gemmes enflammées,

Des rubis, des grenats, des coraux

Roulent en colliers dénoués,

Tombent, en guirlandes rompues, du ciel dans l'eau.

Et les feux de l'horizon qui étincelle

Cerclent la mer d'un anneau d'or,

Comme une fiancée redoutable et belle

Qui, charmeresse, se couche dans les dentelles

De l'écume, légères et frêles

Et, respirant doucement — s'endort.

III: Evening Seascape
For Georges Rodenbach[32]

The sea and the sky have adorned themselves

In a glow of red, in a glow of pink,

In a glow of crimson—in a singing scale

—It's—as if linen had been spattered with blood, amidst roses,

The remnants

Of some gallant drama.

Then, flaming gems,

Rubies, garnets, corals,

Rolling in unstrung necklaces,

Fall, in broken garlands, from the sky into the water.

And the fires of the horizon that sparkles

Circle the sea in a golden ring,

Like a redoubtable and lovely bride,

A charmer who lies down in the lace

Of the foam, light and fragile,

And, breathing softly—falls asleep.

---

[32]Rodenbach (1855–98) was a Belgian symbolist poet and novelist.

Les lampes

Il est des lampes fraternelles

Aux lueurs patientes ;

Il en est de cruelles

De gaies et d'impudentes.

Lampe résignée

Qui baigne d'une teinte falote

L'étoffe riche aux mains lassées

De l'ouvrière pâlotte.

Lampes parées, comme des Princesses Charmantes,

Au-dessus des nappes éblouissantes,

Dans l'argent ciselé, dans le cristal joyeux,

Vous mirez vos feux.

Lampe du penseur solitaire

Guide ironique dans le désert

D'insondables mystères. —

Lampes éclairant

Le Drame, le Crime et le Sang !

Lampe au lit du malade languissant

Quand toute notre âme à son âme fuyante se suspend.

Lamps

There are fraternal lamps
With patient lights;
There are cruel lamps,
Gay and impudent lamps.

There are resigned lamps
That bathe with a dull tinge
The rich cloth in the weary hands
Of the pale seamstress.

Lamps adorned, like Princess Charmings,
Above gleaming tablecloths,
In chiseled silver, in joyous crystal,
You mirror your fires.

Lamp of the solitary thinker,
Ironic guide in the desert
Of immeasurable mysteries.—

Lamps lighting
Drama, Crime, and Blood!

Lamp at the bedside of the languishing invalid.
When all our soul to his fleeing soul clings.

Lampe, de rose et de dentelle voilée

Qui fait un diamant

D'un pleur éclos dans des yeux d'amants

En de divines extases liés.

Lampes de fêtes, aux reflets chatoyants

Sur des épaules nues que la danse entraîne.

Lampe, intime soleil vigilant

Qui brille sur les bonnes heures, sereines.

Lampe qui vit naître et mourir

Douter, souffrir, rire et pleurer.

Et toi, leur sœur pieuse,

Vacillante lumière :

Lampe veilleuse

De sanctuaires

Vous êtes les humbles étoiles de la terre.

Lamp, veiled in pink and lace,

Turning into a diamond

A tear budding in the eyes of lovers,

Bound together in divine ecstasies.

Party lamps, casting shimmering reflections

On naked shoulders led off by the dance.

Lamp, an intimate sun watching

As it shines on the calm happy hours.

Lamp that sees us enter the world and leave the world,

Sees us doubt, suffer, laugh, and cry.

And you, their pious sister,

Trembling light:

Night light

Of sanctuaries,

You are the humble stars of the earth.

GÉRARD D'HOUVILLE

(1875–1963)

pseudonym of Marie de Régnier,
née Marie Louise Antoinette de Heredia

Translations by Anne Atik

Marie de Heredia was born in Paris, the middle of three daughters, to Cuban parents. The child of the Parnassian poet José-Maria de Heredia, she grew up surrounded and encouraged by writers. Leconte de Lisle read the poems she began to write at age six, and her parents schooled her at home. Early on, she displayed the flamboyance, wit, and intelligence that, with later accomplishments, would make her into a celebrity of the literary world.

Marie met many other poets at her father's salon, including both her future husband and the father of her only child. Against her will, José-Maria arranged Marie's marriage, in 1895, to the affluent symbolist poet Henri de Régnier. Although she never divorced, Marie had numerous and often highly public affairs with both men and women, both brief and long-lived, over the next thirty years. Her first lover of note was the writer Pierre Louÿs, who in 1898 became the father of her son, Pierre (called Tigre), an illustrator and writer who predeceased her. In 1899 Louÿs married Marie's younger sister (although his liaison with Marie endured until 1903). Louÿs was followed, notoriously, by Georgie Raoul-Duval, a model for Rézi in Colette's *Claudine en ménage* (1902), and Raoul-Duval was followed by a poet nine years younger than Marie. She was also linked amorously and intellectually to Gabriele d'Annunzio. In 1922 she settled down with the journalist André Chaumiex until his death in 1955.

Houville's literary career was at least as impressive as her love life. Between 1894 and 1907, she published over sixty poems anonymously and (after 1902) pseudonymously in *La revue des deux mondes* (the poems in this volume were chosen from among these), but her collected poems, entitled *Poésies*, did not appear until 1931. Although Houville's poetry bears signs of her Parnassian heritage when impersonal in voice and neoclassical in construction, her obsession with death is nearly decadent. Her subjective poems, often sensual and sometimes mythical, range in landscape from the pastoral to the urban.

In 1903, she published a highly successful novel, *L'inconstante*, which was followed by many more. As a journalist, she wrote articles for *Figaro* under the pseudonym the Flâneur, and in 1907 she began her literary chronicle for *La revue des deux mondes*. She became a member of the jury for the future Prix Femina in 1909. She won several important literary prizes. The Académie Française awarded her the Grand Prix de Littérature for her novels in 1918, the first such recognition for a woman. She was also the first woman elected to the Académie Mallarmé (1937), and in 1958 she won the Académie Française's Grand Prix de Poésie.

For further reading, see Engelking, "Secret Rebellion" and "Voice"; Fleury; Laubier.

Ciel nocturne

Vos invisibles mains, ô fileuses de l'ombre,
Des voiles constellés entremêlent sans bruit
Les fils étincelants, et tournent dans l'air sombre
Les funèbres fuseaux des rouets de la nuit.

Dans la trame éclatante où palpitent les astres
Ensevelissez les destins mystérieux,
D'héroïques espoirs et d'orgueilleux désastres,
Ou la cendre d'un songe à jamais glorieux.

Mais, pour le mal secret d'une âme tendre et fière
Et pour l'obscur tourment dont souffre un cœur troublé,
Silencieuses sœurs, douces à ma prière,
N'ourdissez pas les fils du suaire étoilé.

Fileuses, attendez que la lune illumine
Le ciel pur, du reflet de sa pâle clarté,
Et chargeant vos fuseaux de la lueur divine,
Filez diligemment un linceul argenté.

Afin que la douceur de l'inutile rêve
Repose ensevelie au plus nocturne pli,
Aux rouets ténébreux entremêlez sans trêve
Le rayonnant silence et l'éternel oubli.

Nighttime Sky

Your invisible hands, O shadow spinners,[33]
Noiselessly weave spangled veils
With gleaming threads, and in grim air sley
The mournful spindles of night's spinning wheels.

You, in the brilliant weft where stars quiver,
Mysterious destinies entomb,
Heroic hopes and haughty disasters,
Or the ash of an ever glorious dream.

But, for the secret wound of a tender and proud
Soul, for the dim torment of a troubled heart,
Silent sisters, who to my prayer are lenient,
Don't warp the threads of the star-studded shroud.

Spinners, wait till the moon illumines
The clear sky with its lambent light
And, divine light laden in your spindles,
Zealously spin a silver winding-sheet.

That the sweetness of the fruitless dream, buried
In the most nocturnal fold, remain,
Weave when at the dismal wheels, unflagging,
Radiant silence and oblivion.

---

[33]The Fates (the Parcae in Roman mythology, the Moirae in Greek, akin to the Norse Norns): three sisters, goddesses who control human destiny, are represented as spinners of fate.

L'ombre

Au seuil noir de l'oubli, souterraine exilée,
Seule avec mon miroir familier, j'y revois
Le prestige lointain de ma vie écoulée ;
Nul écho dans le vent ne me redit ma voix.

Le rameur qui m'a pris l'obole du passage
Et qui jamais ne parle aux ombres qu'il conduit,
Me laissa ce miroir aimé de mon visage ;
Je ne suis pas entrée entière dans la nuit.

Mon front encor fleuri par ma mort printanière
Sur l'immobile flot se pencha, triste et doux ;
Mais nulle forme pâle, image coutumière,
Ne troubla l'eau sans plis, sans moire et sans remous.

Les cygnes, loin des flots où sombre la mémoire,
Les cygnes léthéens ont fui, vols oubliés,
Las d'avoir si longtemps cherché dans l'onde noire
Le flexible reflet de leurs cols repliés.

Ô pâles sœurs ! petites âmes fugitives,
Ne tendez pas les bras vers les flots oublieux,
Détournez-vous du fleuve aux ténébreuses rives ;
Vos yeux toujours en vain y chercheraient vos yeux.

The Shadow

At oblivion's black sill, subterranean, exiled,

Alone with my familiar mirror, I reminisce

About the distant glamour of my life flown by;

No echo in the wind repeats my voice.

The boatman who took my coin for the passage,

Who never speaks to the shades ferried across,[34]

Left me this mirror in which my face loved to gaze:

I haven't entered entire in darkness.

My forehead, still garlanded by my springtime death,

Bent over the immobile stream, sad and tender,

But no pale form, the customary image,

No eddy or shimmer, stirred the seamless water.

The swans, far from the streams where memory founders,

The Lethean swans have fled, flights forgotten,

Weary of searching so long in the black waves

For their coiled necks in a pliant reflection.

O pale sisters! Dear fugitive souls,

Don't stretch out your arms to forgetful streams.

Turn away from the river to its gloomy banks;

Your eyes will always search in vain for your eyes.

---

[34]Phlegyas was condemned to ferry souls across the mythological river Styx, which divided earth and the underworld.

Mes sœurs, ne brisez pas aux roches de la grève
Les fidèles miroirs amis de vos destins ;
De ce qui vous fut doux gardez encor le rêve
Et de vos sorts divers les reflets incertains.

Restez auprès de moi qui vous suis fraternelle,
De moi qui fus vivante et déjà m'en souviens
Et qui, pourtant heureuse et par l'amour plus belle,
Hélas ! craignis d'errer sur les bords stygiens.

J'ai connu le frisson de l'aile irrésistible
Et le grand vol obscur s'est fermé sur mon front,
Je sais la route aveugle et l'empreinte invisible ;
Vous y venez vers moi et d'autres y viendront.

Le sable noir n'est pas foulé par vos pieds d'ombre,
Car nul pas ne se grave au sable du Léthé.
Venez vers la songeuse ; ou puisez l'oubli sombre
Aux flots indifférents qui n'ont rien reflété.

My sisters, don't smash on the rocks of the strand

The faithful mirrors, friendly to your lots;

Hold on to the dream of whatever you held dear

And the unknown reflections of your divers fates.

Stay near me, I feel a kinship towards you,

I, who was alive and now remember what it was like

And who, although happy and made lovelier by love,

Alas! was afraid to wander on the Stygian bank.

I knew the thrill of the irresistible wing

And the great obscure flight closed down on my brow.

I know the blind route and the invisible stamp:

You're coming towards me and others will, too.

The black sand is untouched by your feet of shadow,

For on Lethe's sands no step can leave a sign.

Approach the dreamer; or, out of indifferent streams

That reflected nothing, draw dark oblivion.

La robe bleue

Vous en souvenez-vous, Mère au si beau visage,
Ma Mère aux bras si blancs, vous en souvenez-vous ?
Lorsque j'avais été trop longtemps triste et sage
Vous me preniez un peu, le soir, sur vos genoux.

Quelquefois vous portiez une robe très bleue
En satin d'Orient que brodaient des vols d'or ;
Tout un golfe d'Asie ondoyait dans sa queue
Et mes rêves d'enfant y sont bercés encor.

Vous fumiez... et l'odeur de la pale fumée
Venait se mélanger à vos divers parfums ;
Et je vous respirais, ô ma mère embaumée,
Avec le front caché dans mes lourds cheveux bruns.

Comme vous sentiez bon, ô mère nonchalante !
Vous étiez, ténébreuse et pleine de clarté,
Semblable à quelque vague à la fois sombre et lente
Qui mire obscurément les astres de l'été.

Vous étiez le voyage et toutes ses merveilles,
Et votre robe bleue et son or et ses plis
Tropicaux, vous baignait et vous rendait pareille
À quelque grand navire aux féminins roulis.

The Blue Dress

Do you remember, my lovely-faced mother,
Dear mother with such white arms, do you remember?
If I'd been pensive too long a while, too quiet,
You took me on your lap just for a bit, at night.

You sometimes wore a dress of very deep blue
Oriental satin trimmed with golden skeins;
An entire Gulf of Asia rippled in its train,
And my childhood dreams are cradled there, anew.

You smoked . . . and the pale smoke's odor
Merged with the different perfumes in the air;
And it was your scent I inhaled, fragrant mother,
My forehead hidden in my dark, heavy hair.

How lovely you smelled, nonchalant mother!
You were at once gloomy and full of light,
Like a wave that is both slow and somber
Reflecting darkly the summer starlight.

You were both the voyage and all its awes;
And in your blue dress, with its gold, its blazing folds
Bathing you, your every motion
Was like a great ship's womanly undulation.

Vous étiez le départ à l'espoir nostalgique

Et le port qui palpite en ses tranquilles eaux ;

Vos seins arrondissaient leurs caps aromatiques

Où vos manches volaient comme de lents oiseaux.

C'est ainsi que j'ai vu des îles bienheureuses,

L'étrange enchantement de nocturnes pays...

Mères aux douces mains, mères voluptueuses,

Ouvrez à votre enfant les premiers paradis.

Pour que plus tard, déçu par les bonheurs du monde,

Il sache que jadis, à votre cœur lié,

Il avait, dès vos flancs et vos forces profondes,

Atteint le noir rivage où tout est oublié.

You were the departure for a nostalgic hope

And the port beating in its calm waters;

Your breasts rounded their aromatic capes

And, like slow-moving birds, your sleeves fluttered.

That's how I saw these blissful isles,

The strange enchantment of nocturnal lands . . .

Sensuous mothers, mothers with soft hands,

Let your child enter her first paradise.

So that later, the world's joys falling short,

She'll know that, once bound to your heart,

From out of your deep strength and flanks,

She'd reached the black shore where all is forgot.

Celle qui passe: Bas-relief du Parthénon

Ô toi, qui, près de nous, du fond lointain de l'âge,

T'arrêtes pour croiser les lacets sur ton pied,

Quel peut être ton nom ? Tu n'as plus de visage.

Était-il doux, hautain, calme, tendre, effrayé ?

Nous ne saurons jamais si sa splendeur égale

Ton buste qui se penche, et ton bras replié.

De ton geste éternel renouant ta sandale,

Levant ta jambe haute et ton genou divin,

Fugitive à jamais liée au marbre pâle,

D'où viens-tu donc ? quel dieu t'attend sans doute en vain ?

Tu ne peux plus presser ta marche impatiente,

Et tu n'atteindras pas le vieux bonheur humain.

La volupté de ton attitude me hante.

Alerte est ton repos, rapide est ton arrêt ;

Ta tunique de pierre est toute transparente.

Mais, va. Laisse le nœud inutile et secret.

On arrive toujours trop tôt dans l'ombre noire ;

Partout la tombe s'ouvre, et le sépulcre est prêt.

She Who Passes: Parthenon Bas-Relief

O you, from a distant time's depths, who, near us

Stop to cross the laces over your foot,

What can your name be? You no longer have a face.

Was it soft, haughty, tender, frightened, calm?

We'll never know if its splendor was equal to

Your bent-over·bust and your folded arm.

With your eternal gesture of retying your sandal,

Raising high your leg and your knee divine,

Fugitive bound fast to the pale marble,

Whence are you, then? Which god awaits you, doubtless in vain?

You can no longer hasten your impatient step,

And old human happiness is beyond your span.

I'm haunted by your voluptuous stance.

Alert, your rest. Rapid, your halt.

Your tunic of stone is diaphanous.

But go. Let it alone, the useless and secret knot.

One always arrives too soon in the black shade;

The grave opens everywhere, and the tombstone is cut.

Houville is describing *Nike Adjusting Her Sandal* (c. 410 BCE), a fragment of the relief parapet from the Temple of Athena Nike at the Acropolis. Nike, the goddess of victory, is shown bending to tie or untie her sandal. The sculpture is damaged, and Nike's face is missing (line 3).

Ô passante, à quoi bon, marchant vers sa victoire,

Hâter ton féminin et délicat effort ?

Tes genoux entr'ouverts enchantent ma mémoire.

Entends-moi... Reste ainsi... La vieillesse et la mort,

Plus loin, guettent ta force et ta jeunesse lasse ;

Déjoue, en t'arrêtant, la traîtrise du sort,

Tu ne dois pas me fuir... Tu te nommes la Grâce.

O passerby, why try, as you head to its victory,

To step up your effort, feminine and fine?

Your parted knees enchant my memory.

Listen to me . . . Stay so . . . Old age and death

Lie ahead in wait for your strength and weary youth;

Foil, by pausing, fate's treacherousness.

You must not elude me. Your name is Grace.

Vœu

Je n'ai rien voulu des hommes
Oublieux et mensongers ;
Sous les raisins et les pommes
Je dors au fond des vergers.

Satyres, gais petits faunes,
Ô vous qui veniez des bois
Dérober mes pêches jaunes,
Juteuses entre vos doigts,

C'est à votre folle bande
Que je lègue mon tombeau ;
Vous y porterez l'offrande
Des grappes et du miel chaud ;

Le citron par qui s'éclaire
L'arbre sombre où luit son or,
La grenade funéraire,
Seul fruit que je goûte encor,

Incarnates et coniques,
Les figues que l'été fend
Et les fraises impudiques
Qui pointent en rougissant,

Wish

I didn't want anything from men
Who were forgetful and false.
I sleep under apples and grapes
In the orchard's depths.

O you who came from the woods,
Fauns small and gay, satyrs,
Who made off with my yellow peaches,
Juicy between your fingers,

It's to your madcap company
That I bequeath my tomb;
You'll carry there the offering
Of fruit and honey, warm,

Lemon sparkling on the somber
Tree, its gold giving off a glint,
The funereal pomegranate,
The one fruit I still can taste,

Incarnate and conical,
Figs that summer has split,
And immodest strawberries
That turn red when they peep out,

Auprès des corbeilles blondes

Et des vases pleins de lait,

Dans le creux des coupes rondes

À quoi mon sein ressemblait.

Enfants du profond feuillage,

Près de vous que n'ai-je pu

Vivre la beauté de l'âge

D'un corps libre, heureux et nu !

De ma joueuse jeunesse

Songez aux chers jours passés...

J'étais peut-être faunesse

Par mes longs yeux retroussés.

Close by the golden baskets
And vases full of milk,
In the round cups' hollow,
Which my breasts were like.

Children of the deep foliage,
Near you, how I have lived
That beautiful age when one's body
Is free, happy, nude!

Think of my frisky youth,
Of the dear days gone.
With my long, upturned eyes
I was, perhaps, a faun.

Le potier

Aujourd'hui je suis triste. Écoute, ô cher potier,
Je t'apporte le don de mon corps tout entier,
Si tu veux avec art, dans ta durable argile,
Peut-être, éterniser une forme fragile.
Dans une terre rose et semblable à ma chair,
Modèle le contour de mon bien le plus cher :
Mes petits seins égaux aux deux pointes aiguës.
Qu'il reste au moins cela des grâces ingénues
Que j'offre à ton désir, si de chaque côté
De l'amphore funèbre où toute ma beauté
Doit dormir, poudre éparse et cendre inerte et grise,
Au lieu de l'anse, creuse à la main qui l'a prise,
Tu renfles la rondeur de ce double contour
Presque enfantin et prêt à peine pour l'amour.
...Et celui qui, pensif, sous le sol séculaire,
Trouvera quelque jour mon urne funéraire,
Saura que je fus femme, et femme tendrement,
Amoureuse et malicieuse par moment,
Et se demandera devant la terre sombre
Pourquoi tant de clarté dut naître pour tant d'ombre.

The Potter

I'm sad today. O dear potter, listen,
I'll bring you my whole body as token
If, in your lasting clay, you'll artfully
Model a frail form for eternity.
In pink earth, similar to my flesh, fashion
The contour of my dearest possession:
My small twin breasts, with two keen points.
At least that will remain of the artless graces
I offer your desire, if at both sides equally
Of the funeral amphora, where all my beauty
In a thick powder and gray, inert ash reposes,
Instead of the handle, hollow to the hand that holds it,
You swell out the roundness of this double curve
Almost childlike, and hardly ready for love.
. . . And he who, pensive, finds my funeral urn
One day, under the ancient ground, will learn
That I was a woman, and tenderly woman,
Loving and mischievous in turn,
And in front of the dark earth, will want to know
Why so much light was born, for so much shadow.

Avril

Ô ma vie ! il n'est rien dans les villes du monde
Que ne puisse t'offrir la beauté de ce soir !
Paris, avant la nuit, se regarde au miroir
Du fleuve, — et quand le pont s'ouvre en arche profonde
La Seine rose y fait un bruit étrange et noir.

Je longerai longtemps le quai crépusculaire,
Car rien ne m'émeut plus que cette heure et ces lieux ;
Ils dorment dans mon âme et vivent dans mes yeux,
Toute rumeur a fui la berge solitaire,
Et les passants tardifs seront silencieux.

J'aime ce fleuve étroit, et sa courbe imprécise,
Et les vieux monuments reflétés dans ses eaux ;
Mieux qu'Amsterdam, luisante au cœur de ses canaux,
Que l'opale irisée où je revois Venise,
Plus que le bord des mers ces quais me semblent beaux.

Tout près, le vieux jardin régulier et tranquille
Allonge sa terrasse aux arbres reverdis...
Que de fois, accoudée aux balustres tiédis,
J'ai regardé bouger le reflet de la ville,
Quand les bruits des bateaux lointains sont assourdis !

April

O my life! There's nothing in the cities of the world
That, to you, this beauteous evening can't offer.
Before night, Paris looks at itself in the mirror
Of the river—and when the bridge's deep arch is opened,
The sound of the pink Seine is strange and somber.

Lingeringly, I'll skirt the twilit quay,
For nothing moves me more than this hour and this spot;
They sleep in my soul and live in my sight.
The solitary steep bank is now empty of sound,
And late-night passersby are mute.

I love this narrow river and its random twists,
And the old monuments reflected in its waters;
More than Amsterdam gleaming in its canals,
More than the iridescent opals recalling Venice,
And I find the seashore less lovely than these quays.

An old garden nearby, regular and calm,
Stretches its terrace against newly green trees.
How many times, leaning on a warmed balustrade,
I watched the city's reflections go by in a stream
As the muffled sound of far-off boats faded.

C'est la même fraîcheur de ce nouveau feuillage,
La même acidité d'avril et du vent vert,
Le même charme obscur de ce jardin désert ;
J'y songe au même instant, j'ai le même visage,
Et j'y respire encore un narcisse entr'ouvert.

J'ai dû vivre cette heure et son amère ivresse ;
Je retrouve le goût de l'air soudain glacé,
Le frisson du soir brusque et du soleil baissé,
Et, dans ce flot transi qui passe avec paresse,
Mes yeux pourraient revoir les yeux de mon passé.

J'entends le même écho, la même voix peut-être ;
L'or d'un couchant pareil aux toits du Louvre luit.
Ai-je cru le temps mort comme on sait que l'eau fuit ?
Quelque chose est en moi qui germe et va renaître,
Puisque tout recommence et que rien ne finit.

There's the same freshness in this new foliage,

The same pungent April and the same sharp green wind,

The same dim charm on this deserted garden's ground.

I see it all this instant, I have the same visage,

And still breathe a daffodil there, that's half opened.

I must have lived this hour and its bitter intoxication;

I find the taste of the air again, suddenly ice cold,

The thrill of this evening brusque and the light begun to fade.

And, in this chilling flood that passes in slow motion,

My eyes may still see what my eyes once beheld.

I hear the same echo, the same voice, perchance;

The sunset's gold like the Louvre's roofs glows.

Did I think time had died, as one knows water flows?

Something in me buds, its bloom a renaissance.

Because all begins again and nothing's ever closed.

Apparition

D'un petit pas glissant au parquet qui miroite
Ou plus lent, sur la laine en fleur des longs tapis,
Vous avancez, lascive et lasse, et chaude et moite,
Crispant vos doigts aigus, simiesque Balkis.

Entrez. Je reconnais vos grâces étrangères :
Malice langoureuse, œil trop grand, nez qui bat,
Buste étroit balancé sur les jambes légères...
Vous êtes bien ce soir la reine de Saba.

Je vous connais, ô parfumée, ô belle, ô sombre !
Qui, dans vos brunes mains, m'apportez tant de maux
Qu'ils courberaient, plus lourds que des trésors sans nombre,
Vos esclaves, vos onagres et vos chameaux.

Je vous connais. Je sais tout ce qui se dérobe
Sous l'étoffe et sous l'or des joyaux suspendus,
Et je vois piétiner sous la traînante robe
Vos petits pieds de bouc fantasques et fendus.

Mais, comme à Salomon jadis vous apportâtes
Les plus mystérieux et les plus purs parfums,
Vous venez pour m'offrir d'étranges aromates
Dans la troublante odeur de vos cheveux si bruns,

Apparition

With a small, sliding step on the shimmering floor,
Or, even slower, on the long rugs' woolen flower,
Lewd and torpid, hot and moist, you advance
Tensing your pointy fingers, apelike Balkis.[35]

Come in. I recognize your foreign graces:
Languid teasing, too-large eyes, twitching nose,
On slender legs balancing your narrow bust . . .
Indeed you're the Queen of Sheba tonight.

I know you, fragrant, lovely, somber one!
Who, with your brown hands load me with so much bane
That it'd weigh down, more than countless treasures,
Your slaves, your camels, and wild asses.

I know you. I know all that you hide
Under that robe and dangling jewels' gold,
And spy your small goat feet, as they stamp,
Capricious and cleft, under your trailing wrap.

But just as of old you brought Solomon
The most mysterious, purest perfume,
You come to me with strange scents to proffer
In the disturbing fragrance of your brown hair.

---

[35]Name given in the Koran to the Queen of Sheba, who, drawn by the
wisdom of Solomon, traveled to Israel laden with gifts

Dans la coupe des seins doublement renversée,

Dans les flacons égaux de vos bras onduleux,

Les baumes différents de la chair nuancée

Et l'ondoyant sachet d'un corps voluptueux ;

Et ce souffle lointain, salin et balsamique,

Haleine maléfique ou philtre ardent et frais,

Qui semble avoir passé sur la mer Arabique

Pour enivrer mon rêve et pour troubler ma paix.

In the twice reversed goblet of your breasts
In your flowing arms' symmetrical flasks,
The various balms of your many-hued flesh
And a voluptuous body's lithe sachet;

And that balsamic and salty, distant breeze,
Fresh, ardent philter, or malignant breath,
As though it had crossed the Arabian Sea
To disturb my peace and excite my dream.

Salomé

Son corps svelte vêtu d'une soie à rosaces
Traîne l'obscur velours d'un ourlet empourpré
Sur le dallage blanc des plus hautes terrasses
Où l'arabesque luit dans le marbre nacré.

Au rebord du balcon où son rêve l'exile
Elle étend ses bras frais et joue avec ses doigts ;
Son attitude semble une danse immobile,
La fleur de ses cheveux s'effeuille à ses pieds froids.

Sans doute courtisane et surtout enfantine ;
Être doux et pervers et toujours trop aimé ;
Insensible sourire, orgueil de la narine,
Charme de ce qu'on sent perfide, Salomé.

Sa taille ploie, et sous le long sourcil qui s'arque,
Son regard est cruel, innocent et lascif ;
Est-ce d'avoir dansé devant le vieux tétrarque
Ou d'avoir soupesé le plat deux fois massif ?

Salomé

Her svelte body dressed in silk rosette
Trails the dark velvet of an empurpled hem
On the balcony's slabs of white
Whose pearled marble beams an arabesque's gleam.

Exiled by her dream to the terrace's edge,
She plays with her fingers, her cool arms spread;
Her stance like that in an immobile dance,
The flower in her hair, at her cold feet, shed.

Undoubtedly courtesan, childish, above all;
Far too pampered, creature sweet and perverse;
A nostril too proud, an insensitive smile,
Salomé, charm of false-heartedness.

Her waist bends, and under her brow, long and arched,
Her glance is cruel, innocent, and lewd;
Is it for having danced before the old tetrarch
Or pondered the platter's twice heavy load?

In the New Testament, Salomé danced before Herod in return for the head of John the Baptist on a silver platter. A decadent icon of fatal femininity, she was featured in numerous literary works during the second half of the nineteenth century, including Flaubert's short story "Hérodias," Mallarmé's long poem "Hérodiade," Jules Laforgue's story "Salomé," and Oscar Wilde's play *Salomé* (written in French). Salomé was also painted by the decadent artist Gustave Moreau and was the subject of an opera by Jules Massenet. See Marchal.

Elle regarde au loin. D'un argent mat et terne,

La lune, au ciel couvert, s'arrondit lentement.

Elle écoute. Le vent gronde dans la citerne

Ou quel râle lointain en monte sourdement ?

Quel morne chef coupé, — souvenir ou présage, —

Flotte dans le halo de l'astre pluvieux ?

Mais Salomé n'a pas détourné son visage,

Nul effroi ne la trouble et n'obscurcit ses yeux.

Qu'importe que la tête horrible roule, et saigne,

Et pèse un poids trop lourd à son geste ingénu,

Et que son pas dansant de ce sang noir s'imprègne

Et qu'un Roi paternel convoite son corps nu ?

Sa figure naïve est puérile et claire

Entre l'écartement lisse de ses bandeaux,

Et sa robe revêt la grâce singulière

D'un torse adolescent qui cambre un souple dos.

Elle s'attarde ainsi sur la terrasse blanche.

— Qu'est-ce que tout cela, petite fille ? Rien. —

Et songe, en admirant son sein rond et sa hanche,

Qu'elle se trouve belle et qu'elle danse bien.

She gazes far off. Of a dull and matte silver,

The moon rounds slowly in the overcast sky.

She listens. Does the wind growl in the cistern

Or a rattle rumble from it, rising high?

What grim severed crown—relic or omen—

Floats in the halo of the watery star?

But Salomé doesn't alter her mien,

Her eyes don't darken, she's not troubled by fear.

So what if the horrible head bleeds and rolls,

And weighs too heavy for her artless stroke,

And that her dancing step is seeped in black blood,

And that a fatherly king lusts to see her nude?

Puerile and clear is her naive face

Between the silky veils' gap,

And her dress is endowed with the singular grace

Of a youthful torso's arched supple back.

On the white terrace she lingers thus.

"Nothing," she replies to "What's all this, little girl?"

And muses, admiring her hip and round breast,

That she finds herself beautiful and dances well.

Stances

Qu'êtes-vous devenue, enfant songeuse et triste
        Aux sombres yeux ?
Vous dont plus rien en moi maintenant ne persiste,
        Rêves ou jeux ?

Qu'êtes-vous devenue, enfant paisible et tendre
        Au cœur pensif ?
Dans quel étroit tombeau repose votre cendre,
        Corps grêle et vif ?

Vous êtes morte, au fond de moi, vous êtes morte,
        Petite enfant !
C'est moi qui vous abrite, et moi qui vous emporte,
        Tout en vivant.

Ah ! vous aviez si peur de cette ombre lointaine
        Qui fait la mort,
Et l'écartiez déjà d'une main incertaine,
        Tremblant très fort.

Vous étiez douce et caressante et souvent sage ;
        Je vous revois,
Mais les yeux clos, car je n'ai plus votre visage,
        Ni votre voix.

Stanzas

What's become of you, child, sad dreamer
> With somber eyes?
You of whom nothing remains, neither
> Dreams nor games?

What's become of you, child, your heart tender,
> Pensive, calm?
In what narrow tomb do your ashes lie, your slender
> Vibrant frame?

You have died, small child, you have died
> Deep down in me!
It is I, still alive, in whom you abide,
> Who bear you away.

Ah! You so feared that distant shadow, death's usher,
> And even then
Pushed it away, all atremble,
> Your hand uncertain.

You were gentle and often wise, and endearing.
> I see you once more,
But with eyes closed, your face and voice not appearing
> To me anymore.

Ainsi je vais mourir tout le long de ma vie,

Jusqu'à ce jour

Où, de l'espoir qu'on rêve au regret qu'on oublie,

Tristesse, amour,

Je ne serai plus rien dans la nuit sûre et noire

Qu'un poids léger,

Et pourrai sans reflet, sans ombre, et sans mémoire,

Ne plus changer.

Thus will I die all my life that's left,

        Until the day arrive

When from dreamt-of hope to forgotten regret,

        Sadness, love,

In the black, final night I'll be nothing else

        Than a trifling weight, stripped

Of shadow, reflection, memory, changeless

        At last.

Épitaphe

Je veux dormir au fond des bois, pour que le vent

Fasse parfois frémir le feuillage mouvant

Et l'agite dans l'air comme une chevelure

Au-dessus de ma tombe, et selon l'heure obscure

Ou claire, l'ombre des feuilles avec le jour

Y tracera, légère et noire, et tour à tour,

En mots mystérieux, arabesque suprême,

Une épitaphe aussi changeante que moi-même.

Epitaph

I want to sleep in the deep of the woods, so that at times

The wind will stir the foliage till it rustles,

And shake it out in the air like tresses

Above my tomb, and according as the hour

Is dark or light, the leaves' shadows together

With day will write, light and dark by turns,

Supreme arabesque, in words full of mystery,

An epitaph as changeable as I.

Renée Vivien

(1877–1909)

pseudonym of Pauline Mary Tarn

Translations by Melanie Hawthorne

Born in England of a British father and American mother, Renée Vivien lived in Paris as a child. After reaching her majority, she left England permanently and moved to Paris, where, supported by her independent wealth, she led an eccentric, flamboyant existence. In Paris, Vivien was surrounded by other expatriate Anglophones, most notably her lover, the American Natalie Clifford Barney, in whose salon gathered an impressive array of women writers, including Colette, Gertrude Stein, Alice B. Toklas, and many others of the cultural avant-garde. So active was this community and so visible its lesbian participation, that one critic labeled it Sapho 1900 (Billy).

In flawless French, Vivien wrote prolifically in poetry and prose but made her reputation as a poet. She published her first three collections as R. (or René) Vivien, thus allowing her lesbian love poetry to pass as heterosexual and in so doing attracting critical praise. From 1901 to her death in 1909, she wrote over a dozen collections of poetry. Her poems are darkly decadent, often violent and carnal in their representations of love, which she nonetheless explores using the metaphor of fragile violets, undoubtedly a reference to her childhood friend, Violet Shilleto, who died in 1901. Because of her frequent references to the flower, she is often called "the muse of the violets" (in this volume, see her "Violettes d'automne" ["Autumn Violets"]).

Vivien's poetry frequently scrutinizes the congruities of despair, death, and passion. With nostalgic reverence for an idealized lesbian past, it carries many references to the Sappho myth and the Greek island of Lesbos, to which she regularly traveled. She learned classical Greek and translated Sappho's poetry into French. Vivien frequently pastiches Sappho's direct, fragmented style and occasionally employs a French version of what is known as the Sapphic meter (in this volume, see her "Sur le rythme saphique" ["In the Sapphic Rhythm"]).

Overcome by alcoholism and anorexia, Vivien died at the age of thirty-two.

Her major poetic works are *Études et préludes* (1901), *Cendres et poussières* (1902), *Brumes de fjords* (1902), *Évocations* (1903), *Du vert au violet* (1903), *La Vénus des aveugles* (1904), *À l'heure des mains jointes* (1906), *Flambeaux éteints* (1907), *Sillages* (1908), *Dans un coin de violettes* (1910), *Le vent des vaisseaux* (1910), and *Haillons* (1910). Of the poems selected for this anthology, "Sonnet II" and "Amazone" first appeared in *Études et préludes*; "Violettes d'automne," "Aigues-marines," "Roses du soir," and "Le bloc de marbre" in *Évocations*; "La fourrure," "À la perverse Ophélie," "Les succubes disent . . . ," and "Faste des tissus" in *La Vénus des aveugles*; "Attente," "Vous pour qui j'écrivis," and "Le pilori" in *À l'heure des mains jointes*; "Sur le rythme saphique" in *Sillages*; and "Pèlerinage" in *Haillons*. For further reading, see Bartholomot Bessou; Benstock; Engelking, "Renée Vivien's Sapphic Legacy" and "Renée Vivien"; Jay; Marks; Perrin; Sanders; Schultz, "Terms."

Sonnets (II)

Sous un ciel ambigu, l'olivier et l'acanthe
Mêlent subtilement leurs frissons bleus et verts,
Et dans l'ombre fleurit, comme un songe pervers,
L'harmonieux baiser de l'amante à l'amante.

Les cheveux au brun roux d'automne et d'amarante
Et les pâles cheveux plus blonds que les hivers
Confondent leurs reflets. Sur les yeux entr'ouverts
Passe une joie aiguë ainsi qu'une épouvante.

Le crépuscule rose a baigné l'horizon.
Les désirs attardés craignent la trahison
Et le rire sournois de l'aurore importune.

Les doigts ont effeuillé les lotos du sommeil,
Et la virginité farouche de la lune
A préféré la mort au viol du soleil.

Sonnets (II)

Under a cryptic sky, the olive and the acanthus
Casually mingle their shivers of blue and green,
And in the shade there blossoms, like a twisted dream,
The harmonious kiss that women exchange, thus.

Hair the rusty brown of autumn and purple amaranthus
And pale hair more blond than wintry skies
Confound their lights. Over half-open eyes
Passes a joy as sharp as awfulness.

On the horizon rosy dawn has appeared.
By lingering desires betrayal is feared
With the cunning laughter of dawn come too soon.

As fingers caress, sleep's lotus night is done
And the wild virginity of the moon
Would rather die than be raped by the sun.

Amazone

L'Amazone sourit au-dessus des ruines,
Tandis que le soleil, las de luttes, s'endort.
La volupté du meurtre a gonflé ses narines :
Elle exulte, amoureuse étrange de la mort.

Elle aime les amants qui lui donnent l'ivresse
De leur fauve agonie et de leur fier trépas,
Et, méprisant le miel de la mièvre caresse,
Les coupes sans horreur ne la contentent pas.

Son désir, défaillant sur quelque bouche blême
Dont il sait arracher le baiser sans retour,
Se penche avec ardeur sur le spasme suprême,
Plus terrible et plus beau que le spasme d'amour.

Amazon

The Amazon, she smiles from up above the ruins,
As all the while the sun, war-weary, goes to sleep.
The ecstasy of murder made her nostrils flare:
Exultant, she is now death's peculiar lover.

She loves the lovers who give her drunken pleasure
With their wild agony and with their proud demise,
And she scorns the sweetness of saccharine touches;
Dishes without horror do not satisfy her.

Her desire, faltering on some pale, bloodless mouth
From which it extracts an irrevocable kiss,
Leans with ardor over the final spasm of death,
More terrible, more fine than is the spasm of love.

Violettes d'automne

L'air pleure le printemps fervent...
Les arbres souffrent dans le vent,
Sans opulence et sans couronne...
Ah ! les violettes d'automne !

Tu viens, toi que je n'aime plus,
Portant les regrets superflus,
Et plus pâle qu'une madone...
Ah ! les violettes d'automne !

Je songe à nos mauvais adieux.
Nos souvenirs sont dans tes yeux
Que la fraîcheur du jour étonne...
Ah ! les violettes d'automne !

J'ai vu, sous des midis plus beaux,
Des roses jaillir des tombeaux
Où l'aube de l'espoir rayonne...
Ah ! les violettes d'automne !

Mais notre désastreux amour
N'aura ni réveil ni retour,
Ni sanglots dans sa voix atone...
Ah ! les violettes d'automne !

Autumn Violets

The air cries out for fervent spring . . .
Wind-tossed the trees are suffering,
No longer rich, they have no crown . . .
Oh! the violets of autumn!

You come, the one I love no more,
Bearing superfluous remorse,
Paler than the Virgin Mary . . .
Oh! the violets of autumn!

I think back to our bad good-byes.
Our memories are in your eyes
That by the light of day are stunned . . .
Oh! the violets of autumn!

I saw, beneath a finer noon,
Roses sprouting above a tomb
Where the dawning light of hope shone . . .
Oh! the violets of autumn!

But our disastrous love will bring
No new start, no new quickening,
No sobbing in her voice, no tune . . .
Oh! the violets of autumn!

Toi qui fus, par les soirs d'été,

Ma Maîtresse et ma Volupté,

L'ardeur du baiser t'abandonne...

Ah! les violettes d'automne!

Aigues-marines

Des gouttes d'eau — de l'eau de mer —

Mêlent leur lumière fluide,

Glauque et pareille aux flots d'hiver,

À tes longs doigts d'Océanide.

Comment décrire le secret

De leurs pâleurs froides et fines?

Ton regard vert semble un reflet

Des cruelles aigues-marines.

Ton corps a l'imprécis contour

Des flots souples aux remous vagues,

Et tes attitudes d'amour

Se déroulent, comme les vagues...

You were all summer's evenings through

My Mistress and my Pleasure too,

The ardor of your kiss has gone . . .

Oh! the violets of autumn!

Aquamarines

Drops of water—salt seawater—

Mix their fluid light that glimmers,

Glaucous like the waves of winter,

With your long sea nymph–like fingers.

How can I describe the secrets

Of their paleness, cold and refined?

Your greenish glance, it seems, reflects

Aquamarines: hard and unkind.

Your body has the vague outlines

Of undercurrents, supple swells;

And when you love, your pose combines,

Unfurling tides and rolling waves . . .

Roses du soir

Des roses sur la mer, des roses dans le soir,
Et toi qui viens de loin, les mains lourdes de roses !
J'aspire ta beauté. Le couchant fait pleuvoir
Ses fines cendres d'or et ses poussières roses...

Des roses sur la mer, des roses dans le soir.

Un songe évocateur tient mes paupières closes.
J'attends, ne sachant trop ce que j'attends en vain,
Devant la mer pareille aux boucliers d'airain,
Et te voici venue en m'apportant des roses...

Ô roses dans le ciel et le soir ! Ô mes roses !

Evening Roses

Roses on the ocean, roses in the twilight,

And you come from afar, hands weighed down with roses!

I breathe in your beauty. Sunset seems to highlight

A rain of golden ash with rosy dust exposed.

Roses on the ocean, roses in the twilight.

In evocative dream my eyelids are closed.

I wait, not knowing quite what I wait for in vain,

Before the sea like shields of brass I stand again,

Then suddenly you're here, you're bringing me roses.

Oh roses in the evening sky! Oh my roses!

Le bloc de marbre

Je dormais dans le flanc massif de la montagne...
Ses tiédeurs m'enivraient. Auprès de mon sommeil
Sourdait l'ardent effort des fleurs vers le soleil.
Rien ne troublait la paix large de la montagne.

Je dormais. Je semblais un astre dans la nuit,
Et l'ondoyant avril que l'amour accompagne
Tremblait divinement sur l'or de la campagne,
Sans rompre mon attente obscure dans la nuit.

Blancheur inviolée au fond de l'ombre éteinte,
J'ignorais le frisson du nuage, et le bruit
Des branches et des blés sous le vent qui s'enfuit
En sifflant... Je dormais au fond de l'ombre éteinte,

Lorsque tu m'arrachas à mon calme éternel,
Ô mon maître ! ô bourreau dont je porte l'empreinte !
Dans la douleur et dans l'effroi de ton étreinte,
Je vécus, je perdis le repos éternel...

Je devins la Statue au front las, et la foule
Insulte d'un regard imbécile et cruel
Ma froide identité sans geste et sans appel,
Pâture du regard passager de la foule.

The Block of Marble

I slept fast in the side of a massive mountain:
Intoxicating warmth. Beside me in my sleep
Flowers burning to reach the sun began to peep.
Nothing disturbed the ample peace of the mountain.

I slept. I seemed to be a lone star in the night,
And shimmering April accompanied by love
Over golden country trembled godlike above,
Without interrupting my dark wait in the night.

Inviolate whiteness amidst the dull shadows,
I could never know the cloud's frisson, and the sound
Of the branches and wheat as the wind raked the ground
While it whistled . . . I slept amidst the dull shadows.

When you tore me away from my eternal calm,
O master, tormentor, on me you left your brand!
As in the pain and fear of the grip of your hand
I lived, and living so, lost all eternal calm . . .

I became the Statue, weary-browed, and the crowd
Insults with the look of a cruel imbecile
My cold identity—no action, no appeal—
Food for the passing contemplation of the crowd.

Et je suis la victime orgueilleuse du temps,

Car je souffre au delà de l'heure qui s'écoule.

Mon angoisse domine altièrement la houle

Gémissante qui meurt dans l'infini du temps.

Je te hais, créateur dont la pensée austère

A fait jaillir mon corps en de fiévreux instants,

Et dont je garde au cœur les rêves sanglotants...

Je connais les douleurs profondes de la terre,

Moi qui suis la victime orgueilleuse du temps.

And now I am the proud victim of passing time,

For I suffer beyond the mere minutes that pass.

My anguish haughtily controls the surging mass

That groaning dies in the infinity of time.

I hate you, creator whose austere thought gave birth

To my body in an act of feverish art,

Whose sobbing dreams I keep locked deep inside my heart . . .

I have tasted of the deepest pains of the earth,

I who now am the proud victim of passing time.

La fourrure

Je hume en frémissant la tiédeur animale

D'une fourrure aux bleus d'argent, aux bleus d'opale ;

J'en goûte le parfum plus fort qu'une saveur,

Plus large qu'une voix de rut et de blasphème,

Et je respire, avec une égale ferveur,

La Femme que je crains et les Fauves que j'aime.

Mes mains de volupté glissent, en un frisson,

Sur la douceur de la Fourrure, et le soupçon

De la bête traquée aiguise ma prunelle.

Mon rêve septentrional cherche les cieux

Dont la frigidité m'attire et me rappelle,

Et la forêt où dort la neige des adieux.

Car je suis de ceux-là que la froideur enivre.

Mon enfance riait aux lumières du givre.

Je triomphe dans l'air, j'exulte dans le vent,

Et j'aime à contempler l'ouragan face à face.

Je suis fille du Nord et des Neiges, — souvent

J'ai rêvé de dormir sous un linceul de glace.

Ah ! la Fourrure où se complaît ta nudité,

Où s'exaspérera mon désir irrité ! —

De ta chair qui détend ses impudeurs meurtries

Montent obscurément les chaudes trahisons,

Et mon âme d'hiver aux graves rêveries

S'abîme dans l'odeur perfide des Toisons.

Fur

I tremble as I sniff the bestial tepidness
Of a pelt of silvery blue, opaline blue;
I savor its perfume stronger than any taste,
Larger than any voice of blasphemy and rut,
And also I inhale, with similar fervor,
The Woman whom I fear and the Wild Things I love.

My hands of pleasure slide over, all aquiver,
The sweetness of the Furry Fleece, and sensing
The prey I track sharpens the pupils of my eyes.
My northern fantasy seeks out the kind of skies
Whose frigid coldness both draws me and calls me back,
And the forest in which sleeps the snow of good-byes.

For I am one of those whom cold intoxicates.
My childhood laughed out loud at glinting lights of frost,
I triumph in the air, exulting in the wind,
I face the hurricane I like to contemplate.
I am the daughter of the North and Snows, often
I've dreamed of sleep beneath a winding-sheet of ice.

Ah! the Fur in which your nudity takes pleasure
And which exasperates my excited desire!
From your flesh that loosens its ravaged shamelessness
The heated treacheries rise darkly up to me,
And my wintry soul with solemn reveries
Dives into the perfidious smell of Fleeces.

À la perverse Ophélie

Les évocations de ma froide folie

Raniment les reflets sur le marais stagnant

Où flotte ton regard, ô perverse Ophélie !

C'est là que mes désirs te retrouvent, ceignant

D'iris bleus ton silence et ta mélancolie,

C'est là que les échos raillent en s'éloignant.

L'eau morte a, dans la nuit, les langueurs des lagunes,

Et voici, dispensant l'agonie et l'amour,

L'automne aux cheveux roux mêlés de feuilles brunes.

L'ombre suit lentement le lent départ du jour.

Comme un ressouvenir d'antiques infortunes,

Le vent râle, et la nuit prépare son retour.

Je sonde le néant de ma froide folie.

T'ai-je noyée hier dans le marais stagnant

Où flotte ton regard, ô perverse Ophélie ?

To the Perverse Ophelia

The recollections of my cold dementia
Revive the reflections above the stagnant marsh;
Your gaze is floating there, perverse Ophelia!

It is there my desires find you again, tying
Blue irises around melancholy silence,
It is there that echoes jeer as they are dying.

The dead water at night, a languorous lagoon,
And here, dispensing all the agony and love,
Is autumn whose red hair with brownish leaves is strewn.

The shadow slowly stalks the slow departing day.
A distant memory of ancient misfortune,
The wind howls, and the night returning makes its way.

I plumb the nothingness of cold dementia.
Did I drown you last night here in the stagnant marsh?
Your gaze still floats there now, perverse Ophelia.

Shakespeare's Ophelia and in particular her watery, flowery, mad death inspired a number of nineteenth-century writers and artists, most famously the painters Eugène Delacroix (*La mort d'Ophélie* [1838, 1843, 1844, 1853]) and John Everett Millais (*Ophelia* [1852]), the sculptor Auguste Préault (*Ophélie* [1842, 1876]), and the poets Arthur Rimbaud ("Ophélie" [1870]) and Jules Laforgue (who made numerous references to her).

Ai-je erré, vers le soir, douloureuse, et ceignant

D'iris bleus ton silence et ta mélancolie,

Tandis que les échos raillent en s'éloignant ?

L'eau calme a-t-elle encor les lueurs des lagunes,

Et vois-tu s'incliner sur ton défunt amour

L'automne aux cheveux roux mêlés de feuilles brunes ?

Ai-je pleuré ta mort dans l'énigme du jour

Qui disparaît, chargé d'espoirs et d'infortunes ?...

— Ô rythme sans réveil, ô rire sans retour !

Did I wander at dusk, in my pain, and tying

Blue irises around melancholy silence,

While all around echoes jeer as they are dying?

Do the calm waters still glimmer like a lagoon,

Do you still see it bend above your now dead love

This autumn, whose red hair with brownish leaves is strewn?

Did I grieve your death in the enigma of day

That disappears carrying hopes and misfortune? . . .

Unrevivable rhythm, laughter flew away!

Les Succubes disent...

Quittons la léthargie heureuse des maisons,
Le carmin des rosiers et le parfum des pommes
Et les vergers où meurt l'ondoiement des saisons,
Car nous ne sommes plus de la race des hommes.

Nous irons sous les ifs où s'attarde la nuit,
Où le souffle des Morts vole, comme une flamme.
Nous cueillerons les fleurs qui se fanent sans fruit,
Et les âcres printemps nous mordront jusqu'à l'âme.

Viens : nous écouterons, dans un silence amer,
Parmi les chuchotis du vêpre à l'aile brune,
Le rire de la Lune éprise de la Mer,
Le sanglot de la Mer éprise de la Lune.

Tes cheveux livreront leurs éclairs bleus et roux
Au râle impérieux qui sourd de la tourmente,
Mais l'horreur d'être ne ploiera point nos genoux.
Dans nos yeux le regard des Succubes fermente.

The Succubae Say . . .

Let us leave the happy lethargy of our homes,
The carmine rosebushes and the scent of apples,
Orchards where the seasons' undulation dies, for
We no longer belong to the race of mankind.

We'll go beneath the yews where night is lingering,
Where the breath of the Dead is flying like a flame.
We shall pick the flowers that wither without fruit,
And the acrid springtimes will bite us to the soul.

Come: now we shall listen, in a bitter silence,
Amidst the whispering of the brown-winged evening,
To the laugh of the Moon, enamored of the Sea,
And the sob of the Sea, enamored of the Moon.

Your hair will render up its glints of blue and red
To the imperious groan that springs from torment,
But we shall not flinch at the horror of being.
In our eyes the gaze of the Succubae ferments.

Succubae were female demons thought to descend on and have sexual intercourse with men as they slept.

Les hommes ne verront nos ombres sur leurs seuils

Qu'aux heures où, mêlant l'ardeur de nos deux haines,

Nous serons les Banshees qui présagent les deuils

Et les Jettatori des naissances prochaines.

Nos corps insexués s'uniront dans l'effort

Des soupirs, et les pleurs brûleront nos prunelles.

Nous considérerons la splendeur de la Mort

Et la stérilité des choses éternelles.

Men will only see our shadows on their thresholds

At those times when, mixing our twin hatreds' ardor,

We shall be the Banshees who tell of coming death

And the *Jettatori* of imminent new births.[36]

Our sexless bodies will unite in the effort

Of sighs, and tears will burn the iris of our eyes.

And we shall contemplate the splendor that is Death

And the sterility of such eternal things.

---

[36]In Gaelic folklore, banshees are wailing female spirits whose arrival in a household foretells the death of one of its members. *Jettatori*, in Italian, literally means "casters of the evil eye."

Faste des tissus

Estompe ta beauté sous le poids des étoffes,
Plus souples que les flots, plus graves que les strophes.

Elles ont la caresse et le rythme des mers,
Et leur frisson s'accorde au blanc frisson des chairs.

Revêts le violet des antiques chasubles,
Parsemé de l'éclair des ors indissolubles.

L'encens apaise encor leurs plis religieux ;
Elles aiment les Purs et les Silencieux.

Évoque, Océanide aux changeantes prunelles,
Le vert glauque où frémit l'écume des dentelles.

Jadis la gravité du velours se plia
Sur tes seins de pavot et de magnolia.

Le satin froid, où la ligne se dissimule,
Gris comme l'olivier fleuri de crépuscule,

Et la moire, pareille au sommeil de l'étang,
Où stagnent les lys verts et les reflets de sang,

Feast of Fabrics

Veil your beauty under the weight of draperies,
More supple than the waves, more solemn than a verse.

They have the caress and the rhythm of the seas,
And their shimmer matches the white shimmer of flesh.

Put on the violet of ancient chasubles,
Scattered with flashes of indissoluble golds.

The scent of incense still calms their religious folds;
They love those who are Pure as well as Silent Ones.

Evoke, you ocean nymph with ever-changing eyes,
That glaucous green sea where the lacy foam quivers.

Back then the heaviness of velvet fell in folds
Upon your breast of poppy and magnolia.

Cold satin, where contours are cleverly disguised,
Gray like the olive tree that blossoms in the dusk,

And watered silk, like the slumber of a still pond,
Where green lilies stagnate along with glints of blood,

Le givre et le brouillard des pâles broderies,

Où les tisseuses ont tramé leurs rêveries,

Parèrent savamment ta savante impudeur

Et ton corps où le rut a laissé sa tiédeur.

Ressuscite pour moi le lumineux cortège

De visions, et sois l'arc-en-ciel et la neige,

Sois la vague, ou la fleur des bocages moussus,

Ô Loreley, selon la couleur des tissus.

Mes rêves chanteront dans l'ombre des étoffes,

Plus souples que les flots, plus graves que les strophes.

The hoarfrost and the fog of pale embroideries,

In which the women wove a warp and weft of dreams,

—All skillfully adorned your wise immodesty

Along with your body, where rut has left its warmth.

Bring back to life for me the luminous parade

Of my visions, and be the rainbow and the snow,

Be the wave, or the flower of some mossy copse,

Lorelei,[37] according to the fabric's color.

My dreams will sing in the shadows of draperies,

More supple than the waves, more solemn than a verse.

---

[37]In popular legend, the Lorelei was a siren of the Rhine whose singing attracted sailors and led to shipwreck.

Attente

En cette chambre où meurt un souvenir d'aveux,

L'odeur de nos jasmins d'hier s'est égarée...

Pour toi seule je me suis vêtue et parée,

Et pour toi seule j'ai dénoué mes cheveux.

J'ai choisi des joyaux... Ont-ils l'heur de te plaire ?

Dans mon cœur anxieux quelque chose s'est tu...

Comment t'apparaîtrai-je et que me diras-tu,

Amie, en franchissant mon seuil crépusculaire ?

Des violettes et des algues vont pleuvoir

À travers le vitrail violet et vert tendre...

Je savoure l'angoisse idéale d'attendre

Le bonheur qui ne vient qu'à l'approche du soir.

En silence, j'attends l'heure que j'ai rêvée...

La nuit passe, traînant son manteau sombre et clair...

Mon âme illimitée est éparse dans l'air...

Il fait tiède et voici : la lune s'est levée.

Expectation

In this room a remembered confession has died,
The scent of the jasmine from yesterday is gone . . .
For you alone I've dressed, my finest I've put on,
And just for you alone, my hair has been untied.

I've chosen some jewels . . . with luck they'll please you more.
Inside my anxious heart, the words have gone away . . .
How will I look to you, what are you going to say,
My love, as you approach my crepuscular door?

Violet and seaweed through stained-glass windows rain,
Painting the floor purple, tender green in color . . .
I savor the perfect anguish of waiting for
The joy that comes only when evening falls again.

In silence I await the hour of my vision . . .
The night passes, trailing its mantle dark and clear . . .
My boundless soul disperses through the atmosphere . . .
It is warm, and now here: the moon has arisen.

Vous pour qui j'écrivis

Vous pour qui j'écrivis, ô belles jeunes femmes !
Vous que, seules, j'aimais, relirez-vous mes vers
Par les futurs matins neigeant sur l'univers,
Et par les soirs futurs de roses et de flammes ?

Songerez-vous, parmi le désordre charmant
De vos cheveux épars, de vos robes défaites :
« Cette femme, à travers les sanglots et les fêtes,
A porté ses regards et ses lèvres d'amant. »

Pâles et respirant votre chair embaumée,
Dans l'évocation magique de la nuit,
Direz-vous : « Cette femme eut l'ardeur qui me fuit...
Que n'est-elle vivante ! Elle m'aurait aimée... »

It Was for You I Wrote

It was for you I wrote, beautiful young women!
You alone whom I loved, will you reread my lines
Some future morning when it snows upon the world,
Some future evening full of roses and of flames?

Will you think, surrounded by the sweet disorder
Of your disheveled hair, and your unfastened dress:
"That woman, in the midst of sadness and in joy,
Still wore the looks and lips that lovers always wear."

All pale and smelling of your softly perfumed flesh
In night's evocative magic, will you then say:
"That woman, she had an ardor that eludes me . . .
Would she were still alive! For she would have loved me . . ."

Le pilori

Pendant longtemps, je fus clouée au pilori,
Et des femmes, voyant que je souffrais, ont ri.

Puis, des hommes ont pris dans leurs mains une boue
Qui vint éclabousser mes tempes et ma joue.

Les pleurs montaient en moi, houleux comme des flots,
Mais mon orgueil me fit refouler mes sanglots.

Je les voyais ainsi, comme à travers un songe
Affreux et dont l'horreur s'irrite et se prolonge.

La place était publique et tous étaient venus,
Et les femmes jetaient des rires ingénus.

Ils se lançaient des fruits avec des chansons folles,
Et le vent m'apportait le bruit de leurs paroles.

J'ai senti la colère et l'horreur m'envahir.
Silencieusement, j'appris à les haïr.

Les insultes cinglaient, comme des fouets d'ortie.
Lorsqu'ils m'ont détachée enfin, je suis partie.

Je suis partie au gré des vents. Et depuis lors
Mon visage est pareil à la face des morts.

The Pillory

For a long time I was nailed to the pillory,
And seeing my distress, the women laughed at me.

The men picked up some mud and flung it with their hands,
It spatters over me, on head and cheek it lands.

Then tears rose up inside, they surged like waves at sea,
But pride made me repress the sobs that rose in me.

I saw these things as though it were an awful dream
Where horror never ends, and chafing torments teem.

It was a public square and everyone had come,
And women stood and jeered, their laughter simple, dumb.

They all were throwing fruit and singing crazy songs,
And carried on the wind came the words of the throngs.

I felt a rage within, and horror seized my soul.
I silently began to learn to hate them all.

The insults stung my cheeks, like nettles used to flay.
And when they took me down at last, I ran away.

Blown by the wind I've been an outcast since I fled,
And now my face is like the faces of the dead.

Sur le rythme saphique

Pour moi ce qu'on désire
Je l'ai méprisé.
—*Sapho*

Pour moi, ni l'amour triomphant, ni la gloire,

Ni le souffle vain d'hommages superflus.

Mais la paix d'un coin dans une maison noire

   Où l'on n'aime plus.

Je sais qu'ici-bas jamais rien ne fut juste,

Je fus patiente en attendant la mort.

J'ai tu ma douleur, et quoiqu'il fût injuste

   J'ai subi mon sort.

Pour moi, ni l'accueil bienveillant ni les fêtes,

Mais l'apaisement d'un très profond soupir,

Le silence noir qui succède aux défaites

   Et le souvenir.

In classical Greek prosody, a system of quantitative verse, the Sapphic meter was a hendecasyllable having a fixed pattern of long and short syllables. Vivien employs the French hendecasyllable, in which a caesura follows the fifth syllable.

In the Sapphic Rhythm

> *What others desire*
> *I disdain.*
> —Sappho

Not for me a love triumphant, or glory,

Or empty breath of vain and hollow homage.

But a peaceful corner in a darkened house

        Where love is no more.

I know that here below things were never just,

With patience I waited for my death to come.

I silenced my pain, and though it was unjust,

        I suffered my fate.

Not for me, warm greetings or festivities,

But the peaceful calm of a very deep sigh,

Black silence that comes in the wake of defeats

        And my memories.

Pèlerinage

Il me semble n'avoir plus de sexe ni d'âge,

Tant les chagrins me sont brusquement survenus.

Les Temps se sont tissés... Et me voici pieds nus,

Achevant le terrible et long pèlerinage...

Je sais que l'aube d'or ne sait que décevoir,

Que la jeunesse a tort de suivre les chimères,

Que les yeux ont trompé... Mes lèvres sont amères...

Ah ! que la route est longue et que lointain le soir !

Et la procession lente et triste défile

De ces implorateurs que lasse le chemin.

Parfois on me relève, une me tend la main,

Et tous nous implorons le Divin Soir tranquille !

Pilgrimage

It seems to me I have no longer sex or age,

Thanks to all the sorrows that suddenly did land.

Time has spun itself up . . . And now barefoot I stand

Finishing the long and terrible pilgrimage.

I know the golden dawn can only disappoint,

That yearning youth can err in following its dreams,

My eyes have been deceived . . . My lips are bitter streams . . .

Oh how the road is long, dusk still a far-off point!

The slow and sad parade of people is weaving,

Wearied by the pathway, beseechers in a band.

Sometimes one helps me up, someone gives me her hand,

Together we implore the calm Holy Evening!

Works Cited in the
Headnotes and Footnotes

Abélès, Luce, ed. *La dame aux éventails: Nina de Callias, modèle de Manet.* Paris: Réunion des musées nationaux, 2000.

Ackermann, Louise. "My Life." Introd. and trans. Gretchen Schultz. Lloyd, *Nineteenth-Century Women* 64–74.

———. *Œuvres:* Ma vie, Premières poésies, Poésies philosophiques. 1874. Paris: L'Harmattan, 2005.

———. *Pensées d'une solitaire.* Paris: Lemerre, 1882.

Ambrière, Francis. *Le siècle des Valmore.* 2 vols. Paris: Seuil, 1987.

Baale-Uittenbosch, Alexandrina Elisabeth Maria. *Les poétesses dolentes du Romantisme.* Haarlem: De Erven F. Bohn, 1928.

Badesco, Luc. *La génération poétique de 1860, la jeunesse des deux rives.* 2 vols. Paris: Nizet, 1971.

Banville, Théodore de. *Petit traité de poésie française.* 1872. Geneva: Slatkine Rpts., 1972. Vol. 8 of *Œuvres.*

Barbey d'Aurevilly Jules-Amédée. *Les œuvres et les hommes.* 1860–1909. 26 vols. Geneva: Slatkine, 1968.

Barre, André. *Le symbolisme: Essai historique sur le mouvement symboliste en France de 1885–1900.* 1911. New York: Franklin, 1968.

Bartholomot Bessou, Marie-Ange. *L'imaginaire du féminin dans l'œuvre de Renée Vivien: De mémoires en mémoire.* Clermont-Ferrand: PU Blaise Pascal, 2004.

Baude de Maurceley, Charles. *La vérité sur le salon de Nina de Villard.* 1929. Ed. Michael Pakenham. Paris: La Vouivre, 2000.

Baudelaire, Charles. *Œuvres complètes.* Ed. Claude Pichois. 2 vols. Paris: Gallimard, 1975–76.

Beizer, Janet. *Ventriloquized Bodies: Narratives of Hysteria.* Ithaca: Cornell UP, 1994.

Bellet, Roger, ed. *Femmes de lettres au XIXe siècle: Autour de Louise Colet.* Lyon: PU de Lyon, 1982.

Bénichou, Paul. *Les mages romantiques.* Paris: Gallimard, 1988.

———. *Le temps des prophètes: Doctrines de l'âge romantique.* Paris: Gallimard, 1977.

Benstock, Shari. *Women of the Left Bank: Paris, 1900–1940.* Austin: U of Texas P, 1986.

Berger, Anne. "The Maternal Idol in a System of Bourgeois Poetics." *On the Feminine.* Ed. Mireille Calle. Trans. Catherine McGann. Atlantic Highlands: Humanities, 1996. 135–47.

Bersaucourt, Albert de. *Au temps des parnassiens: Nina de Villard et ses amis.* Paris: La Renaissance du Livre, [1921].

Bertrand, Marc. *Une femme à l'écoute de son temps: Marceline Desbordes-Valmore.* Lyon: Cigogne, 2007.

————. Introduction. Desbordes-Valmore, *Œuvre* 6–24.

Billy, Andre. *L'époque 1900*. Paris: Tallandier, 1951.

Bood, Micheline, and Serge Grand. *L'indomptable Louise Colet*. Paris: Horay, 1986.

Boutin, Aimée. "Inventing the 'Poétesse': New Approaches to French Women Romantic Poets." *Romanticism on the Net* 29-30 (2003). 27 Nov. 2007 <http://www.erudit.org/revue/ron/2003/v/n29/007725ar.html>.

————. *Maternal Echoes: The Poetry of Marceline Desbordes-Valmore and Alphonse de Lamartine*. Newark: U of Delaware P, 2001.

————. "'Transnational Migrations: Reading Amable Tastu with Felicia Hemans." *The Cultural Currency of Nineteenth-Century French Poetry I*. Ed. Joseph Acquisto and Adrianna M. Paliyenko. Spec. issue of *Romance Studies* 26.3 (2008): 210-20.

Boutin, Aimée, and Adrianna M. Paliyenko. "Nineteenth-Century French Women Poets: An Exceptional Legacy." *Women in French Studies* 10 (2002): 77–109.

Bowman, Frank Paul. *French Romanticism: Intertextual and Interdisciplinary Readings*. Baltimore: Johns Hopkins UP, 1990.

Brahimi, Denise. *Théophile et Judith vont en Orient*. Paris: La Boîte à Documents, 1990.

Braswell, Suzanne F. "Breaking the Silence: Antiphonal Voices in the Poetry of Delphine Gay de Girardin." Nesci, *Delphine de Girardin* 24–39.

Brogniez, Laurence. "Marie Krysinska et le vers-libre: L'outrage fait aux Muses." Planté, *Masculin/Féminin* 421–36.

Caws, Mary Ann. *Glorious Eccentrics: Modernist Women Painting and Writing*. New York: Palgrave-Macmillan, 2006.

Charlton, D. G. *Positivist Thought in France during the Second Empire*. Oxford: Clarendon, 1959.

Citoleux, Marc. *La poésie philosophique au XIXe siècle: Mme Ackermann d'après de nombreux documents inédits*. 1906. Geneva: Slatkine, 1973.

Coligny, Charles. "*Les muses parisiennes*: Mme Malvina Blanchecotte." *Revue fantaisiste* 1.2 (1861): 107–15.

Cros, Charles, et al. *Dixains réalistes*. 1876. Ed. Michael Pakenham. Paris: Des Cendres, 2000.

Czyba, Luce. "Tragique et stoïcisme dans l'œuvre poétique de Louisa Siefert." Planté, *Masculin/Féminin* 317–27.

Danahy, Michael. "Marceline Desbordes-Valmore and the Engendered Canon." *Yale French Studies* 75 (1989): 129–47.

Dante Alighieri. *The Inferno*. Trans. Robert Hollander and Jean Hollander. New York: Doubleday, 2000.

Deforges, Régine, ed. *Poèmes de femmes des origines à nos jours*. Paris: Le Cherche Midi, 1993.

Delumeau, J., and Y. Lequin, eds. *Les malheurs des temps: Histoire des fléaux et des calamités en France*. Paris: Larousse, 1987.

Denommé, Robert. *The French Parnassian Poets*. Carbondale: Southern Illinois UP, 1972.

Desbordes-Valmore, Marceline. *Les veillées des Antilles*. 1821. Ed. and introd. Aimée Boutin. Paris: L'Harmattan, 2006.

———. *Œuvre poétique intégrale*. Ed. Marc Bertrand. Lyon: André, 2007.

———. *Les œuvres poétiques*. Ed. Marc Bertrand. 2 vols. Grenoble: PUG, 1973.

Engelking, Tama Lea. "Renée Vivien and the Ladies of the Lake." *Nineteenth-Century French Studies* 30.3-4 (2002): 362–79.

———. "Renée Vivien's Sapphic Legacy: Remembering the 'House of Muses.'" *Atlantis: A Women's Studies Journal / Revue d'études sur la femme* 18.1-2 (1992–93): 125–41.

———. "The Secret Rebellion of a Literary Daughter: The Poetry of Gérard d'Houville." *French Literature Series* 16 (1989): 94–109.

———. "A Voice of Her Own: Gérard d'Houville's Thread and Literary Tradition." *Women in French Studies* 9 (2001): 28–39.

Finch, Alison. *Women's Writing in Nineteenth-Century France*. Cambridge: Cambridge UP, 2000.

Fleury, Robert. *Marie de Régnier, l'inconstante*. Paris: Plon, 1990.

Fontana, Michèle. "'Un démon dans une honnête femme': Louise Ackermann face à la critique." Planté, *Masculin/Féminin* 409–20.

Gauthier, Xavière. *La vierge rouge: Biographie de Louise Michel*. Paris: De Paris, 1999.

Gautier, Théophile. *Emaux et camées*. 1852. Ed. Claudine Gothot-Mersch. Paris: Gallimard, 1981.

Geoffroy, Daniel. *Élisa Mercœur: Nantaise romantique*. Maulevrier: Herault, 1990.

Giacchetti, Claudine. *Delphine de Girardin, la muse de Juillet*. Paris: L'Harmattan, 2004.

Goulesque, Florence R. J. *Marie Krysinska: Une femme poète symboliste, la Calliope du Chat Noir*. Paris: Champion, 2001.

Gray, Francine du Plessix. *Rage and Fire: A Life of Louise Colet*. New York: Simon, 1994.

Greenberg, Wendy. *Uncanonical Women: Feminine Voice in French Poetry, 1830–1871*. Amsterdam: Rodopi, 1999.

Harismendy-Lony, Sandrine. "Entre paraître et disparaître: Le 'Testament' de Nina de Villard." *Nineteenth Century French Studies* 30.1–2 (2001): 81–91.

———. "Nina de Villard, *singulière* Parisienne." *Nineteenth-Century French Studies* 27.1-2 (1998–99): 200–13.

Hugo, Victor. *Poésies*. Ed. Bernard Leuilliot. 3 vols. Paris: Seuil, 1972.

Jasenas, Eliane. *Marceline Desbordes-Valmore devant la critique*. Paris: Minard, 1962.

Jay, Karla. *The Amazon and the Page: Barney and Vivien*. Bloomington: Indiana UP, 1988.

Jenson, Deborah. "Gender and the Aesthetic of 'le Mal': Louise Ackermann's *Poésies philosophiques.*" *Nineteenth-Century French Studies* 23.1-2 (1994–95): 175–93.

———. "Louise Ackermann's Monstrous Nature." *Symposium* 53.4 (2000): 234–48.

———. *Trauma and Its Representations: The Social Life of Mimesis in Postrevolutionary France.* Baltimore: Johns Hopkins UP, 2001.

Johnson, Barbara. "Gender and Poetry: Charles Baudelaire and Marceline Desbordes-Valmore." *Displacements: Women, Tradition, Literatures in French.* Ed. Joan DeJean and Nancy K. Miller. Baltimore: Johns Hopkins UP, 1991. 163–81.

———. "The Lady in the Lake." *A New History of French Literature.* Ed. Denis Hollier. Cambridge: Harvard UP, 1989. 627–32.

Kelly, Dorothy. "Delphine Gay de Girardin." Sartori and Zimmerman 188–97.

Knapp, Bettina Liebowitz. *Judith Gautier: Writer, Orientalist, Musicologist, Feminist: A Literary Biography.* Dallas: Hamilton, 2004.

Krysinska, Marie. *Rythmes pittoresques: Mirages, Symboles, Femmes, Contes, Résurrections.* 1890. Ed. and introd. Seth Whidden. Exeter: U of Exeter P, 2003.

Laforgue, Jules. *Mélanges posthumes.* 1903. Paris: Ressources, 1979.

Lassère, Madeleine. *Delphine de Girardin: Journaliste et femme de lettres au temps du romantisme.* [Paris]: Perrin, 2003.

Laubier, Marie de. *Marie de Régnier, muse et poète de la belle époque.* [Paris]: Bibliothèque Nationale de France, 2004.

Leconte de Lisle, Charles. *Articles, préfaces, discours.* Ed. Edgard Pich. Paris: Société d'Édition "Les Belles Lettres," 1971.

Lejeune, Paule. *Louise Michel l'indomptable.* Paris: L'Harmattan, 2002.

Lloyd, Rosemary, ed. *Nineteenth-Century Women Seeking Expression: Translations from the French.* Liverpool Online Ser. Critical Editions of French Texts 2. Liverpool: U of Liverpool, 2000. 27 Nov. 2007 <http://www.liv.ac.uk/www/french/los/Women.pdf>.

Lloyd, Rosemary, and Brian Nelson, eds. *Women Seeking Expression: France, 1789–1914.* Melbourne: Monash Romance Studies, 2000.

"Louise Michel: Increvable anarchiste: Extrait du procès de la communarde Louise Michel." *Le drapeau noir.* 11 Feb. 2008 <http://www.drapeaunoir.org/commune/michel/proces.html>.

Maclellan, Nic. *Louise Michel.* Melbourne: Ocean, 2004.

Mallarmé, Stéphane. *Œuvres complètes.* Ed. Henri Mondor. Paris: Gallimard, 1945.

Marchal, Bertrand. *Salomé entre vers et prose: Baudelaire, Mallarmé, Flaubert, Huysmans.* Paris: Corti, 2005.

Marieton, Paul. *Josephin Soulary et la pléiade lyonnaise: Victor de Laprade, Pierre Dupont, Jean Tisseur, Louisa Siefert, Paul Chenavard.* Paris: Flammarion, 1884.

Marks, Elaine. "'Sapho 1900': Imaginary Renée Viviens and the Rear of the Belle Époque." *Yale French Studies* 75 (1988): 175–89.

Marzouki, Afifa. *Amable Tastu, une poétesse à l'époque romantique*. Tunis: Faculté des Lettres de la Manouba, 1997.

Mercœur, Élisa. "Mémoires sur la vie d'Élisa Mercœur." *Œuvres complètes*. Vol. 1. Paris: Pommeret, 1843. xvii–clxxxviii.

Michel, Louise. *À travers la vie et la mort: Œuvre poétique*. Ed. Daniel Armogathe and Marion Piper. Paris: La Découverte, 2001.

Mihram, Danielle. "Judith Gautier." Sartori and Zimmerman 170–77.

Molènes, Paul de. "Les femmes poètes." *La revue des deux mondes* July 1842: 48–76.

Morgan, Cheryl A. "Death of a Poet: Delphine Gay's Romantic Makeover." *Symposium* 53.4 (2000): 249–60.

Mortelette, Yann. *Histoire de Parnasse*. Paris: Fayard; 2005.

Nesci, Catherine, ed. *Delphine de Girardin*. Spec. issue of *Dix-Neuf* 7 (2006): 1–150. 13 Feb. 2008 <http://www.sdn.ac.uk/dixneuf/previous.htm#7>.

———. Introduction. Nesci, *Delphine de Girardin* 1–10.

Noblet, Agnès de. *Un univers d'artistes: Autour de Théophile et de Judith Gautier: Dictionnaire*. Paris: L'Harmattan, 2003.

Paliyenko, Adrianna M., ed. *Engendering Race: Romantic-Era Women and French Colonial Memory*. Spec. issue of *L'Esprit Créateur* 47.4 (2007): 1–132.

———. "In the Shadow of Eve: Marie Krysinska and the Force of Poetic Desire." Lloyd and Nelson 159–79.

———. "Is a Woman Poet Born or Made? Discourse of Maternity in Louisa Siefert and Louise Ackermann." *Esprit Créateur* 39.2 (1999): 52–63.

———. "Re-reading *la femme poète*: Rimbaud and Louisa Siefert." *Nineteenth-Century French Studies* 26.1-2 (1997–98): 146–60.

Perrin, Marie. *Renée Vivien: Le corps exsangue: De l'anorexie mentale à la création littéraire*. Paris: L'Harmattan, 2003.

Planté, Christine, ed. *Masculin/Féminin dans la poésie et les poétiques du XIXᵉ siècle*. Lyon: PUL, 2002.

———. *La petite sœur de Balzac: Essai sur la femme auteur*. Paris: Seuil, 1989.

———. Preface. *Tablettes d'une femme pendant la Commune*. By A.-M. Blanchecotte. Tusson: Du Lérot, 1996. v–xvi.

Plötner, Bärbel. "Les débuts d'Élisa Mercœur et d'Émile Souvestre dans le *Lycée armoricain*." Planté, *Masculin/Féminin* 177–90.

Porter, Laurence M. *The Crisis of French Symbolism*. Ithaca: Cornell UP, 1990.

———. *The Renaissance of the Lyric in French Romanticism: Elegy, "Poëme," and Ode*. Lexington: French Forum, 1978.

Poussard-Joly, Catherine. *Madame Tastu, ou "La muse oubliée": Biographie*. Palaiseau: Société Historique de Palaiseau, 1995.

Racine, Jean. *Théâtre complet*. Paris: Garnier, 1960.

Richardson, Joanna. *Judith Gautier: A Biography*. New York: Watts, 1987.

Rimbaud, Arthur. *Complete Works, Selected Letters: A Bilingual Edition*. Trans. Wallace Fowlie. Ed. Seth Whidden. Chicago: U of Chicago P, 2005.

———. *Œuvres complètes.* Ed. Antoine Adam. Paris: Gallimard, 1972.

Sainte-Beuve, Charles. *"Rêves et réalités,* par Madame M. B. (Blanche-cotte), ouvrière et poète." *Causeries du lundi.* Vol. 15. Paris: Garnier, n.d. 327–32.

Sanders, Virginie. *"Vertigineusement, j'allai vers les étoiles": La poésie de Renée Vivien.* Amsterdam: Rodopi, 1991.

Sartori, Eva, and Dorothy Zimmerman, eds. *French Women Writers.* Lincoln: U of Nebraska P, 1991.

Schaffer, Aaron. *The Genres of Parnassian Poetry.* Baltimore: Johns Hopkins UP, 1944.

Schapira, Marie-Claude. "Amable Tastu, Delphine Gay, le désenchantement au féminin." Planté, *Masculin/Féminin* 191–205.

Schultz, Gretchen. *The Gendered Lyric: Subjectivity and Difference in Nineteenth-Century French Poetry.* West Lafayette: Purdue UP, 1999.

———. "Loathsome Movement: Parnassian Politics and Villard's Revenge." *Moving Forward, Holding Fast: The Dynamics of Nineteenth-Century French Culture.* Ed. Barbara T. Cooper and Mary Donaldson-Evans. Amsterdam: Rodopi, 1997. 169–81.

———. "Terms of Estrangement: Renée Vivien's Construction of the Lesbian Subject." *The Rhetoric of the Other: Lesbian and Gay Strategies of Resistance in French and Francophone Contexts.* Ed. Martine Antle and Dominique Fisher. New Orleans: UP of the South, 2002. 79–100.

Scott, Clive. *Vers Libre: The Emergence of Free Verse in France, 1886–1914.* Oxford: Clarendon, 1990.

Siefert, Louisa. *Souvenirs rassemblés par sa mère; Poésies inédites.* Paris: Fischbacher, 1881.

Staël, Germaine de. *De l'Allemagne.* 1813. Paris: Hachette, 1958.

Stivale, Charles J. "Louise Michel's Poetry of Existence and Revolt." *Tulsa Studies in Women's Literature* 5.1 (1986): 41–61.

Thomas, Edith. *Louise Michel ou la Velleda de l'anarchie.* Paris: Gallimard, 1971.

Verlaine, Paul. "Les poètes maudits." *Œuvres en prose complètes.* Ed. Jacques Borel. Paris: Gallimard, 1972. 666–78.

Vincent, Patrick. *The Romantic Poetess: European Culture, Politics, and Gender, 1820–1840.* Hanover: UP of New Hampshire, 2004.

Wagener, Françoise. *Madame Récamier, 1777–1849.* Paris: Flammarion, 2000.

Whidden, Seth. Introduction. Krysinska 1–20.

———. "Marie Krysinska: A Bibliography." *Bulletin of Bibliography* 58.1 (2001): 1–10.

———. "Marie Krysinska's Prefaces and Letters: Not 'du Voyant' but 'd'une Défiante'." Lloyd and Nelson 180–93.

Zayed, Georges. "Un salon parnassien d'avant-garde: Nina de Villard et ses hôtes." *Aquila* 2 (1973): 177–229.

Notes on the Translators

Anne Atik is the author of two books of poetry, *Words in Hock* (1974) and *Offshore* (1991); *Drancy*, a special edition with the painter Kitaj (1989); and *How It Was: A Memoir of Samuel Beckett* (2001). Her poems have appeared in *Literary Imagination*, *Pequod*, *New World Writing*, the *Nation*, *London Jewish Quarterly*, *American Poetry Review*, *Partisan Review*, and *Ploughshares*. She has translated francophone poets in *African Heritage*, Raymond Queneau, and Jules Supervielle. From the Hebrew she translated poems by T. Carmi. She lives in Paris.

Michael Bishop is Emeritus McCulloch Professor of French and Contemporary Studies at Dalhousie University, Canada. He specializes in modern and contemporary French and francophone literature, art and culture, with an emphasis on poetry. His publications include books on René Char, Michel Deguy, Jacques Prévert, André du Bouchet, and women poets in France since 1960. His latest books offer translations and *inédits* of Gérard Titus-Carmel, Yves Bonnefoy, and Christian Jaccard.

Mary Ann Caws is distinguished professor of English, French, and comparative literature at the Graduate Center, City University of New York. She is the author of *Marcel Proust: Illustrated Lives* (2003), *To the Boathouse: A Memoir* (2004), *Pablo Picasso: Critical Lives* (2005), *Henry James: Illustrated Lives* (2006), *Extraordinary Women* (2006), and *Glorious Eccentrics: Modernist Women Painting and Writing* (2006). She edited *The Surrealist Painters and Poets* (2001), *Manifesto: A Century of Isms* (2001), *The Yale Book of Twentieth Century French Poetry* (2004), and *Surrealism* (2004).

Melanie Hawthorne is professor of French at Texas A&M University and coordinator of the Program in Comparative Literature. Her most recent translation is *Monsieur Vénus,* by Rachilde (2004). Her other translations include *The Juggler,* by Rachilde, and works by Gisèle d'Estoc and Marie Lenéru.

Rosemary Lloyd is Rudy Professor of French emerita at Indiana University; Fellow emerita of New Hall, Cambridge; and affiliate professor of Adelaide University. She specializes in the nineteenth- and twentieth-century novel and poetry. Her translations include selections from the correspondence of Baudelaire and of Mallarmé, Baudelaire's prose poetry, and an anthology of nineteenth-century texts, *Revolutions in Writing*. Her *Baudelaire's World* (2002) is a study of translations of Baudelaire's work and includes many of her own translations.

J. S. A. Lowe is the author of the chapbook *DOE* (2008). Her poems have appeared in *AGNI, American Scholar, Chicago Review, Denver Quarterly, Fish Drum, Poetry Daily, Salamander,* and *Tricycle*. She is a teaching associate and graduate student in poetry at Arizona State University.

Laurence M. Porter teaches French and comparative literature at Michigan State University. He translated Marceline Desbordes-Valmore, Madame de Staël, Joseph de Maistre, and Victor Hugo's *Les misérables*. His most recent publications are the chapter "Maryse Condé, Historian of the Black Diaspora" in *An Introduction to Maryse Condé* (2006) and the monograph *Women's Vision in Western Literature: The Empathic Community* (2005).

Christopher Rivers is professor of French at Mount Holyoke College. He is the translator and editor of Adolphe Belot's 1870 novel *Mademoiselle Giraud, ma femme* (2002). His translation of a memoir originally published in French by the first black heavyweight champion of the world, Jack Johnson, was recently published. He is currently working on a cultural biography of the great French boxer Georges Carpentier.

Gretchen Schultz is associate professor of French studies at Brown University. She is the author of *The Gendered Lyric:*

Subjectivity and Difference in Nineteenth-Century French Poetry (1999). She translated texts by Ackermann and Krysinska and wrote articles on Baudelaire, Desbordes-Valmore, Louÿs, Verlaine, Villard, and Vivien, among others.

Patricia Terry's verse translations include *The Song of Roland, Renard the Fox,* and *Poems of the Elder Edda.* She collaborated with Mary Ann Caws on translations of Reverdy, Breton, Desnos, and numerous other nineteenth- and twentieth-century poets. She is retired from the University of San Diego.

Rosanna Warren is the author of a chapbook (*Snow Day* [1981]) and three collections of poems: *Each Leaf Shines Separate* (1984), *Stained Glass* (winner of the Lamont Poetry Award from the Academy of American Poets; 1993), and *Departure* (2003). She edited and contributed to *The Art of Translation: Voices from The Field* (1989) and is cotranslator, with Stephen Scully, of Euripides's *Suppliant Women* (1992). She is Emma MacLachlan Metcalf Professor of the Humanities at Boston University.

Modern Language Association of America
Texts and Translations

Texts

Anna Banti. *"La signorina" e altri racconti*. Ed. and introd. Carol Lazzaro-Weis. 2001.

Adolphe Belot. *Mademoiselle Giraud, ma femme*. Ed and introd. Christopher Rivers. 2002.

Dovid Bergelson. אָפּגאנג. Ed. and introd. Joseph Sherman. 1999.

Elsa Bernstein. *Dämmerung: Schauspiel in fünf Akten*. Ed. and introd. Susanne Kord. 2003.

Edith Bruck. *Lettera alla madre*. Ed. and introd. Gabriella Romani. 2006.

Isabelle de Charrière. *Lettres de Mistriss Henley publiées par son amie*. Ed. Joan Hinde Stewart and Philip Stewart. 1993.

Isabelle de Charrière. *Trois femmes: Nouvelle de l'Abbé de la Tour*. Ed. and introd. Emma Rooksby. 2007.

François-Timoléon de Choisy, Marie-Jeanne L'Héritier, and Charles Perrault. *Histoire de la Marquise-Marquis de Banneville*. Ed. Joan DeJean. 2004.

Sophie Cottin. *Claire d'Albe*. Ed. and introd. Margaret Cohen. 2002.

Marceline Desbordes-Valmore. *Sarah*. Ed. Deborah Jenson and Doris Y. Kaddish. 2008.

Claire de Duras. *Ourika*. Ed. Joan DeJean. Introd. DeJean and Margaret Waller. 1994.

Şeyh Galip. *Hüsn ü Aşk*. Ed. and introd. Victoria Rowe Holbrook. 2005.

Françoise de Graffigny. *Lettres d'une Péruvienne*. Introd. Joan DeJean and Nancy K. Miller. 1993.

Sofya Kovalevskaya. Нигилистка. Ed. and introd. Natasha Kolchevska. 2001.

Thérèse Kuoh-Moukoury. *Rencontres essentielles*. Introd. Cheryl Toman. 2002.

Juan José Millás. *"Trastornos de carácter" y otros cuentos*. Introd. Pepa Anastasio. 2007.

Emilia Pardo Bazán. *"El encaje roto" y otros cuentos*. Ed. and introd. Joyce Tolliver. 1996.

Rachilde. *Monsieur Vénus: Roman matérialiste*. Ed. and introd. Melanie Hawthorne and Liz Constable. 2004.

Marie Riccoboni. *Histoire d'Ernestine*. Ed. Joan Hinde Stewart and Philip Stewart. 1998.

Eleonore Thon. *Adelheit von Rastenberg*. Ed. and introd. Karin A. Wurst. 1996.

Translations

Anna Banti. *"The Signorina" and Other Stories*. Trans. Martha King and Carol Lazzaro-Weis. 2001.

Adolphe Belot. *Mademoiselle Giraud, My Wife*. Trans. Christopher Rivers. 2002.

Dovid Bergelson. *Descent*. Trans. Joseph Sherman. 1999.

Elsa Bernstein. *Twilight: A Drama in Five Acts*. Trans. Susanne Kord. 2003.

Edith Bruck. *Letter to My Mother*. Trans. Brenda Webster with Gabriella Romani. 2006.

Isabelle de Charrière. *Letters of Mistress Henley Published by Her Friend*. Trans. Philip Stewart and Jean Vaché. 1993.

Isabelle de Charrière. *Three Women: A Novel by the Abbé de la Tour*. Trans. Emma Rooksby. 2007.

François-Timoléon de Choisy, Marie-Jeanne L'Héritier, and Charles Perrault. *The Story of the Marquise-Marquis de Banneville*. Trans. Steven Rendall. 2004.

Sophie Cottin. *Claire d'Albe*. Trans. Margaret Cohen. 2002.

Marceline Desbordes-Valmore. *Sarah*. Trans. Deborah Jenson and Doris Y. Kaddish. 2008.

Claire de Duras. *Ourika*. Trans. John Fowles. 1994.

Şeyh Galip. *Beauty and Love*. Trans. Victoria Rowe Holbrook. 2005.

Françoise de Graffigny. *Letters from a Peruvian Woman*. Trans. David Kornacker. 1993.

Sofya Kovalevskaya. *Nihilist Girl*. Trans. Natasha Kolchevska with Mary Zirin. 2001.

Thérèse Kuoh-Moukoury. *Essential Encounters*. Trans. Cheryl Toman. 2002.

Juan José Millás. *"Personality Disorders" and Other Stories*. Trans. Gregory B. Kaplan. 2007.

Emilia Pardo Bazán. *"Torn Lace" and Other Stories*. Trans. María Cristina Urruela. 1996.

Rachilde. *Monsieur Vénus: A Materialist Novel*. Trans. Melanie Hawthorne. 2004.

Marie Riccoboni. *The Story of Ernestine.* Trans. Joan Hinde Stewart and Philip Stewart. 1998.

Eleonore Thon. *Adelheit von Rastenberg.* Trans. George F. Peters. 1996.

Texts and Translations in One Volume

جدید اردو شاعری کا انتخاب / *An Anthology of Modern Urdu Poetry.* Ed., introd., and trans. M. A. R. Habib. 2003.

An Anthology of Spanish American Modernismo. Ed. Kelly Washbourne. Trans. Washbourne with Sergio Waisman. 2007.

An Anthology of Nineteenth-Century Women's Poetry from France. Ed. Gretchen Schultz. Trans. Anne Atik, Michael Bishop, Mary Ann Caws, Melanie Hawthorne, Rosemary Lloyd, J. S. A. Lowe, Laurence Porter, Christopher Rivers, Schultz, Patricia Terry, and Rosanna Warren. 2008.